Sara Miller McCune founded SAGE Publishing in 1965 to support the dissemination of usable knowledge and educate a global community. SAGE publishes more than 1000 journals and over 800 new books each year, spanning a wide range of subject areas. Our growing selection of library products includes archives, data, case studies and video. SAGE remains majority owned by our founder and after her lifetime will become owned by a charitable trust that secures the company's continued independence.

Los Angeles | London | New Delhi | Singapore | Washington DC | Melbourne

Jean McNiff

Action Research

All You Need to Know

Los Angeles | London | New Delhi
Singapore | Washington DC | Melbourne

Los Angeles | London | New Delhi
Singapore | Washington DC | Melbourne

SAGE Publications Ltd
1 Oliver's Yard
55 City Road
London EC1Y 1SP

SAGE Publications Inc.
2455 Teller Road
Thousand Oaks, California 91320

SAGE Publications India Pvt Ltd
B 1/I 1 Mohan Cooperative Industrial Area
Mathura Road
New Delhi 110 044

SAGE Publications Asia-Pacific Pte Ltd
3 Church Street
#10-04 Samsung Hub
Singapore 049483

Editor: Mila Steele
Editorial assistant: John Nightingale
Production editor: Victoria Nicholas
Copyeditor: Aud Scriven
Proofreader: Elaine Leek
Marketing manager: Sally Ransom
Cover design: Shaun Mercier
Typeset by: C&M Digitals (P) Ltd, Chennai, India
Printed in the UK

Library of Congress Control Number: 2016953527

British Library Cataloguing in Publication data

A catalogue record for this book is available from
the British Library

ISBN 978-1-47396-746-5
ISBN 978-1-47396-747-2 (pbk)

Contents

Acknowledgements

Books do not just come into being of their own accord. They are more the creation of multiple people talking together and sharing ideas, whether in everyday settings, lecture theatres or texts. This book is no exception: it arises from multiple conversations with companions in all walks of life and through multiple experiences, including focused conversations of learning and teaching and often over teacups.

Specific individuals deserve special mention and thanks. These are my two editors at Sage, Mila Steele and John Nightingale, and the fine production team, especially Victoria Nicholas, who always had words of encouragement in working with and making sense of the original manuscript. I also have to thank all contributors of case studies and other material for permission to use their work, and for their very valuable feedback on different aspects of the book. And of course, Peter, always there, always kind.

I hope you enjoy reading the book as much as I have enjoyed writing it. I hope the ideas are useful for finding ways of taking social and epistemological action in the world. It is the responsibility of all to use their space in the world for good: I hope the book has a place in this.

Open thy mouth, judge righteously, and plead the cause of the poor and needy. Proverbs, 31: 9

Introduction

This book is a reasonably comprehensive guide to action research. It is written for all practitioners enrolled on university-accredited courses, across disciplines and settings, who are new to action research and wish to use it as a main methodology for their studies. It is also written for lecturers teaching those courses. Readers will therefore include experienced academics, new and early career researchers, students on undergraduate and postgraduate courses, and practitioners involved in workplace-based research. The aim of the book is to help you see what doing action research involves, why you should do it, and when, where, and how to do it. The book takes the form of a practical workbook though also with a strong philosophical basis. References to key literatures provide the means of integrating what other researchers and scholars have said into your own thinking and writing. This enables you to fulfil the scholarly criterion to have engaged critically with the literatures, and show how this has possibly influenced your thinking and practices. A key theme throughout is the idea that practitioners have something to say from which others can learn: doing your research and producing a text in the form of an assignment, dissertation or conversation with another person enables you to say it. Seeing how to do this is the main focus.

The book also helps you to find your way around the complex contemporary field of action research. The field has expanded considerably in the last two decades: the term 'action research' is everywhere and books and papers abound concerning what it means and how to interpret and use it. This variety, in my view, is healthy: it requires people to think carefully about ideas and how they communicate and justify these to others. Yet it is also where the idea of action research is contested, especially in universities that now openly state they are about marketisation and profit, with the result that both the concept and practices of action research are often co-opted and distorted. In many institutions, it has stopped being understood as a democratic practice for everyday life (as was common from about the 1930s to the 1980s, and still is today in many quarters) and is now viewed as a technique for achieving specific results. This shift goes against everything many researchers, including myself, stand for, including celebrating the capacity of people to think for themselves as they work together and find ways to create new futures that are right for them.

This diversity provides a backdrop to the book because it raises questions about the what, why and how of action research. It especially raises questions about the need to interrogate the visions that inspire our actions. How we see the world and how we think it should work are inspired by our values. Sowell (1987: 7–8) speaks about how different values inform different kinds of vision: 'constrained visions' that see reality in terms of maintaining the status quo, and 'unconstrained visions' that see everything as open to change. Yet, he says, visions also have to be considered in relation to interests: in whose interests is it to promote a certain idea? Also, visions can often conflict with interests: are we prepared to forgo a holiday and give the money to charity, or perhaps welcome destitute people into a middle-class area? Pluralism is great in theory but not always in practice. Engaging with these issues requires some personal interrogation: we do not often think about our visions, says Sowell, yet we pay a good deal of attention to our interests.

A core message of the book is that all people are able to and should do action research, not as an instrumental technique for getting other things done, which links with the marketisation agenda of many universities, but as a way of taking action in the world and speaking for themselves as they provide explanations for what they are doing. This issue is especially pressing these days when the higher education sector (containing the people who will accredit your work) is under increasing pressure to secure market edge. A favoured strategy of institutions in achieving this edge is to identify themselves as a community of 'experts'. Their job is to generate knowledge and theory for use by so-called practitioners in workplaces: thus practitioners become identified as technicians whose job is to apply the theory provided by experts. The traditional divide of thinkers and doers, of theory and practice is intensified. Further, because higher education is still seen as the main institution for legitimating what counts as knowledge and theory, the situation becomes a self-perpetuating cycle of power (Dyrberg, 1997), where participants do not and are not allowed to choose how or what to think. And many dissenting academics, too, who identify themselves as practitioners in a workplace called 'a university', find themselves caught up in the same struggle: while they may wish to promote the idea that all people are capable of thinking and acting for themselves they are under the same corporate pressures to conform. The penalties for not conforming can be severe.

It is possible to see the bureaucratic rhetoric of 'expertise' everywhere in contemporary policy and academic literatures: Hattie (2015) recommends leaving theory to the academics; Taber (2013) says that teachers cannot generate theory; Rafferty (1996, 2010) argues that 'correct' nursing knowledge should be acquired from a university, not from a bedside. At the same time, happily, it is also possible to see powerful counter-bodies of literature that challenge the status quo: Hilde Hiim (2015, 2016) and colleagues challenge the irrelevance of many so-called 'academic' texts for workplace practices; Andy Convery and colleagues, Joseph Shosh and colleagues and many others (all in this book) explain why practitioners' knowledge should be seen as powerful forms of theorising; and many other voices are heard in the book that tell the same story. They demand, even by their very presence, that those who wish to stifle dissent do not have the final word but have to negotiate spaces with equally informed and articulate workplace practitioners. This book therefore becomes part of those critical literatures that both challenge the status quo and also provide practical and theoretical resources to show how transforming the challenge into reality can be achieved.

The book argues that, if a main criterion for being a knowledgeable and worthwhile person is the capacity to create knowledge and generate theory, then everyone is able to do so. A basic condition of being human is that we accept life as meaningful, so we seek to understand and understand better; we generate descriptions and explanations for these processes as theories of everyday living. So-called 'ordinary' people are able to generate theory, albeit of a different kind from that normally generated by traditionalist academics. In a traditionalist academy the acceptable form of theory is abstract; it involves speaking about concepts and practices from an outsider perspective and developing arguments that hang together linguistically. Just as useful for the practical business of everyday life, however, are the personal and dynamic theories that practitioners produce from within practices as they ask, 'How do I/we work with this situation we are in? How do we make sense of it? What do we need to know and do to improve things? How do I/we offer explanations to show and explain what I/we are doing?' This form of theorising also tends to take a personalised embodied form, often using innovative forms of representation including multimedia and dynamic forms such as performance. Producing this kind of theory is the business of action research. Practitioners in all walks of life, including in higher education, can and should generate their own personal and collective theories of practice to show how they hold themselves accountable for what they are doing.

So it emerges that there are several sets of reasons for doing action research:

- First, you can improve learning in order to improve practices.
- Second, you can advance knowledge and theory, that is, new ideas about how things can be done and why. All research aims to generate knowledge and theory. As a practitioner-researcher, you aim to generate theories about learning and practice, both your own and other people's.
- Third, you can explain how you are contributing to new understandings for yourself, for others and for the world.

This highlights the need for you to become politically savvy about the politics of knowledge production in order to critique those scholarly literatures, including many action research texts that talk a great deal about improving practices but substantially less about improving learning as the basis of improving practice; and they talk even less about how this may be seen as the grounds for new theory and an important contribution to the history of ideas. The literature tends to reinforce the portrayal of practitioners as doers who are competent for improving practices. They are not, however, competent to be involved in debates about knowledge. Consequently, in wider debates, including policy debates, practitioners tend to be excluded, on the assumption that they are good at practice but should leave it to official theorists to explain what, how and why people should learn, and how they should use their knowledge. So strong is this discourse that many practitioners have come to believe it themselves, and collude in their own subjugation by refusing to believe that they are competent theorists, or by dismissing 'theory' as above their heads or irrelevant.

I disagree. I believe that practitioners can, and should, get involved. I also believe that theory generation itself should be seen as a pluralistic practice: all forms are welcome, including traditionalist abstract forms about practices and practical dynamic forms conducted within practices, and each should recognise the other as an ally, not an enemy. This is why doing action research is so important. You can show both how you have learned to improve practice, in terms, say, of achieving better working conditions or increased opportunities for learning, and can now produce your own personal or collective theories about why it worked (or did not, as the case may be), and you can also show how you have incorporated conventional abstract theories about practices into your own. Theorising practices in this way shows that you are producing thoroughly grounded ideas that can influence others' learning. Your practice, both in practical workplace spaces and in the conceptual spaces of theory generation, is the grounds for your own theory of practice.

This pluralistic, non-absolutist view of theory is uncommon in the mainstream literatures, which largely maintain that theory should be expressed as sets of propositions or statements about practices, produced by official knowledge-creators in universities and think tanks. Such kinds of theories do exist, of course, and are important for a range of practices. However, this is not the only kind of theory available or recognised. People's personal theories of practice are just as important as abstract theories, but they tend not to be seen as such in the mainstream literatures. In my view, there should be room enough for both kinds, and discussions about how one can contribute to the development of the other.

We need to remember that the world is made of stories. Loy writes:

> According to a Hindu myth the world is upheld by the great elephant Maha Pudma, who is in turn supported by the great tortoise Chukwa.
>
> An Englishman asked a Hindu sage what the great tortoise rests upon.
>
> 'Another turtle,' was the reply.
>
> And what supports the turtle?
>
> 'Ah, Sahib, after that it's turtles all the way down.' (Loy, 2010: 4)

We live by stories. But that's a story, too. No one has the true story. But that's also a story. We choose the stories we believe. But that's another story again. It's stories all the way down.

I agree with Foucault's idea that knowledge is power. As a practitioner you should regard yourself also as a researcher, capable of creating your own theories by studying your living practices. You have important things to say, both in relation to the world of work and relationships, and also in relation to the world of ideas and theory. This book aims to help you voice those things in such a way that others will listen and want to hear more. It also aims to help you take your rightful place both as a publicly acknowledged competent professional and as a brilliant knower.

Here are some notes to assist you in reading the book.

A note on the structure of the book

This book is organised into seven parts, which deal with:

- what you need to know about action research;
- why you need to know it and how it can help you as a self-reflective and self-critical practitioner-researcher;
- how you can do action research, and learn to critique it as you go;
- how you can test the validity of your emergent knowledge claims (what you think you have found out), and act on critical feedback;
- how you can disseminate your knowledge for public use, and develop it further, acting on your own and others' critical responses;
- how you can represent and communicate your knowledge;
- how you can reflect on and explain the significance and potential implications of what you have achieved, so that other people can learn with and from you; and use this as the basis for new or ongoing enquiries.

The chapters follow a coherent sequence, and each deals with a separate issue. The material is organised like this so that you can see action research as an integrated whole while focusing on particular issues as needed. The chapters are reasonably concise, with examples and case studies throughout. The book also becomes a workbook: it shows how you can use and develop the ideas in your own contexts.

Working with the text can itself be seen as you engaging in your action enquiry about how you can learn about action research and generate your own ideas about how to do so and what some of the implications may be for your practice. On page 129 you can read how doing action research involves asking a range of questions, such as the following (you may have questions of your own to add to the list, and you can modify these questions as suits your own purposes):

• What is my concern? What do I want to investigate further?
• Why am I concerned? Why do I want to investigate this?
• What is my research question?
• How do I regularly gather data and generate evidence to show what the situation is like both now and as it develops?
• What can I do about the situation? What will I do?
• How do I evaluate what I am doing in relation with others?
• How do I test the validity of my emerging knowledge and knowledge claims?
• How can I check whether any conclusions I come to are reasonably fair and accurate?
• How do I modify my practices and thinking in light of my evaluation?

These questions should be seen not simply as straightforward questions but more as heuristics, ways of identifying and engaging with a particular topic or field of enquiry. They can be supplemented by other questions: see Chapter 9.

The introduction to each part draws your attention to where you are in this action–reflection cycle. As you read and work with the ideas, you may become aware of your own process of becoming increasingly critical, and more aware of the values base of what you are doing in your real-life setting. You are invited to engage with these ideas, and to transform your understanding about how you can make your contribution to the field. While you may read the book initially to learn more about how to do action research, think also about what you can achieve through your own enquiry, and how this can benefit yourself and others, because this is really what it is all about.

A note on some terminology

I confess to an ongoing dilemma about using some terminology, including the terms 'academic', 'practitioner' and 'workplace'. I tend to use the term 'academic' to refer to people working in higher education contexts, in the Academy, whose job is to engage in higher education-oriented work. The word 'academic' tends to refer more to a form of practice rather than an organisational role. I use the term 'practitioner' to refer to anyone involved in a practice, including academics, usually in a formal workplace though also in informal workplaces such as gardens. From this perspective, an academic is a practitioner in an academic setting. Also, once a work-based practitioner enrols on a programme of studies, by default they become an academic too. I do not use the terms to denote position power, more to indicate how people are positioned in workplace settings.

I use the term 'dissertation' to refer to the text you will produce, although this may take the form of an assignment. However, most people on courses will produce some kind of dissertation so this term is used throughout.

I use the word 'traditionalist' to refer to those kinds of research that err towards a positivist perspective. In other texts I have tended to use the term 'social science', but this could be misleading: some people see action research as a form of social science, and the term 'social science' itself is given many meanings.

A note on the research base of the book

The case studies in the book take different forms: some have been written especially for the book; others are in the public domain and drawn from a range of research projects that I have supported or otherwise been involved with; some case studies have been slightly edited with their authors' permission. The projects in question include my own authored texts and edited collections: the series of International Conferences on Value and Virtue in Practice-Based Research, held at York St John University, UK; other projects from South Africa, Ireland, Northern Ireland, Norway, Qatar and Cambodia; and works from people registered on master's and doctoral courses. The case studies come from around the world and from a range of settings and sectors; they are from practitioners and academics alike, many working collaboratively. Inevitably, the teaching profession is the most prominently represented, since my work is mainly to do with the professional education of teachers, though I also work with people in medicine, nursing and healthcare and in business. Permission to publish their work here has been sought from and granted by all contributors. All in all, the case studies communicate Bakhtin's (1981) idea of heteroglossia, a living unification of multiple voices, that, while representing often widely divergent thinking, now speak with a single voice that calls for greater understanding and accountability in the interests of a more stable and person-centred global order.

All are invited – you too. If you would like to get involved, please contact me: I am easily reachable. You can find me at jeanmcniff@mac.com. My website is www.jeanmcniff.com

Finally …

This book is part of my own writing and dissemination programme, as I pursue my research into how to encourage practitioners to believe in themselves, and produce their theories (descriptions and explanations) of practice that will contribute to new learning. Many examples of these ideas appear on my website and in other texts (see the list of references).

Certain ideas inspire my own life, which inevitably come through in this book. I believe passionately in the right of all to speak and be listened to, and I believe in the need for individual practitioners, working collectively, to show how they hold themselves accountable for what they do. I aim to do the same. It is the responsibility of each of us to think for ourselves. No one can die for you, so no one can live for you. I believe that each of us lives a life that we did not ask for but was freely given. We each occupy our own space on earth: no one else can occupy it, so it becomes a personal responsibility to use it well. Each life matters.

Thank you for reading the book. Time is limited and you have a lot to do, so I hope you find it worthwhile.

PART I

What do I need to know?

This part is about the main contemporary issues in action research. It explains that action research is about practitioners creating new ideas about improving their work and putting those ideas forward as their personal theories of practice. This is different from traditionalist research in which official researchers produce theory, which they then expect practitioners to apply to their practices. Given the power-constituted nature of these issues, we are therefore immediately into issues of power and politics, about what counts as knowledge and who counts as a knower.

Part I discusses these ideas. It contains the following chapters.

I suggested in the Introduction that you could regard working with the book as your action enquiry into how you can learn about action research and how to do it. At this point in your action–reflection cycle you are asking, 'What is my concern?' You are saying that you need to find out what the main ideas of action research are so that you have a good grasp of the basics in order to begin your action research from an informed position.

What is action research?

The action research family is wide and diverse, and different people hold different perspectives about what action research is, what it is for, who can do it and how. You need to know about these debates so that you can decide for yourself which approach to take and then get actively involved. Taking part also helps you appreciate why you should do action research and how this can help you contribute actively to shaping the future for yourself, for others and for the world.

This chapter is organised into four sections that deal with these issues:

1. What action research is and is not
2. Different approaches to action research
3. Purposes of action research
4. When and when not to use action research

1. What action research is and is not

Action research is a practical form of enquiry that enables anyone in every job and walk of life to investigate and evaluate their work. They ask, 'What am I doing? Do I need to improve anything? If so, what? How do I improve it? Why should I improve it?' They produce their accounts of practice to show: (1) how they are trying to improve what they are doing; this involves first thinking about and learning how to do it better; (2) how this enables them to give meaning to their lives; and (3) how they are trying to influence others to do the same thing. These accounts stand as their own practical theories of practice, from which others can learn if they wish.

From this perspective, action research has become increasingly popular around the world as a way for all people to take action in their personal and social situations with a view to improving them. It has also become popular as a form of professional learning across the professions and disciplines, including in business and management (Coghlan and Shani, 2016) and leadership studies (Branson et al., 2016; Davids and Waghid, 2017). It is particularly well developed in education, specifically in teaching, and in professional education, mainly in teacher education (Ellis and McNicholl, 2015) and nurse education (McDonnell and McNiff, 2016). A major attraction of action research is that everyone can do it, so it is for 'ordinary' practitioners as well as for principals, managers and administrators. It is not a case that only professional researchers can do action research: students and plumbers also can and should do action research (McNiff, 2016a). You can gain university accreditation for your action enquiries, as some of the case studies in this book show. In a practice setting, action research can therefore be a powerfully liberating form of professional enquiry because it means that practitioners themselves investigate their practices as they find ways to live more fully in the direction of their personal and social values. They are not told what to do; they decide for themselves what to do, in negotiation with others. This can work in relation to individual as well as collective enquiries. More and more groups of practitioners are getting together to investigate their collective work and put their stories of learning into the public domain. Your story can add to these and expand and strengthen them.

This is what makes action research distinctive. Practitioners research their own practices, which is different from most traditionalist forms of research where a professional researcher does research *on* rather than *with* practitioners. Traditionalist researchers tend to stand outside a situation and ask, 'What are those people over there doing? How do we understand and explain what they are doing?' This kind of research is often called outsider or spectator research: the kind of theory they generate is usually abstract and conceptual and is communicated through words. Action researchers, however, are insider researchers. They see themselves as part of the context they are investigating, and ask, individually and collectively, 'Is my/our work going as we wish? How do we improve it where necessary?' If they feel their work is already reasonably satisfactory, they evaluate it and produce evidence to show why they believe this to be the case. If they feel something needs improving, they work on that aspect, keeping records and producing regular oral and written progress reports about what they are doing. The kind of theory they produce is dynamic and developmental and communicated through their actions as well as their words.

Many varieties of action research are available these days and most are counted as legitimate within their own traditions, so researchers adopt different positionalities in relation with others in the research field (see page 14 of this book, which presents a summary of these positionalities). Remember, however, that regardless of the approach you choose, you will need to justify your stance and explain why you have chosen it.

Here are some examples of traditionalist research (outsider) questions and action research (insider) questions to show the difference between them.

Traditionalist research (outsider) questions

- What is the relationship between nurses' practice-based knowledge and the quality of patient care?
- Does management style influence worker productivity?
- Will a different seating arrangement increase audience participation?

Action research (insider) questions

- How do I study my nursing practice for the benefit of the patients?
- How do I improve my management style to encourage productivity?
- How do I encourage greater audience participation through trying out different seating arrangements?

Notional action plans

Like all research, action research aims to be a disciplined, systematic process which at some point you make public (even if this is only handing in an assignment to your supervisor). As in all research it follows a notional action plan. Here are some of those action plans that show the process of everyday enquiry: they are notional in that you should see them as heuristics, ways of understanding a topic that you intend to investigate further.

A notional action plan can take this form:

- Take stock of what is going on.
- Identify a concern.
- Think of a possible way forward.
- Try it out.
- Monitor the action by gathering data to show what is happening.
- Evaluate progress by establishing procedures for making judgements about what is happening.
- Test the validity of claims to knowledge.
- Modify practice in light of the evaluation.

This action plan can then be turned into a set of questions that you can elaborate on as appropriate to your context, as follows:

- What is my concern? What issue do I wish to investigate?
- Why am I concerned? Why is this an issue? Why do I wish to investigate it?
- What is my research question? Have I several questions relating to different aspects of my research?
- How do I show the situation as it is and as it develops? What kind of data do I need to gather to show what is going on?
- What can I do about it? What will I do about it? What actions will I take?
- How do I evaluate what I am doing? How do I analyse and interpret my data to generate evidence?
- How do I test the validity of my claims to knowledge? How do I show that people can believe what I say?
- How do I check that any conclusions I come to are reasonably fair and accurate? How do I avoid jumping to conclusions?
- How do I write a good quality report? How do I disseminate my findings so that other people can learn from and with me?
- How do I modify my ideas and practices in light of the evaluation? How will I use the learning I have acquired from doing my research to inform new practices? (See also McNiff, 2016b.)

In practical terms, this means you would identify a particular concern, try out a new way of doing things, gather, analyse and interpret the data on an ongoing basis, reflect on what was happening, check out any new understandings with others, and in light of your reflections try a different way that may or may not be more successful. As a nurse, for example, you would monitor and evaluate how you were relating to patients, and how they were responding to you (Higgs and Titchen, 2001; McDonnell, 2017; Rolfe, 1998). This would help you find the best way of working with patients to encourage their self-motivation towards recovery.

The process of 'observe – reflect – act – evaluate – modify – move in new directions' is generally known as action–reflection, although no single term is used in the literature. Because the process tends to be cyclical, it is often referred to as an action–reflection cycle (see Figure 1.1). The process is ongoing because as soon as you reach a provisional point where you feel things are satisfactory, that point itself raises new questions and it is time to begin again. Good visual models exist in the literature to communicate this process (Elliott, 1991; McNiff, 2013).

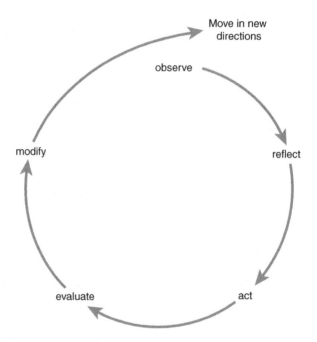

Figure 1.1   A typical action-reflection cycle

Here are some examples of action enquiries undertaken by real people:

- Colleen McLaughlin and Nazipa Ayubayeva (2015) developed an action research project into how they could support educational reform in Kazakhstan.
- Andrew Townsend and Pat Thomson (2015) worked with a collaborative team comprising staff from a water heritage museum, a university, teachers and artists: the aim was to improve educational practices through the use of art installations.

- Anbarah Al-Abdallah (2013), working in Qatar, wanted to help her learners develop greater proficiency in maths.
- Mzuzile Mpondwana (2008) wanted to find ways of developing better relationships among people living and working in a South African township.
- Susanne Winther (2016) from Denmark wanted to support a smoother transition from intensive care units to general wards.
- Each asked questions of the kind, 'How do I do this? How do I learn to do it better?'

2. Different approaches to action research

The action research family has been around for a long time, at least since the 1920s, and has become increasingly influential. As often happens, however, different family members have developed different opinions and interests, some have developed their own terminology, and some have formed breakaway groups, some of which have in turn become mainstreamed. You need to decide which kind of action research is best for you, which means developing at least a working knowledge of the field and taking a critical perspective to some key issues. These include the following:

- Different views of what action research is about and which perspective to take.
- Different forms of action research and different names and terminology.

Different views of what action research is about and which perspective to take

There is general agreement among the action research community that action research is about:

- action: taking action to improve practices, which is rooted in improving understanding; and …
- research: finding things out and coming to new understandings, that is, creating new knowledge. In action research the knowledge is about how and why you should act in the world and to evaluate the effects of your actions.

There is disagreement about:

- the balance between taking action and doing research: many texts emphasise the need to take action but not to do research, and this turns action research into a form of personal-professional development but without a solid research/knowledge base that clarifies the reasons and purposes for the action;
- who does the action and who does the research, that is, who creates the knowledge about what is done and whether it has achieved its goals.

Furthermore, because knowledge contributes to theory, that is, explanations for how and why things happen, it becomes a question of who does the action and who generates the theory (explanations) about the action. To help clarify, take the example of a video shoot.

On most video shoots, some people are positioned, and frequently position themselves, as actors and agents (doers), while others see themselves as directors and producers (thinkers). Similarly, practitioners in workplaces are often seen as actors whose job is to do things, while 'official' researchers in research institutions such as universities are seen as directors and producers whose job is to provide the scripts for the practitioner-actors to speak, and to direct what they do. The directors and producers also provide explanations for what the actors are doing and why they are doing it. The hidden assumptions are that the actors are good at acting but are not able to theorise (explain) what they are doing, whereas the directors are good at theorising what the actors are doing and writing reports about it. Theory and practice are seen as separate, and theory is generally seen as more prestigious than practice. This attitude is commonplace in a good deal of (though not all) conventional social science research, where a researcher writes reports about what other people are doing. Ironically it is also now common-place in certain forms of action research (see below). The difference between a conventional social science scenario and an action research scenario is that in social science research the aim is to demonstrate a causal relationship ('If I do this, that will happen'), whereas in action research the aim is to improve thinking and practice. The issue is always about the nature of relationships: who decides on what needs improving and how this should be done.

It can be useful here to draw on the ideas of positioning theory (Harré and van Langenhove, 1999) and critical discourse analysis (Fairclough, 2003). In any social encounter, according to Harré and van Langenhove, people are positioned, or position themselves, in certain ways: for example, as speakers or listeners, or as insiders and outsiders. 'Positions' are not the same as 'roles': roles are more about job descriptions whereas positions are to do with relationships. Positions are therefore flexible and fluid, depending on the nature of the relationships and the interactions of participants. Relationships and positions are always created through what people say and do and how they say and do it (they are discursively constructed). Jørgensen and Phillips (2002: 1) comment that 'our ways of talking do not neutrally reflect our world, identities and social relations but, rather, play an active role in creating and changing them'. Writers in the field of critical discourse analysis, including Fairclough (2003) and Laclau and Mouffe (1985), also emphasise that we negotiate who we are and who we become through what we say and do; however, this calls for critical reflection because it may become a case of one person imposing their ideas on another.

Herr and Anderson (2005: 32–45) used these kinds of concepts in drawing up a typology of researcher positionalities in research:

- Insider, studying their own practices: this involves self-study, autobiography, ethnomethodology.
- Insider, working collaboratively with other insiders.
- Insider, working collaboratively with outsiders.
- Reciprocal collaboration between insider–outsider teams.
- Outsiders working collaboratively with insiders.
- Outsiders studying insiders.
- Multiple positionalities.

These issues have also given rise to different perspectives and terminologies in the action research literatures. Further, other issues about types of knowledge and theory enter the debate: these are developed in Chapter 2.

Now, consider different forms of action research within the action research community itself.

Different forms of action research and different names and terminology

Until about the 1980s action research was a reasonably integrated field and the action research family was quite close-knit: these days it has fragmented into different groups, sometimes looking like tribes, and these also tend to use their own language and occupy their own territories or sectors, such as work-based learning or higher education. Some believe that the proper way to do research is for an external researcher to watch and report on what other practitioners are doing, as on the film set cited earlier. This is generally referred to as second- or third-person action research (see below). It is probably still the most common form of action research around and is the main form used in higher education settings, although first-person accounts are becoming increasingly accepted. There are also those who believe that a practitioner is able to offer their own explanations for what they are doing. This is referred to variously as first-person action research or self-study action research. Many people link this form with autoethnography (for example, Hunt, 2016); this view links with the long tradition of autobiography as philosophy (see Mathien and Wright, 2006). However, the differences between outsider and insider groupings are often not clear, because people often tend not to take a definitive stance, but position themselves somewhere between the two.

What is notable, however, is the different forms of theory (explanations) used. As mentioned above, traditionalist forms of theory tend to offer explanations about what 'they' are doing, and take a more conceptual form: they also tend to speak about action research as a technique to be applied. Person-centred forms of theory are more about what 'I' am doing as a living person. 'I' speak about action research as something I do, part of 'my' experience. 'My' theories take on a dynamic transformational form: the explanations the person offers for their life and practices are within the way they live and practise. So it is quite common nowadays to understand the word 'theory' in two ways: as an abstract propositional form about what is happening for other people, and as an embodied personal form about what is happening for me.

The language and definitions of action research are also in transition.

Reason and Bradbury (2008), for example, have developed a useful typology, which they call 'first-, second- and third-person action research'. They say that 'First-person research is the kind of research that enables the researcher to foster an inquiring approach to his or her own life, to act choicefully and with awareness, and to assess effects in the outside world while acting ...', that second-person research is when the practitioner can 'inquire face-to-face with others into issues of mutual concern ...', and that third-person research looks at influencing wider social systems, and to create '... a wider community of inquiry involving persons who, because they cannot be known to each other ... have an impersonal quality' (2008: 6). Others speak about participatory action research: this term was first used when action research came to prominence around the 1940s and 1950s and referred to groups who wished to reclaim lands and property taken from them; it was associated with the work of Orlando Fals Borda and shares the same heritage as scholars such as Paulo Freire. Today, the vocabulary of participatory action research continues to be used when emphasising the participative and collaborative nature of action research.

Other names, reflecting political commitments or positioning, include feminist participatory action research (Reid and Frisby, 2008), educational action research, practitioner action research and practice-based action research. At a tangent there is action learning, which emphasises the actions of work-based learning rather than theory-generation (though action learning is shifting more and more towards action research these days), and action science, which takes a more scientific stance towards demonstrating causal relationships. Furthermore, many of these different groupings cross over or draw on other traditions such as narrative enquiry, appreciative enquiry and complexity theory, so it is difficult to see where one piece of scholarly territory ends and another begins.

Added to this, many people within these groupings prefer to speak only about reflective practice. However, taken on its own, reflective practice could be seen as people reflecting on what they are doing without necessarily taking action to improve it. You can sit all day reflecting on what you are doing but this is no use when trying to improve social situations with justification, which means drawing on a research base that demands personal accountability.

So here is a wonderful rich tapestry of people, all working with the same purpose of finding how to create a more socially just world from their different values and methodological commitments, and united in terms of what they stand for and against. It would be difficult for any beginning researcher to enter this world and immediately make sense of who is doing what and why, because there is no clearly delineated route map, and people who are active in the field move around and change perspective. Perhaps the best advice for beginning action researchers is to read as much as possible and keep a level head when dealing with different terminology. Keep in mind also that the key issues are about the politics of knowledge and theory, namely who counts as a knower, who is able to offer explanations, and about what, what counts as knowledge, and who makes decisions about these things. Keep in mind the difference between visions and interests and what Sowell said (1987: 8): 'We will do almost anything for our visions, except think about them'. Sowell's aim was to get people to think about their visions and why they hold them. This book does the same.

It is especially rewarding to see the same kind of commitment to diversity in community and to critical thinking reflected at an organisational level, too, as shown in the following accounts.

Pen Green, UK. Felicity Norton, Deputy Head of Centre and Coordinator of the Research, Training and Development base and Teaching School, writes:

'Pen Green, an integrated children's centre, nursery school, research and training base, established in 1983, is located in Corby, Northamptonshire, a former steel town with a rapidly rising though disadvantaged population. The centre offers high quality early years education and care, adult education, family support, health services, research and development, a range of short courses and higher education courses from Foundation Degree to PhD. The research base was established in 1996 to promote practitioner research in the early years. It now also has a strong publishing base.

'The content of Pen Green's programmes is influenced by constructivist approaches to teaching and learning for children and adults. This reflects a belief in engaging parents, families, the wider community and other agencies and professionals in equal and respectful partnerships. The multidisciplinary staff team, including teachers, social workers, health workers and early years practitioners, have developed a model of cooperative working that respects the learning and support needs of parents, and their children's right to high quality early years education with care. The Centre is recognised nationally and internationally for its commitments to developing quality services for children and their families, and to developing leadership capacity throughout organisations and across the sector. This same commitment is reflected throughout the development of its programmes and its focus on specific teaching and learning strategies, including:

- the central importance of personal experience in learning;
- the importance of the learning climate;
- the involvement of learners in the identification of learning needs;
- the involvement of learners in the development of the learning experience, with tutors acting as guides and content resources;
- the mutual responsibility of learners and teachers for managing and developing learning experiences.

These principles acknowledge important factors relating to learner aspiration, commitment, motivation and involvement. All teaching teams are committed to an approach that encourages self-reflection, action research, and respect for practical wisdom.'

The Early Learning Initiative (Dublin, Ireland). Josephine Bleach, Director writes (adapted from Bleach, 2016):

'The Early Learning Initiative (ELI) is a community-based educational project in the National College of Ireland (NCI), and shares the learning from its action research-based process with local, national and international audiences. We, at ELI, believe that, if our work and action research as a methodological approach to organisational and community development are to influence wider practices, policy and theory, the learning from the process needs to be shared with others. A core element of this is to show how we learned together to realise our underpinning values as living practices ... The NCI is an Irish third level learning, teaching and research institution, with a long-standing commitment to widening participation in higher education (Bleach, 2013). As a third-level provider, it has a unique relationship with its local community in the Dublin Docklands and believes that early intervention is critical if educationally disadvantaged young people and their families from the area are to access third level education. The ELI is an integral part of NCI's mission to "change lives through education" (ELI, 2012). It is a potent symbol in its local community, providing pre-school, primary and second level students and their families with a visual reminder that they have a right to third level education and that with support it is within their reach.'

This brings us to ideas about the purposes of research in general and action research in particular.

3. Purposes of action research

The purpose of all research is to generate new knowledge. Action research, as part of a life of enquiry, generates the kind of knowledge that contributes to sustainable personal, social and planetary wellbeing.

As noted above, the term 'action research' contains the words 'action' and 'research'. The action piece of action research is about taking action for improving practices. The 'research' piece of action research is about offering descriptions and explanations for what you are doing as and when you take action. Another word for 'descriptions and explanations' is 'theory'. Like all research, the purpose of action research is (1) to generate new knowledge, which (2) feeds into new theory. When you generate new knowledge, you say that you know something now that you did not know before: for example, 'I now know more about car mechanics', or 'I understand better how to dance properly'. Saying that you know something is called a knowledge claim, or a claim to knowledge. You need this knowledge in order to explain what you are doing and why you are doing it (to theorise what you are doing). You say, 'I can describe and explain how and why I have learned about car mechanics' or 'I can describe and explain how and why it is important to dance properly'. Being able to explain what you are doing and why you are doing it also enables you to be clear about its significance for your field: this is important when it comes to saying why your research should be believed and taken seriously by others, especially peers.

By doing your action research you are hoping, therefore, to make knowledge claims such as the following:

- I have improved my practice as a teacher, and I can describe what I have done and explain why I have done it.
- I am a better manager than before because I have studied what I am doing, and I can explain how and why my practice is better.

Action research has always been understood as people taking action to improve their personal and social situations, and offering explanations for why they do so. Arendt (1958) states that 'action' is the highest form of human achievement and is the basis of liberal democracy: like Dewey (1933), she says that taking action involves active thinking. Some show the potentials of action research for achieving these aims through their work and writings (for example, Brydon-Miller, 2008; Heron and Reason, 2001; Noffke and Somekh, 2009). New work is emerging about ecoliteracy (Sinclair, 2017) and sustainable improvement (Chambers, 2008; Sterling, 2001). Educational action research is widely seen as a methodology for real-world social change. People communicate their ideas as theories of real-world practice, by explaining what they are doing, why they are doing it and what they hope to achieve. These personal theories are dynamic, in-the-world theories; they change and develop as people themselves change and develop. The aim of practitioners using an action research approach is to generate their personal and collective theories about how their learning has improved practices and is informing new practices for themselves and others.

The best accounts show the transformation of practice into personal theories. The individual practitioner asks, 'What am I doing? How do I understand it in order to improve it? How can I draw on ideas in the literature and incorporate these into my own understanding? How do I transform those ideas into action?' Asking these questions can help practitioners find practical ways of living in the direction of their educational and social values. The examples throughout this book show how this can be done, including this one from Sally Aston and Maria James, both of St Mary's University, Twickenham, UK:

VALUES: RHETORIC OR REALITY – LAMINATED OR LIVED?

'In our Pecha Kucha presentation, we share how we strive to live our values in our practice. If, as Gibbs says, this acknowledgement can develop "an inner knowing of being true to oneself in who we are" and an "inner peace in being meaningfully connected with self in time and place" (2006: 18), then this self-knowledge becomes an imperative on an organisational and individual basis. We have, historically, adopted our own personal values as standards of judgement for research, seeking to move from a state of incongruity to a greater sense of shalom and dynamic stability. This sense has begun to be developed in our professional practice through: articulating our educational values; striving to live more in the direction of them; and asking others to use them as standards of judgement by which our claims might be judged. A new potential initiative that we will introduce concerns the value and virtues of applying for the Values Based Education International Kitemark for our School of Education.'

4. When and when not to use action research

You can use action research for many purposes, but not for all.

When to use action research

Use action research when you want to evaluate whether your work is contributing to your own or other people's learning, or whether you need to do something different: you could see this as acting for yourself, for others and for the world. For example, you may want to do this for the following reasons.

- For yourself, to contribute to your understanding:

  o Patient waiting times in the hospital are too long. How are you going to find out why, so that you can do something about the situation?
  o Your students are achieving remarkably high scores. Why? Is it your teaching, their extra study, or a new classroom environment?

- For others, to contribute to their understanding:

  o How do you learn to encourage people to be more positive?
  o How do you learn to improve your own timekeeping?

- For the world, to contribute to wider thinking through the literatures and media:

  o How do you promote efforts to develop more inclusive pedagogies?
  o How do you communicate ideas about basic patient care?

When not to use action research

Do not use action research if you want to draw comparisons, show statistical correlations or demonstrate a cause-and-effect relationship. For example:

- You want to see whether adults who are accompanied by children are more likely to wait at pedestrian crossings than those who are not accompanied by children, so you would do an observational study and include statistical analyses of a headcount.
- You want to show the effects of good leadership on organisational motivation. You could interview a sample of employees and analyse their responses. You could probably also interview a sample of business leaders and get their opinions on the relationship between their leadership and the quality of employees' motivation.

These are standard social science topics where researchers ask questions of the kind, 'What are those people doing? What do they say? How many of them do it? How do we account for what they think?' Action research questions, however, take the form, 'How do I understand what I am doing? How do I improve it? How do I account for what I think?' They place the emphasis on the researcher's intent to take action for personal and social improvement.

A point to remember is that these kinds of social science topics can be included within practitioner-researchers' personal theories of practice. Action research projects that ask questions in the form of 'How do I ...?' usually (though not always) need to contain pieces of empirical research that respond to questions in the form of 'What is happening here?' This kind of fact-finding then acts as the basis for taking action to improve real-world situations.

Here is an example to show how 'How do I ...?' questions often begin with 'What is happening here?' questions, which then act as the basis for focused social action.

Table 1.1 Turning 'How do I ...?' questions into social intent

'How do I/we ...?' questions	'What is happening here?' questions	'What shall we do about it?' questions
How do I/we coordinate our adult community learning programme?	• How many colleagues are involved in the programme? • What is their background? • In what ways are they involved in the programme?	• What strategies will help us to coordinate our programme successfully? • How can we learn more about coordinating community learning programmes?
How do I/we encourage students to read more educational books?	• What kind of books do students read at present? • How many categories of books are in the college library? • How much time is given to independent reading in the curriculum?	• How do I/we encourage students to read more widely? • How do we persuade the librarian to buy in more educational books? • Can we as a team redevelop the curriculum to ensure a broader reading base?

Summary

This chapter has set out some core issues in action research. It has explained that, unlike traditionalist forms of social science, action research places the individual 'I' at the centre of an enquiry. Different forms of action research have emerged over the years which prioritise different aspects. Action research can be useful when investigating how to improve learning and take social action. It is inappropriate for investigations that aim to draw comparisons or establish cause-and-effect relationships.

The next chapter deals with the interesting and contested question of who can do action research, who says, and whose interests it serves to perpetuate mythologies.

——————— EXERCISES ———————

- Check that you are reasonably clear about what action research is and what it is not. Be aware that different books say different things, so what you are reading here is one person's view of action research. Decide for yourself: do you accept it or not? If so, why? If not, why not?
- Talk with your colleagues and see what they say. Do you agree with them? If so, why? If not, why not?
- Write out some 'outsider'- and 'insider'-type questions. Compare what you have written with what colleagues have written.
- Also write out two situations when you would not use an action research approach and two situations when you would.

Who can do action research?

Anyone and everyone can do action research. You do not need any specialised equipment or knowledge. All you need is curiosity, creativity and a willingness to ask critical questions of others and of yourself. You can do action research virtually anywhere – in institutional settings, in homes and on safaris.

Investigating your work and finding ways to improve it means that you now become a knowledge creator and an actor (recall Arendt's 1958 idea, outlined in Chapter 1, that the most important thing anyone can do is to think and act in relation to their commitments). This idea has implications for the politics of knowledge and action, because not all people would agree that workplace practitioners should be knowledge creators or actors. Some people think that practitioners should concern themselves only with workplace practices, and not get involved in research, generating knowledge or taking action in the social world. More enlightened others think that practitioners should credit themselves as working with their intellects and contributing to policy debates. All this amounts to practitioners turning a politics of resistance into a politics of action as they ask, 'What can we do about the situation?' The question also arises: whose interests are served by perpetuating the mythology that practitioners cannot do research, think for themselves or take focused action, or that those currently positioned as 'professional' academic researchers should not see themselves also as practitioners?

This chapter is organised into four sections, which address the following issues:

1. Who is a practitioner?
2. Why is practitioner knowledge important?
3. What is special about practitioners' theories of practice?
4. How can practitioners contribute to new practices and new theories?

The chapter provides examples of the realisation of what Rorty (1999) calls 'social hope', in that academics in higher education actively position themselves as practitioners working with so-called workplace practitioners to form communities of collaborative enquiry. This immediately raises the thorny question of 'Who is a practitioner?'

1. Who is a practitioner?

The contested nature of the territory is illustrated by a famous metaphor by Donald Schön about the topography of professional landscapes.

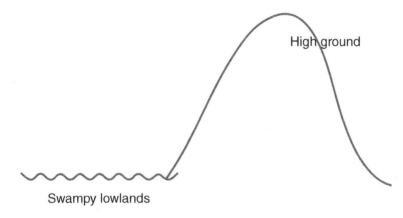

Figure 2.1 The topography of professional landscapes

The topography of professional landscapes

In his book *The Reflective Practitioner* (Schön, 1983: 42), and again in 1995, Schön developed a metaphor that was to become an enduring theme in the literatures, with special relevance for practitioner research. He wrote about the topography (the contours and different heights) of professional landscapes, where there is a high, hard ground and a swampy lowlands. The high ground is occupied mainly by those whom Schön calls 'intellectual elites', such as those university and organisational researchers who position themselves as 'experts' and produce 'pure' conceptual theory about disciplines such as nursing, education, management and other matters. This theory is regarded as legitimate both by themselves and by practitioners. Practitioners, such as nurses, teachers and shop-floor workers, occupy the swampy lowlands. They are involved in everyday practices and so create the kind of knowledge that is valuable for conducting everyday lives. However, it is held both by elites and by practitioners that practitioner knowledge should not be regarded as theory, nor should practitioners regard themselves as legitimate knowledge creators. In this metaphor, Schön returns us to the issues addressed earlier. The entire research community, including practitioner-researchers, have too often been persuaded to believe that there are 'real' theorists, desk-workers designated by higher institutional rank, who produce abstract conceptual theory, and there are shop-floor practitioners in workplaces, who create practical knowledge, which is useful knowledge but not 'real' theory. The irony for Schön is that the knowledge produced in the swampy lowlands is the kind of knowledge that is of most benefit for everyday living, while the knowledge produced on the high ground is often far removed from the practicalities of everyday living, and so often does not touch ordinary people in a meaningful and relevant way. Its remoteness is accentuated by the kind of language used. Professional elites tend to use their own language to talk to one another. This language can often be obscure and in code, and in Schön's opinion (which is shared by other researchers such as Jenkins, 1992; and Thomas, 1998) the elites deliberately keep it that way.

Schön maintains that practitioners in the swampy lowlands should create their own knowledge through investigating their practices, and submit their emergent personal theories to the same rigorous processes of testing and critique as happens in the creation of high-ground theory. This would be important if practitioners wanted to demonstrate the validity of their arguments, and have their ideas accepted as bone fide theory by the high-ground research community and the wider public.

Schön's ideas have been influential over the years, and still hold true in many quarters today, but things have changed considerably with the advent of action research. In some places the topography is beginning to level out. Many people working in higher education and managerial positions now perceive themselves as practitioners in a workplace with responsibility for supporting people in other workplaces, while also generating their personal theories of practice about how they do this. Self-study forms of action research and autoethnography, as recognised forms of practice, have legitimised the positioning of those practitioners who are supporting other practitioners, and creating democratic communities of practice committed to a scholarship of educational enquiry.

This changing topography has highlighted the need for all to regard themselves as practitioners and to study their practice collaboratively, in a disciplined and scholarly way, and to make their accounts of practice public, so that others in their communities and elsewhere can learn and benefit. Here are some examples to show the realities of these situations. They are significant in that higher education practitioners identify themselves as knowledge workers alongside other knowledge workers whose studies they support (as do the academic practitioners in Pen Green and the ELI, outlined in Chapter 1).

This example comes from Andy Convery who has been working for the last ten years as a University Programme Leader, managing a partnership of college tutors who, in their roles as teacher-trainers, have been teaching pedagogical skills to trainee vocational teachers in order to help them teach their crafts to young people. Arrangements like these are significant because the form and quality of knowledge gained through Vocational Education and Training are generally deemed as of lower status than knowledge acquired at universities, as are its associated colleges. However, while it was initially Andy's responsibility to ensure that the tutors 'delivered' the programme according to university specifications, it became obvious that those tutors' existing expertise from their experience of vocational teaching was being systematically overlooked in the university-designed programme. Andy and the college tutors therefore decided to co-develop a collaborative project to investigate an issue of national concern in vocational teaching, namely, 'How could they help trainee teachers to develop confidence in promoting diversity in their vocational teaching?' The partnership tutors and Andy together identified and further developed pedagogical practices relevant for different settings. These included changing the existing university-designed assignments to include learner-centred strategies to help trainee teachers think more actively about diversity. The tutors' teaching of diversity to trainee teachers was officially recognised at their next government inspection as the outstanding strength of the programme. The team also presented their work at conferences, thus helping them strengthen their self-identifications as research professionals.

The implications for recognition and accreditation are considerable. Those who are not seeking accreditation for work-based learning come to be regarded as competent and capable professionals. Those who are seeking accreditation come to be seen as practitioner academics whose studies are supported by fellow academic practitioners. Any previously existing hierarchies of power between academics and practitioners are demolished, and power is shared among equals for the benefit of others. While this may seem like a pipe-dream to some, it has been made a reality by the likes of Andy Convery and his colleagues.

2. Why is practitioner knowledge important?

Practitioner knowledge is central to practical and theoretical evolution. To help appreciate why and how this may be the case it can be helpful to think about how knowledge can take many different forms. At a minimum you need to know about three forms: know-that, know-how and personal knowledge:

- **Know-that**, also called propositional and technical rational knowledge, is to do mainly with facts and figures. Knowledge exists 'out there', separate from the knower, whose job is to discover it and pass it on to others. Know-that is the most valued form in most institutional settings, and especially beloved in higher education contexts. Demonstrating the validity of factual knowledge claims means producing empirical data to show what is happening in a situation.
- **Know-how**, also called procedural knowledge, refers to procedures, skills and technical capabilities, and involves practical procedural knowing. 'I know how to do this' refers to actions in the world; the validity of knowledge claims can be tested by, for example, demonstrating that you can ride a bike or draw pictures.
- **Personal knowledge**, also linked with tacit knowledge (Polanyi, 1958, 1967), refers to a subjective, intuitive form of knowing that comes from contact with the living world. This kind of knowledge cannot be rationalised. Often we cannot articulate what we know: we just know. Polanyi (1967) uses the example that we can identify a person's face out of a million other faces, though we cannot explain how we have done this. Try asking someone how it is that they can touch their nose without looking, or how a pianist knows when a note sounds just right.

In many academic and organisational contexts these forms of knowledge are put into hierarchies, with know-that at the top and personal knowledge at the bottom. Sadly this is happening more and more in many professions in the UK and elsewhere: for example, nursing, which has become an elitist profession requiring university accreditation, prioritises know-that; the profession has moved away both from the personal knowledge of hands-on care and from the patient, whose needs are now largely attended to by unqualified healthcare assistants, supervised by a qualified nurse.

Practitioners doing action research acknowledge the value of all kinds of knowledge. They draw on abstract propositional knowledge and theories as they produce their personal theories of practice. In the example above, through developing innovative teaching strategies, the tutors were able both actively to test the appropriateness of established theories-in-the-literatures about Diversity Education, and also develop their own personal and collective theories of Diversity Education.

It is this kind of internal capacity that gives action research its strength for theoretical evolution. Evolution refers to the idea that living systems have the internal capacity for independent and interdependent self-renewal: this is also a core feature of complexity theory (Lewin, 1993; Waldrop, 1992; Wheatley, 1992). Reliance on any external agency means that a system may collapse if that agency is withdrawn, whereas internal capacity implies the creation of renewable resources for growth.

Practitioners' personal theories constitute these renewable resources. All are free to say what needs to be done to enable themselves and others to grow in ways that are right for them. This was the idea that first inspired action research as a methodology for social change. Lewin (1946), one of the originators of the idea of action research, believed that if all members of a workforce were involved collaboratively in creating and implementing strategy, the organisation itself would grow. This view has been further developed by a range of respected theorists, including:

- Amartya Sen (1999), winner of the 1998 Nobel Prize in Economic Science, who talks about the need to move from seeing the development of capital in primarily monetary terms to seeing it as a process in which human beings take ownership of the production of their own futures.
- Richard Rorty (1999), who believes that research should not only be about creating knowledge for its own sake but also should be used for developing new futures. Knowledge thereby becomes a resource for social hope.
- Hannah Arendt (1958), who also argues that power lies in the conversational power of people when they come together to plan how they might organise their own lives (she also says that when power is vested in the hands of an individual or a minority it becomes violence).

Yet while it is possible to speak analytically about different kinds of knowledge, as is happening here, in reality knowledge cannot exist without knowers, and knowledge emerges in a whole range of ways, primarily through dialogue. Dialogue occurs when we speak with others, whether in face-to-face conversations or at a distance through emails and other social media, and with ourselves, as when we talk to ourselves or write or think. Dialogue is different from simple conversation in that it involves actively listening to the other (even when the other is oneself) and trying to achieve mutual understanding. We create knowledge through conversation at several levels: we can create factual knowledge about a topic, or procedural knowledge about the process of speaking with the other; and the experience of sharing ideas can be a form of knowledge creation, too. We think differently when we are in dialogue with another: conversation itself becomes the site for the creation of new knowledge.

Look at what Walker and Solvason (2014: 2) write about why early years researchers should study their own practices:

It is important that [practitioner-researchers should take] an appreciative stance, building upon existing strengths and looking for areas of further development. These areas for improvement apply foremost to yourselves as developing professionals but also to the settings within which you practise, as conduits of quality early years practice. As students, research can enhance your knowledge, understanding and practice, and improve your employability prospects. Settings can be encouraged to embed a culture of research within their day-to-day practice, so that the quality of practice can be enhanced and developed in light of new discoveries. Rather than be a rite of passage, research can become a meaningful undertaking, which continues throughout your career, a skill that is central to early years practice and essential if we are to develop and improve practice for children and families.

Action research has this self-transforming capacity. Practitioners can show how they have contributed to new practices, and how these new practices can transform into new theory. When researchers claim that they have generated new theory, they are saying that they have created knowledge that never existed before. Perhaps pieces of knowledge existed, but what practitioners do with that knowledge and how they have reconfigured it in relation to their own contexts can be seen as their original theorising. This capacity for ongoing creativity contributes greatly to theoretical evolution.

3. What is special about practitioners' theories?

The basis for many practitioners' research is that they are trying to live in the direction of their educational values. If they hold values of justice and compassion, they will try to live in a way that is just and compassionate. They will make practical judgements about the extent to which they can show they are living in the direction of these values.

The Vocational Teaching team, supported by Andy, decided to investigate collaboratively the extent to which they, as teacher-lecturers, were promoting diversity: their longer-term goal was to publish their work and raise the status of their students, themselves and the profession. To start the process, they wrote short accounts of their current teaching practices. Through their writing, reading and discussions they began to question whether they had actually positively tackled racial discrimination and gender inequality: they started to question both their practices (what they were doing) and their values (why they were doing it). They began critically to review and revise those practices and reconsider their values; this led them to change their teaching strategies and focus more on developing empathy rather than technical skills. While they were thus able to develop their propositional knowledge (about the need for inclusion) and their procedural knowledge (teaching strategies for raising awareness), they could do this only through improving their personal knowledge of different contextualising factors. This personal knowledge, generated through and tested in practice, then came to stand as a contribution to the public fund of factual knowledge with potential for informing other practitioners' practices.

(Continued)

(Continued)

Similarly, Jill Wickham, a physiotherapist and university lecturer in physiotherapy, has strong commitments to the capacity of practising physiotherapists to celebrate their practical work-based knowledge. She found that many student physiotherapists could not see the relationship between the practical knowledge they gained on placements in the workplace and the disciplines-based knowledge communicated at the university. This situation denied Jill's values of social justice, and she now works hard to encourage students to appreciate how the theory–practice gap can be demolished. By encouraging them to see their knowledge as integrated, and to learn how to incorporate disciplines-based knowledge into their practical theorising, Jill is contributing to new discourses both in placement contexts and in the university. Furthermore, she is influencing colleagues in the university to appreciate that different forms of knowledge can be integrated within professional education curricula, and she is actively influencing a reconceptualisation of physiotherapy education for a curriculum for higher education within the university.

Like Andy and Jill, many practitioners work in contexts where their values of social and epistemological justice and compassion are denied in practice. Nor are external forces the only sources of this denial. Most of us often deny our own values by acting in a way that is contrary to what we believe in. We then put our best efforts into trying to practise in a way that is consistent with our values, and we assess the quality of our work in those terms. We gather data and generate evidence that we believe show instances of ourselves at work with others in ways that accord with our values, such as justice and compassion, and we invite critical feedback on our perceptions. If other people agree that we are acting in accordance with our values, we can claim greater validity for our knowledge claims as we put those claims forward for public consideration.

This is a rigorous and stringent research process that can be seen as systematic enquiry and an uncompromising testing of the validity of knowledge claims. The account that a practitioner produces contains descriptions of the research (what was done) and explanations (why it was done and what was aimed for). This account then constitutes the practitioner's own personal theory of practice: they can describe what they are doing and explain why they are doing it.

4. How can practitioners contribute to new practices and new theories?

Appadurai (1996: 167) maintains that it is the right of all people to do research. Contrary to its being seen as only a 'high-end, technical activity, available by training and class background to specialists in education, the sciences and related fields', he believes that research should be seen as a right, 'albeit of a special kind'. Research, he says:

Is a specialised name for a generalised capacity, the capacity to make disciplined inquiries into those things we need to know, but do not know yet. All human beings are, in this sense, researchers, since all human beings make decisions that require them to make systematic forays beyond their current knowledge horizons. (1996: 167)

I agree. I also believe that it is the right and, moreover, the responsibility of all, especially professional practitioners, to research, to generate personal theories of practice and to make explicit how and why they have done so. Doing research that enables us to find ways of living our values in practice helps to give meaning to our lives. This view debunks the popular belief that 'theory' is something mysterious, which it is not. We will often say things like 'I have a theory about cats', or 'This is my theory about the way things work'. A theory is a set of ideas about what we claim to know and how we have come to know it. If we can show that our claim to have theorised our practices stands up to public scrutiny in relation to agreed criteria and standards of judgement, we can claim that our claim (and thus our theory) has validity (i.e. has truth value and is trustworthy).

By doing your research, you can claim to have generated your personal theory of practice: that is, you can say with confidence that you know what you are doing and why you are doing it. You are showing that you are acting in a systematic way, not ad hoc, and that you are developing a praxis, which is morally committed practice.

Andy Convery asks: 'What does practitioner action research look like?' He provides the following examples from the research that colleagues and he undertook to encourage more effective working practices by removing some of the existing mental and physical barriers that divided people and their forms of knowledge.

Simon

Whilst studying for his BA in Education and Training, Simon worked as a Physical Training Instructor in a secure forensic psychiatric setting. He wanted to find ways to help patients make best use of the unit's gym facilities to maximise their independence, yet could not understand why so few chose to use the facilities: they just watched television and seemed continually bored. Through interviewing patients, Simon quickly discovered that they felt dis-couraged from using the gym because this appeared to annoy the staff. On further investi-gating staff behaviour, he discovered that the gym was often the last facility to be opened and the first to be closed by staff (including himself): this was because they had to maintain strict institutional schedules. He therefore worked with a small group of gym users to set up a patient-led Activities Committee; they suggested developing more organised timetabled activities to encourage greater use of the gym through enhanced access. When he explained his findings to his colleagues they agreed to keep the gym open for longer periods. Simon's research had alerted the staff to the taken-for-granted nature of organisational practices.

Simon's example illustrates how an individual can research and develop their working knowledge to enable an organisation to fulfil its mission of rehabilitation, recovery and the maintenance of human dignity for some of the most marginalised in society.

Sarah

Sarah was an experienced hospital Ward Manager teaching on a College Access course designed to prepare adults who now wished to go to university. She wanted to investigate why there was a high initial dropout from the otherwise successful programme. She began

(Continued)

(Continued)

by asking some current students whether they had ever considered dropping out. They responded that the critical decision point for students was the receipt of their first feedback on a university-level assignment. It appeared that a major barrier for students was not their knowledge of curriculum content but the difficulties of understanding the academic requirements of university-designed tasks. Sarah therefore initiated a strategy of preparing for assignments by helping adults to develop their own ways of interpreting assessment criteria and 'translating' these into their own language. Some, however, did not want to acknowledge what appeared as a lack of competence, so Sarah organised small groups to discuss how to involve all the participants in their learning; this helped her to offer them more constructive guidance and practical help. Following this initiative, more assignments were submitted on time, with fewer instances of work being referred. In follow-up interviews, the mature students said they felt more confident about which study skills were needed to undertake a university degree programme.

Sarah's example shows what can happen when a higher education practitioner investigates her practice collaboratively with participants. By becoming aware that academic cultures as well as academic content could create barriers for learners' progression, Sarah was able to interrogate her own assumptions and begin to change her practices. She also demonstrated how a reflective action research approach requires an imaginative response to emerging situations.

These are not isolated examples. Increasingly thoughtful and far-sighted educators and administrators in senior positions are working with groups of practitioners and collecting bodies of case study evidence to show the potentials for social change. Look at the work of Joseph Shosh here.

This example is from Dr Joseph Shosh, Professor & Chair, Moravian College Department of Education, and Executive Committee Chair, Action Research Network of the Americas.

'At Moravian College, we agree with Lawrence Stenhouse's (1981) notion that every teacher must have the opportunity to be intimately involved in the research process, so my colleagues and I have developed a graduate program in which every teacher is a researcher. Each semester, more than 100 educators in our eastern Pennsylvania community inquire into their professional practice to begin to answer the questions about teaching and learning that matter most to them, their colleagues, and the young people they serve in our local schools. Knowledge to support student engagement and achievement inside and outside the classroom is constructed through careful analysis of data gleaned through participant observation, surveys, interviews, and student artifacts as teachers engage in dialogue with one another and the authors of published research studies, first and foremost of which are the formal action research reports in the form of new Master of Education thesis studies that are added to the permanent collection each year and freely available for download at www.moravian.edu/education/research.

'Teachers document how the process of conducting their own research improves their professional practice and deepens their thinking about teaching and learning. They question the traditional notion of knowledge existing objectively in isolation outside of the knower and construct their own theoretically rich, practice-based accounts to share what they have learned with colleagues both inside and far beyond our community.

'My own research into my professional practice has continued to evolve as I have studied the influence of my curricular design on the action research projects of teachers, conducted a meta-thematic analysis of the nearly 200 published studies that teachers have authored in our program to date, and examined the university's role in supporting teacher research after master's degree completion. I am currently working with a cadre of teachers who have been designated Leadership Lehigh Valley Teacher Research Fellows to explore character education in our schools and new notions of participatory action research to help our community of nearly one million residents deepen its understanding of and commitment to educating the whole child.'

The examples in this chapter show how practitioners can improve their practices through thoughtful reflection and dialogue with others, and especially by becoming aware of the need to take others' feelings and circumstances into consideration. They also show how practitioners' practical theories of practice can provide a body of evidence that may contribute to wider understandings of the nature of educational practices, with implications for further widespread take-up both in the profession and in public life. On page 44 we consider the idea of 'generalisability' as one of the key criteria proposed by the traditionalist research community for judging quality in research. While many practitioners would not claim that their work is 'generalisable' in that it can be applied to all like situations, they would agree it is generalisable in that others can learn with and from stories of practice and adopt or adapt these to their own practices as deemed appropriate. This is where the power of action research lies, in the capacity of people who come together to find ways of creating better futures.

Now consider how you might do this yourself.

Summary

This chapter has set out a debate about the politics of knowledge, in relation to who should be regarded as a practitioner, and who decides. It has addressed the following questions:

- Who is a practitioner?
- Why is practitioners' knowledge important?
- What is special about practitioners' theories of practice?
- How can practitioners contribute to new practices and new theories?

The chapter maintains that all people who are involved in learning and influencing the learning of others should regard themselves as practitioners, regardless of role or setting.

The next chapter develops some of these ideas by considering some of the main features of action research and their underpinning assumptions.

---------------------------- **EXERCISES** ----------------------------

- Think about how you identify yourself in a workplace or everyday life situation. Do you see yourself as a practitioner? As a researcher? If so, why? If not, why not?
- Explain the importance of these issues to your colleagues. Say whether you have ever experienced the exercise of the politics of knowledge in your workplace or in an everyday life situation.
- Explain to your colleagues why their and your personal theories of practice are important. In what ways are these different from traditionalist perspectives? In what ways are these special?
- Write out your theory of practice and how this can contribute to other people's understandings.

The values base of action research

Although anyone and everyone can do action research, as noted earlier, deciding whether to do it, or what kind to do, depends on certain factors. These include being clear about the values that inform your everyday practices and your research stance, interrogating whether these values may conflict with your personal, social or institutional interests, and if so, deciding how you will deal with the issues. Also important to note is that the socially oriented values base of action research has changed in recent times. Given ongoing trends towards a global neo-liberalist market culture, many institutions, including universities, have adopted a technical instrumental rather than pluralistic perspective; this inevitably influences the nature of their programmes. Action research is caught up in this. Whereas the traditional values of action research included commitments to collaboration and mutual understanding, today those commitments are now equal to the achievement of outcomes and self-service. You need to be aware of these issues, given that you are in an institutional context, since they will influence your choice of research design.

This means that, before you begin a project, you will need to think about the values that inform your work and what you hope to achieve through doing the research. For example, you will need to decide whether you wish to adopt a safe stance by showing how, through doing action research, you identify and achieve specific outcomes, or whether you wish to pursue a more adventurous path, perhaps by challenging orthodox stances in the literatures or by using innovative forms of expression such as poetry or artwork in your dissertation. If so you will need to be confident both about what you are doing and the expectations of your accrediting institution. These are political choices that carry risk. Therefore, considering the overall values base of action research may help you make sense of what you are doing and give you a firm basis for decisions.

The chapter is in two sections:

1. Reasons, aims, purposes and values in action research
2. The contested values base of action research

In this book I focus on how action research can be a way of giving deep meaning to working with others in the interests of a more just and compassionate society. The case studies are of real-life people who have undertaken action enquiries.

1. Reasons, aims, purposes and values in action research

Before committing to an action research approach, consider what is involved methodologically in all kinds of research, including action research, how this distinguishes research as research and not just activity, and how specific values inform your choices. The basic action steps of research are as follows (there are many other refinements but this list will do for now).

- Identify a research issue.
- Identify the research aims.
- Draw up a research design (and plan).
- Gather data.
- Establish criteria and standards of judgement.
- Analyse and interpret the data.
- Come to some provisional conclusions (findings).
- Make a claim to knowledge.
- Submit the claim to critique.
- Explain the significance of the research.
- Disseminate the findings.
- Modify practices in light of the evaluation.
- Link new knowledge with existing knowledge.
- Evaluate the findings.

Now consider how these action steps are informed by specific values (Table 3.1 provides an overview of this schema and its relevance to action research).

Table 3.1 Reasons, aims, purposes and values in research

Research action: what do you do?	Reason for the action: why do you do it?	Purpose of the action: what do you wish to achieve?	Values that inform action research
Identify a research issue.	Be clear about what you hope to find out.	To clarify what the research focus is.	Openness: Need for clarity about why you think the topic is important.

Research action: what do you do?	Reason for the action: why do you do it?	Purpose of the action: what do you wish to achieve?	Values that inform action research
Identify research aims.	To establish the importance of investigating the area.	To say what you hope to achieve through doing the research.	Reflection: Need to articulate your own aims and purposes in doing the research.
Draw up a research design (plan).	To explain how you are going to do the research.	Need to outline practicalities and considerations: e.g. What will you do? Who will be involved? Why them? Which methodology?	Responsibility: Need to be clear about the scope and range of the research.
Gather data.	To gather empirical and subjective data to show what is happening.	Aim to show the situation as it is and as it develops; explain who your data sources are, data-gathering strategies, why you have selected these and not others.	Exercising attention: Gathering data prepares for the generation of evidence that will ground knowledge claims.
Establish criteria and standards of judgement.	Criteria and standards will be central to analysing and interpreting the data for generating evidence and testing the validity of knowledge claims.	Clarify how judgements may be made about procedures for analysis and interpretation in testing the validity of knowledge claims.	Justification for procedures in testing validity of knowledge claims.
Analyse and interpret the data.	To begin to make sense of the data and explore their meanings.	Come to some provisional conclusions about the quality of the research by reading the data critically.	Integrity in analysis and interpretation of data for deeper understanding.
Come to some provisional conclusions (findings).	To begin to draw some provisional conclusions and reach a point of consolidation.	Consolidate thinking and begin to reach provisional conclusions for future thinking and action.	Wisdom of pausing to consolidate thinking in order to provide justification for developing particular ideas and themes.
Make a claim to knowledge.	Need to be clear about what the research is about and whether aims have been achieved.	Need to show understanding that research is about knowledge production; make a contribution to knowledge of the field.	Development of insight through emphasising that research is about knowledge creation and mobilisation.

(Continued)

Table 3.1   (Continued)

Research action: what do you do?	Reason for the action: why do you do it?	Purpose of the action: what do you wish to achieve?	Values that inform action research
Submit the claim to critique.	Need to invite critical feedback on own conclusions.	Avoid making unwarranted claims based on personal opinion; demonstrate awareness of different values positions in the field.	Respect for truth and integrity; demonstrate readiness to act on feedback as appropriate.
Explain the significance of the research.	Need to show that research topic is not trivial.	Show the importance of the topic and its relevance for others' thinking and practices.	Explicitness through sharing the learning for development of own and others' thinking and practices.
Disseminate the findings.	Need to make research findings public; need to inform others.	Communicate the importance of the topic and research to others; make a contribution to knowledge of the field.	Collaboration through involvement of the wider research community in considering the legitimacy of the research for the field of ideas.
Evaluate the findings.	Need to evaluate findings in light of possible critique.	Show the importance of avoiding dogmatism and prejudice.	Responsibility in holding knowledge lightly and maintaining an open mind.
Link new knowledge with existing knowledge.	Demonstrate awareness of existing knowledge of the field and others' perspectives and viewpoints; engagement with the literatures.	Show legitimacy of new knowledge.	Inclusion of others' voices: show research as a collaborative evolutionary practice; show willingness to change perspectives in light of developing insights.
Modify practices in light of the evaluation.	Develop critical stance and new, more context-appropriate, practices.	Need to ensure relevance of new knowledge for the field; need to link practice and theory.	Commitment to new forms; ongoing adaption of knowledge to new scenarios.

Doing this kind of exercise can help you clarify the values base of your research and also show how those values come to act as the golden thread that runs through your research. This idea of a golden thread comes from the Greek legend of Theseus who had to find his way through a maze in order to free prisoners who had been captured by the Minotaur. Ariadne, the goddess who loved Theseus, gave him a golden thread to tie to the entrance so that he could safely retrace his steps. You too will need to wind this golden thread through your research to show how it should be seen as an integrated whole, how your findings and conclusions link with your aims and questions. If your question is 'How do I encourage more democratic practices in our organi-sation?', your research claim would be 'I have encouraged more democratic practices in our organisation'. You would then produce evidence, generated from your data, to show that this statement was believable and not just your opinion. Your research programme would then take the form as shown in Table 3.2 (where the value of participation is used as a running example).

Table 3.2 The place of values in research

Research action: what do you do?	How does your research develop?	Where do values feature in the research?
Identify a research issue.	You identify a research issue to do with lack of participation in organisational planning.	Participation becomes the value that inspires your research.
Identify research aims.	You aim to find ways to involve more people in organisational planning.	Increasing the amount of participation becomes the aim of your research.
Draw up a research design and action plan.	You design the research and draw up an action plan to show how you will involve more people in organisational planning.	The value of participation informs your research design and research plan.
Gather data.	You gather an initial data set to show the amount of participation in action; you take action to encourage more participation; you continue to gather data to show whether participation has increased.	You show how values inform your data-gathering methods.
Establish criteria and standards of judgement.	You identify your values as criteria and standards of judgement: you ask, 'Can I show participation in this event? How much participation is there? What kind of participation?'	Values transform into criteria and standards of judgement.
Analyse and interpret data.	You analyse and interpret the data according to your own identified categories of analysis. You ask, 'Which instances of data show participation in action? How do these instances give meaning to the data and research by showing the realisation of my values?'	Values inform categories of analysis to help you solicit meaning from the data about the extent of the realisation of values.
Come to some provisional conclusions.	You begin to come to some provisional conclusions about the success of your research in terms of demonstrating the achievement of greater participation.	Values are demonstrated to have emerged through practice and thereby give further meaning to the practice in question.
Make a claim to knowledge.	You claim that you have engaged fully with your original research question: that you have encouraged greater participation in organisational planning.	Showing how the value of participation has been realised in practice becomes a core feature of knowledge claims.

(Continued)

Table 3.2   (Continued)

Research action: what do you do?	How does your research develop?	Where do values feature in the research?
Submit the claim to critique.	You invite others to scrutinise your research and get their critical feedback: you stay true to the value of participation throughout the evaluation process.	The value of participation becomes a key principle in processes of critical feedback.
Explain the significance of the research.	You explain why participation is important for organisational planning.	The value of participation acts as a conceptual framework for demonstrating the significance of the research and for the concept of participation.
Disseminate the findings.	You make your findings public: this means handing in your assignment to your supervisor or getting it published as an article or book: or you can identify a wider audience who may like to read your research report.	Participation of all stakeholders and the wider public is important for disseminating your research findings.
Evaluate the findings.	You invite responses from a wider audience about the potentials of your research for developing their own thinking, for themselves, for others, and for the world.	The value of participation becomes a core feature of debates about the need for pluralism and multicultural understanding.
Link new knowledge with existing knowledge.	Your research is approved and your text is placed on the institution's library shelves.	Your make a contribution to knowledge of the field of how to develop participative ways of working.
Modify practices in light of the evaluation.	You show how you have learned about participation through doing your research, especially through working with others.	The value of participation remains central to your work; you continue to find ways of demonstrating how you have realised your value in action.

Also, remember that values are contestable: some people value things that others don't.

At a 2015 presentation at the British Educational Research Association meeting I asked a group of academics 'Would you give Al Capone a PhD?' Their responses were varied, including the following:

- Yes, if he demonstrated methodological rigour.
- Yes, but he would have to produce evidence in support of his knowledge claims.

A discussion also ensued about whether the quality of practices should inform decisions about granting awards. Do gangsters' practices warrant a doctorate? Who decides? The debate was later continued on social media by participants at the meeting under the heading 'Great Ethical Question'.

2. The contested values base of action research

So, given that values inspire our commitments yet are always contested, it may help to think about which values inspire your own research commitments: here are some important areas to think about:

1. Ontological commitments.
2. Epistemological commitments.
3. Methodological commitments.
4. Social commitments.

Ontological commitments

Ontology is the study of being, and is strongly linked with values: you can say, 'My ontological commitments are that I value the environment'. Our ontologies influence how we view ourselves in relation with others. The ontological commitments that underpin action research include the following:

- Action research acknowledges its democratic and egalitarian values base.
- Action research is morally committed.
- Action research is dialogical, inclusional and relational.

Action research acknowledges its democratic and egalitarian values base

Deciding to do research emphasises the need to think critically about different research approaches and not take things for granted. Most universities prefer an objective, traditionalist attitude where research is seen as values-neutral; the researcher stays out of the research so as not to contaminate the findings. This is of course not possible in any kind of research: a researcher is a human being who brings their values with them wherever they go. A traditionalist form of research is also abstract and technical, and aims to demonstrate a cause-and-effect relationship between variables of the form 'If I do this, that will happen'. Reports are usually written in the third person ('the researcher did'). You would use this kind of approach if you wanted to test, for example, the effectiveness of a particular plant food: you would apply the plant food to an experimental group of tomato plants to see if they yielded bigger, better and more tomatoes in comparison with a control group. You would probably not use it if you were trying to improve a practical issue, such as 'How do I manage my finances this week?' Action research acknowledges the importance of subjectivity: authors such as Gadamer (2004) and Senge and Scharmer (2001) emphasise that understanding others begins with understanding yourself as you try to live in the direction of your values.

Reasons for not realising values in practice can come from outside and inside. Sometimes we will deny our own values in practice: we may hold a value such as participation, yet not live according to the value, or we may believe in justice but act in an unjust way.

'My name is Baghran. I am a General Practitioner in a medium-sized southwest town in the UK. Patients often have multiple issues, which could benefit from my spending more time with them during appointments. This clashes with the mandatory requirements to see a certain number of patients in each session. How do I manage the conflicting demands?'

Action research is morally committed

Trying to live in the direction of your values can be difficult, because everything you do, including investigating your practice, involves other people who may have different values from yours. This then involves negotiating meanings and practices, which is easy to say but difficult to do. Al Capone had what many may have called unsociable values yet they were still values. Also, some people saw his practices as morally committed: for example, during the days of the Great Depression, he provided free meals for working men (Eig, 2010). Recognising the contested base of values is called 'agonistics': cruelty is a value as much as kindness and there is no Big Book of Values that tells you what to believe. It is up to you to decide which values you want to live by and be accountable for in negotiation with others who are trying to do the same.

Doing your action enquiry therefore involves explaining what inspires you to act as you do, and what you hope to achieve, in terms of what you understand as 'good' and 'better'. This can be tricky also when working in different cultures, which have their own values system. You have to decide which values system to live by. You may sometimes try to influence the culture because you find that your values are in conflict with it: this is bound to be difficult because, although it is emphasised throughout that there is no one set of 'foundational' values, you have to take a stand somewhere, which is in itself a fundamentalist position. Strong debates exist about these matters, including the justification of trying to impose your own values system on other people: for example, female genital mutilation (FGM) is a crime against women and thereby against humanity, perpetuated through the powerful discourses of male-oriented cultures whose interests FGM might serve, and it should be stopped.

Joyce Wambura (2016), a PhD candidate at York St John University, investigates how the role of discourse in FGM could influence efforts to end the practice and lead to positive change. She writes:

Drawing on critical discourse analysis (Fairclough, 2003, 2015), I seek to address the FGM issue by analysing traditional African female circumcision songs and examining ways in which linguistic choices are employed in elevating the circumcised while alienating the uncircumcised. Focus is on how, through discourse, FGM is normalised and advanced within a sociocultural system and how this, in turn, contributes to its perpetuation.

Whatever you decide, aim to make yours a purposeful, morally committed practice, that is, praxis. Also remember that you cannot hold yourself responsible for other people's decisions: they will decide for themselves. It is your responsibility to hold yourself accountable for yourself, and how you try to influence other people's learning. This has big implications. Do you do this in a coercive way, insisting that people listen to you, or in a more educational way, respecting others' points of view but inviting them to consider other options? This means carefully considering the importance of thinking critically, which is easily said but not so easily done.

Action research is dialogical, inclusional and relational

Action research is conducted in the real world: you are part of that world, together with the other people who inhabit it. Action research is therefore pluralistic and relational, and is grounded in empathetic other-oriented values (Dadds, 1995; Hay, 2006). Empathetic relationships inform the social world, where we are in relation with others, and also the mental world, where ideas exist in relation with other ideas.

Action researchers always see themselves in relation with others, with their ideas and with their environment: Bakhtin (1981) explains how everything is connected and in dialogue with everything else. In action research you do not adopt a spectator approach, or conduct experiments on others: you undertake enquiries with others. Even when we are alone, we are still in the company of others, who are perhaps absent in time and space, but their influence is evident. The pen or computer you are using was created by someone for someone else's use at some time. The ideas you express began as other people's ideas: you have now made them your own. You have mediated them through your unique capacity for creativity, reconfiguring them in your own original way. Your beginnings, which were in other people, now emerge as new beginnings, which other people will turn into their new beginnings and new opportunities. This idea was a key theme in the work of Hannah Arendt, who spoke about a person's natality, the capacity to bring something new to the world. She holds (1958) that we contribute to the world by our very birth. Contributing new ideas and practices for social development then becomes a main responsibility of researchers. It also means, as stated in the Introduction, that if you occupy your space on earth, it becomes your responsibility to use that space well.

This idea of never being alone is key. Although the focus of the enquiry is you, as you ask 'How do I improve what I am doing?', your question assumes that any answer will involve other people's perceptions of your influence in their learning. You are also in company with others who are asking the same question, and who also assume that their answers will involve other people's perceptions of their influence in learning. It is not a case of you as a free-standing 'I', in the company of other free-standing 'I's: on the contrary, each one of you recognises that you are in company, and that you form a community of 'I's, all of whom understand that their claims to educational influence will be evaluated by others within their range of influence.

'My name is Jim. I run a support group for people with obesity issues. We share and discuss strategies and approaches for weight loss and increased activity levels but when each person returns to their environment of family and social structures they meet varying levels of support, from positive to negative peer pressure. How do I encourage them to have confidence in their own decisions, in spite of peer pressure?'

However, nurturing respectful relationships does not mean that everyone should agree on how to conduct social practices. Differences of opinion act as the basis for creative engagement. It does, however, mean that everyone recognises and respects the uniqueness of the other, even though they may act and think in ways that are sometimes radically different. Yet while this is a laudable vision, it is often overtaken by personal and institutional interests, which often require some to obey others: Habermas (1998) speaks about the hypothetical 'inclusion of the other', but the inclusion is often aspirational rather than realised, though there is little doubt that difficulties could be reduced if we all agreed to live according to shared values. This vision may also be undesirable in that it prevents creative dissent and opens the real-world door to totalitarianism when one party seeks to impose their views of 'the good' on another. Having said this, there must be some core values that distinguish what makes us human, such as our avoidance of wanton cruelty. The challenge for action researchers is then to find ways of living in the direction of their values within a context of (1) being with others who do not share the values or the same commitments and (2) being in a context that must recognise basic standards of humanity.

Summary: Ontological values at a glance

The main ontological values discussed are:

- Action research is value-laden and morally committed. This is different from the dominant traditionalist assumption that research should be value-neutral.
- It aims to understand what I/we are doing, and not only what 'they' are doing. This demonstrates a shared commitment towards 'we–I' forms of enquiry.
- It assumes that the researcher is in relation with everything else in the research field, and influences, and is influenced by, everything else. The research field cannot be studied in a value-free way, because the researcher is part of the situation they are studying and brings their own values with them.
- It assumes that we need to negotiate our values and forms of living with others.

Now consider some epistemological values.

Epistemological values

Epistemology is to do with how we understand, acquire and create knowledge. It also has a component for testing the validity of knowledge claims. The epistemological assumptions underpinning action research include the following.

The focus of the enquiry is the 'I' in company with other 'I's

The 'object of enquiry' (some people call it the 'unit of enquiry') refers to the focus of the research, that is, the thing being studied. In first person or self-study forms of action research, the focus of the research is you. You study yourself, not other people. The questions you ask are of the kind 'What am I doing? How do I improve it?', not of the kind 'What are they doing? How do they improve it?' You aim to show how you hold yourself accountable for what you do and think.

This idea of personal accountability has big implications. One is, as noted earlier, that you cannot accept responsibility for what others do and think, but you can and must accept full responsibility for what you do and think. This can be difficult, because it sometimes means being prepared to let go of favourite positions, which may even have become entrenched prejudices, and it also means interrogating what we may take for granted.

Another implication is that you will always need to recognise that you may be mistaken. Testing your ideas rigorously against the feedback of others is not a sufficient safeguard; and public approval does not necessarily mean that practices are socially beneficial, or that what people say can always be believed. Take the case of Galileo. Galileo was threatened with torture to make him recant what he had demonstrated empirically to be true. The most stringent safeguard in the wider field is to take into account the opinions of all whose lives are involved. In your case, this refers to your research participants. In the case of governments, it refers to all citizens of the world.

> 'My name is Evelyn. I run an under-13s football club. My idea is that this allows youngsters a chance to develop skills, confidence and social awareness. I try to do this by rotating players, encouraging them to try out ideas and developing a team spirit. However, certain parents constantly push for the team to win every match, criticise any errors and focus on competition and winning at all costs, rather than participating.'

Knowledge is uncertain

Traditionalist researchers tend to believe that knowledge is certain, and assume the following (Berlin, 1998):

- There is an answer to everything. Knowledge is certain and true, and is 'out there', waiting to be discovered.
- Knowledge can be discovered using specific methodologies such as the 'scientific method', which aims to predict and control outcomes.
- Answers to questions are fixed for all time. All possible answers are compatible and commensurable. Once found, everyone will agree with the answer.

This perspective may be valuable for the natural sciences, such as in genetic engineering, but it does not work in relation to human practices, because humans are unique and unpredictable, and make their own decisions about what to believe.

Action researchers, in contrast, tend to assume the following (Berlin, 1998):

- There is no one answer. Knowledge is uncertain and ambiguous. A question may generate multiple answers, which in turn can generate new questions.
- Knowledge is created as well as discovered. We create knowledge through dialogue with one another. Provisional answers, and the process itself, are always open to critique.
- Any answer is tentative, and open to modification. Answers are often incommensurable and cannot be resolved. Key theorists for this idea are Berlin (1998), Gray (1995), Mouffe (2013) and Rorty (1999).

This means that researchers should not look for a definitive answer or theory that can be applied everywhere. Instead they produce their personal theories (also subject to modification over time) to show what they are learning and invite others to learn with them: and they make a stand according to what they believe is right (Polanyi, 1958). They judge their work not in terms of its generalisability or replicability, which are traditionalist research criteria, but in terms of whether they can show how they are living in the direction of their educational and social values, using those values as their criteria and standards of judgement (see above). It also means that it is legitimate for action researchers to have different aims. In some participatory action research, for example, researchers usually act to resolve a common problem, whereas other researchers may wish to find ways of living in situations where people disagree, often fundamentally, about how they should live.

Knowledge creation is a collaborative process

Although the 'I' is central, the 'I' should never be understood as in isolation. We all live and work in social situations. Whatever we do in our professional practices potentially influences someone somewhere. Action research means working with others at all stages of the research process. At the data-gathering stage you (singular or plural) will investigate your practice in relation with others; at the evaluation stage you will negotiate your findings with others. Research is not a solitary activity. Also, the people you will be working with will possibly be researching their own practices, too, so the situation will become one of collectives of individuals investigating their practices; a question of the 'I/we' investigating the 'I/we' in company with others who are also investigating their individual or collective practices. Eikeland (2006) speaks about the need for communities of enquiry, where all practitioners commit to a negotiated process.

Frequently groups of action researchers will undertake joint enquiries. In this case the focus shifts from 'I' to 'we'. This is particularly helpful when the aim of the research is to improve whole organisational practices (Coghlan and Brannick, 2014). Underpinning such initiatives is the understanding that groups share certain collective values that they wish to realise, though these always need to be negotiated.

Seán, who is a ward manager, is telling his line manager, Caitlin, about how he tries to maintain good staff morale and team cohesion. He tells her that they celebrate each team member's birthday and arrange a monthly night out together. Caitlin praises this but points out that it is important to build cohesion and morale directly around beneficial outcomes for patients. She points out that you can have high morale and cohesion built around poor quality practice too.

Summary: epistemological commitments at a glance

- In first person, self-study forms of action research the object of enquiry is not other people but the 'I' in relation with other 'I's.
- Knowledge is uncertain. Answers are created through dialogue and negotiation. Often answers cannot be negotiated, so people may have to learn to live with a situation. Answers can be communicated through how we live as much as through what we say.
- Knowledge is a property of individuals, so it is often subjective and biased. Individuals have to negotiate their meanings with other knowing individuals.

Methodological commitments

Methodologies refer to the way research is conducted. The main methodological assumptions of action research include the following:

- All practitioners are agents, not recipients or onlookers.
- The methodology is open-ended and developmental.
- The aim of the research is to improve learning with social intent.

All practitioners are agents, not recipients or onlookers

The idea of agency is that people are able to and indeed should take an active part in decisions about how they and others should live. An agent, says Sen, is 'someone who acts and brings about change, and whose achievements can be judged in terms of her [*sic*] own values and objectives, whether or not we assess these in terms of some external criteria as well' (1999: 19). Easterly (2013) challenges dominant views of rural development, which see some people as 'experts', donors of knowledge and other goods, while others become recipients. Arendt (1958) says that exercising agency by taking action is the highest realisation of the human condition.

A main responsibility of agents is to ask questions, and not accept complacency or self-righteous justification, either their own or anyone else's. In this sense, they act as public intellectuals (Said, 1994) and public representatives whose job is to interrupt and question the status quo. Why are things as they are? Are they satisfactory? If not, how can they be changed? For researchers this means always asking questions and not accepting final answers.

Traditionalist forms of research assume that a researcher is a neutral, value-free operative who observes, collects data and generates evidence to support their findings, but should not influence or be influenced by the research itself. Action researchers, on the other hand, accept full responsibility for exercising influence. This involves taking action and considering what influence they may be having on their own and other people's learning. Therefore when you ask 'How do I improve what I am doing?' you are raising questions about two related processes: first in relation to what is going on 'out there' in your social situation; second in relation to what is going on 'in here' in your own thinking. You ask critical questions about why things are as they are. Why do you think as you do? Do you think for yourself, or is your thinking based on what someone else tells you? Who writes your script? How can you show that your own capacity for critique influences other people's capacity also to critique?

The methodology is open-ended and developmental

Unlike traditionalist enquiries, action enquiries do not aim for closure, nor do practitioners expect to find certain answers. The process itself is the methodology (Mellor, 1998) and this is frequently multidimensional, haphazard and experimental. Richard Winter (1998) talks about 'improvisatory self-realisation in action research', involving an entrepreneurialist attitude, and Marian Dadds and Susan Hart (2001) talk about 'methodological inventiveness', where we will try multiple innovative ways until we find the one that is right for us. One step leads to another, and one cycle of action–reflection leads to another, though not necessarily in a pre-specified order. Answers are held as provisional because any answer already has new questions within itself. So it is important always to be open to new possibilities, and never see learning as complete. Doing research is not about producing a completed story, it is more about letting the story evolve. It is as much about the storyteller as about the story.

'My name is Xavier. I am studying my practice as an amateur beekeeper for my BA studies. I also organise meetings for local beekeepers. At each meeting, experienced beekeepers give a lecture and share information from beekeeping magazines and other resources. At each meeting we also ask each member, new and old, to recount some recent experiences. This is because we believe that knowledge of bees is still developing and each of us can add to that body of knowledge.'

At the same time, however, research needs to take the form, as Stenhouse (1983) says, of a systematic enquiry made public: that is, it must demonstrate methodological rigour, and so it must follow through all the action steps of a research programme as outlined above. It must show the traces of the golden thread that runs from beginning to end. The dissertation it generates, the 'making public' part, must describe the processes involved and explain their importance for the overall research design and its findings.

However, be aware that, as well as being exciting, this way of working is also risky. As a researcher you are constantly standing on the edge. The next moment is unknown and so you will commit to the risk of creating a new future. This is a different mental set from traditionalist assumptions that knowledge is given. In action research you always anticipate new problematics. Concrete answers do not pre-exist but are created by real people, in negotiation with others. This can be destabilising for people who are comfortable with being told what to do. Instead of beginning with a hypothesis (which assumes that you know what you will know before you know it), you start with an idea and follow where it leads.

The aim of the research is to improve learning with social intent

Traditionalist researchers aim to show a cause-and-effect relationship between variables, assuming that if people do this, that will happen. It also sees things as 'either this, or that', even though most social situations are full of contradictions and dilemmas that cannot be resolved by technical means. This instrumental view can be witnessed in many workplace and education programmes and practices. Sometimes managers or principals will try to ensure that specific inputs are arranged to achieve targets and produce specific outputs. Many curricula are constructed to generate learning outcomes consistent with official policy. Learners are expected to internalise the message that they should not think for themselves but do as they are told.

However, if you take the view that all people have agency, you also commit to the idea that they can, and should, think for themselves. Managers and educators then need to provide appropriate conditions for this. Their task is to enable people to work with their new knowledge in ways that are right for them, and help them to create their own new futures.

This idea, however, carries conditions. If people wish to create their own futures, they must accept responsibility for the present. In research terms, this means producing their personal theories of practice to show how they are living in the direction of their values, how they are improving their own and other people's learning with social intent, and how they are subjecting those theories to stringent critique.

Summary: methodological commitments at a glance

The dialogical emphasis of action research shows the following:

- In action research you do not do research on others but on yourself, in company with others. Action research is participatory and collaborative in that it takes place in social contexts and involves other people. It is assumed that people know what is best for themselves, so no one should try to think or do for others.
- Action research begins with the experience of a concern and follows through a developmental process which shows cycles of action and reflection. It aims to demonstrate relationships of influence.
- You aim to investigate your practice with a view to improving it. You aim for new beginnings where one state metamorphoses into another. Change is understood as people improving research-based learning to improve practices.

Social commitments of action research

Social purpose refers to why we act in our social contexts and this includes doing research. The main social purposes of action research include the following:

- You aim to improve workplace practices through improving learning.
- You aim to promote the ongoing democratic evaluation of learning and practices.
- You aim to create good social order by influencing the education of others, individually or in groups.

You aim to improve workplace practices through improving learning

Action research is assumed to be research done by workplace practitioners (Garnett et al., 2009; Helyer, 2015). Practitioner-researchers may or may not be supported by higher education personnel or by people in the workplace acting as university tutors and professional mentors. Some workplaces now award their own forms of accreditation. Some academics (though these are probably in the minority) also see themselves as working in workplaces.

The aim is consistently to improve practice through improving learning, produce personal and collective explanatory accounts that show the processes involved, and make these public. In this way practitioners can produce a body of theory that clarifies what is involved in understanding work as a living practice. This is why it is important for you to put your story of practice into the public domain, because you can show how you are contributing to new discourses about how practices may be improved and theory generated.

Xavier continues:

'We have recently developed a website and a blog through which we share our experiences. We also invite input and discussion from the wider community. In this way we form a community of practice (Wenger, 1998) and a comprehensive archive that contains practitioners' accounts as well as news of the latest formal theories of funded research, as reported through the media. We believe, like Alexander Pope, that the proper study of beekeeping is bees.'

You aim to promote the ongoing democratic evaluation of learning and practices

Action research is such a common-sense approach to personal and professional development that, when people first meet the idea, they often say, 'That's what I do in any case. What's different?'

What is different is that in action research you show how you can test the validity of claims to knowledge through the gathering, analysis and interpretation of data and the production of authenticated evidence, and you then make the claims public in order to subject them to critical evaluation.

However, evaluation itself is a problematic concept, involving different views about what it entails. There is common agreement that evaluation aims to establish the value of something; there is little agreement about what is valuable, who should evaluate and why, and what should be evaluated (see Chapter 8).

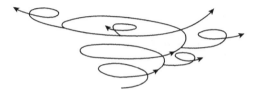

Figure 3.1 A generative transformational evolutionary process: after McNiff (1989)

Traditionalist research perspectives regard evaluation as evaluating a thing or a product from the perspective of an outsider evaluator who makes judgements on an insider's practice. Doing action research, however, is the responsibility of individuals involved in ongoing processes of learning and action, and reflection on the processes. The process is generative and transformational, where the end of one thing becomes the beginning of something else. All organic systems have their own internal generative capacity to transform into ever more fully developed versions of themselves (McNiff, 1989, 2013; see also Figure 3.1). A living system does not work towards a notional perfect end state: it is currently the best it can be but always has the potential to transform into ever more fully realised states. Action research is this kind of generative transformational process, where claims to improved learning and practice generate further learning to improve practices.

The question therefore arises, who evaluates what? In outsider/spectator approaches, an external researcher makes judgements on what other people are doing. From a self-study perspective, the researcher evaluates their own work. Action research is a process in which the 'I' studies the 'I' in company with other 'I's'; therefore evaluation can be seen as the 'I' making judgements about what the 'I' is doing in relation to others. This calls for honesty as well as the capacity to listen to and act on critical feedback. It also calls for the articulation of standards of judgement that draw on the practitioner's own aims and values.

'My name is John. I am a lecturer and researcher in the business school of a university. I also run an action research group with small local businesses, supporting each of them in business development. I make a point of presenting my work at departmental research seminars, attended by colleagues who mainly do conventional social science research. Their critiques of my methodologies keep me aware of the challenges and questions that action researchers need constantly to be aware of, especially in an environment where established orthodoxies seek to maintain their dominance.'

It aims to create good social order by influencing the education of social formations

In action research, the situation changes from an external person studying 'them', to an individual studying 'me', or a collective of individuals studying 'us' in relation with others. Each person asks, 'How do I improve what I am doing for my own and others' benefit?' Each person is seen as an agent with the capacity for influencing their own and others' practices, and with the potential to influence wider social change.

In this book I endorse the idea of how social groupings can work together, and how this can contribute to the creation of good social order. This means seeing all as legitimate participants whose different social and intellectual traditions need to be valued. This can be problematic in contexts in which parties hold different values perspectives and come from different cultural traditions. Further, in politically contested contexts where one party is dominant, that party may mobilise their resources to continue subjugating the other. The subjugated party then comes to be seen, and sometimes to believe, that they are not worthy of being regarded as a legitimate participant, but remain as peripheral and subservient. In many cases, the oppression leads to such frustration that feelings spill over into violence. How, then, do social groupings learn to see the other as someone whose opinion and voice may be different, but who needs to be listened to in any serious commitment to dialogue?

In action research, people hold themselves accountable. They do not make judgements on others without first making judgements on themselves, and they do not expect others to do anything they are not prepared first to do themselves. Each participant learns to recognise themselves as other to the other (Ricoeur, 1992), subject to the same social rules as others.

Summary: social commitments of action research assumptions at a glance

- Action research can be workplace-based, which raises questions about who is seen as a worker, and what is seen as a workplace. It can also take place within non-work-based relationships in the family and community.
- Practitioners evaluate their own work in relation to their values. They do not need 'external' evaluation, but they understand the need for stringent testing and evaluation at all stages of the research, which involves the critical insights and judgements of others.
- Practitioners create their own social order through exercising their capacity to think for themselves and demonstrate how they hold themselves accountable for their educational influence both in their own and one another's learning.

Summary

Action research can be workplace-based, which raises questions about who is seen as a worker and what is seen as a workplace. It can also take place within non-work-based relationships in the family and community.

Practitioners evaluate their own work in relation to their values. They do not need 'external' evaluation, but they understand the need for rigorous testing and evaluation at all stages of the research, which involves the critical insights and judgements of others.

Practitioners create their own social order through exercising their capacity to think for themselves and demonstrate how they hold themselves accountable for their educational influences in both their own and one another's learning.

The next chapter puts all these issues into the context of asking where action research is now, how it has got here, and where it might be heading. And if you are in an institutional context, what you will need to do.

EXERCISES

- Check again that you are clear about the differences between traditionalist forms of research and action research. Now check that you are reasonably clear about the values base of both kinds of research. Which approach will you choose for your enquiry? Why?
- Explain your decision to your colleagues, and say also how your decisions have been influenced by your understanding of the values that inform different approaches to doing research.
- Write out the values that inform your practice, and how you hope to realise these through doing your research.

Critical times for action research

These are critical times for action research because in many ways (though others may disagree) it seems to have lost its way in terms of what it is and what it is for. Also remember that 'action research' is not a thing in itself: it is a term that refers to people who are investigating their practices, and there are also differences of opinion about what investigating practice means and why it is important. This has direct relevance to you as a practitioner in terms of why you do action research and how you do it. To appreciate the implications, it is worth knowing where action research came from and where it is now. However, where it is going is uncertain and largely depends on you, working with others, and how you choose to shape it. These matters are especially important if you are registered on a university course, where the idea of action research takes on a special meaning. It is essential that you have at least a working knowledge of these issues so that you can make an informed judgement about how to act. You also need to know how colonising forces can be subverted and used to create open spaces – new public spheres – where people can discuss, democratically and thoughtfully, how to create new forms of living that achieve their values of participation and enable them to speak for themselves.

The point is to restate continually that, although the democratic and compassionate values of action research are under attack from technically oriented others, it does not have to be like this, and you can do something about it, as millions of people already are. A main strategy is to work in solidarity with others who share the same values and find ways of letting your voice be heard in the world.

The chapter is organised to address these issues as follows:

1. Where did action research come from?
2. Where is it now?
3. Where is it going?

1. Where did action research come from?

It is well documented in the literatures that action research had its roots in popular projects during the early part of the twentieth century: it is, say Herr and Anderson (2005: 8), a 'cover term for several approaches that have emerged from different traditions'. Most of these traditions are linked with one another. Herr and Anderson also cite a range of respected historical overviews, while acknowledging that these are told from specific intellectual or social perspectives, as in the following:

> Anderson, Herr, and Nihlen (1994, practitioner research); Argyris, Putnam and Smith (1985, action science); Chambers (1997, participatory rural appraisal); Cochran-Smith and Lytle (1993, teacher research); Fals Borda (2002, participatory action research); Greenwood and Levin (1998, action research); and Maguire (1987, feminist participatory action research). (Herr and Anderson, 2005: 8)

Accounts drawn from these overviews are presented in the various handbooks and encyclopaedias now available (including Chevalier and Buckles, 2013; Coghlan and Shani, 2016; Noffke and Somekh, 2009; Reason and Bradbury, 2001, 2008; Rowell et al., 2016). Core features of these accounts are the foundational principles of action research: emancipation, collaboration, compassion, dialogue and self-actualisation. They also emphasise that action research celebrates the fact that the local knowledge of practitioners can become public knowledge that will be used by others to inform and improve their own practices.

Rather than give an 'official' history of action research here, I will now offer a brief account of my own contact with action research. It is history interpreted from my perspective.

Personal experience

I first came into contact with action research during the 1980s when I was a deputy head teacher in a large secondary school in Dorset, UK, with a main responsibility for the well-being and good order of the pupils. At that time a new curriculum initiative, called Personal and Social Education (PSE), was introduced, though there were differences of opinion whether it was a subject in itself or a cross-curricular approach (Pring, 1984); so, because of the nature of my job, I was tasked with the responsibility of finding out. An opportunity arose to attend a course run by Leslie Button, whose Active Tutorial approach emphasised the importance of young people researching their practices in collaboration with one another and their teachers in order to develop confidence and self-agency (Button, 1974). What I learned from that course had a lasting effect on me, especially the idea that research was not a specialised activity conducted at universities so much as a practical engagement with real-life issues that could, and should, be undertaken by everyone. Because I wanted to pursue the idea further I enrolled for a university-based doctoral programme where I got to grips with the philosophy of PSE and related literatures, including action research.

Like others at the time, I also struggled with the dilemma of whether PSE was a subject or an approach, and this was evident during the writing up of my thesis. I had produced a nearly complete thesis before the penny dropped. In that first thesis I discussed PSE as a subject, drawing on my research with a group of 12 young people who were doing their action research under my guidance. Now, however, instead of writing about this thing called PSE, I began to see that I was not speaking about a topic so much as speaking about myself, in collaboration with the young people. We were all investigating in action what it meant to be personally and socially educated: doing action research could be seen as a process of personal and social education. I wrote a second thesis out of this new learning, and used the first thesis as data to show how my earlier thinking had changed through the process of reflecting and writing about it. My thesis was accepted in 1989 and I began to become activist in the field.

While still working in school I began writing seriously: the first edition of *Action Research: Principles and Practice* was published in 1988. A lot of luck was involved: it was the right book at the right time. I recall the letter from the publisher who said 'I have to publish this book: I have received three proposals in recent times about this topic'. I took early retirement in 1987 because of a health condition, so, because I still had to earn a living, I purchased and ran a gift shop, with a business partner, in the seaside town where I live. In the shop I sold buckets and spades and flip-flops, while studying and writing up my thesis. It was this experience that made me appreciate the non-difference between academics (me) and practitioners (also me). At the same time I began to develop the writing; I did this while sitting at the till during quiet times. On the strength of the publications I began to get invited to talk in different organisational settings, including higher education, and it was here that I began to feel the full force of the academic establishment. The idea of action research was ridiculed as so much 'navel gazing' and not a proper form of research, and I was ridiculed as not a 'proper academic'. I carried on regardless. I also began to appreciate the immense educational power of writing for the dissemination of ideas as well as the immense disciplinary power of the discourses of the traditionalist university that would brook no challenge to its established epistemology.

During the late 1980s and 1990s a vigorous lobby developed in favour of getting action research accepted as a bona fide form of research (see for example, Carr and Kemmis, 1986; Elliott, 1991). This now began to be taken seriously, given also that new social science literatures were appearing emphasising the changing nature of knowledge and its production: for example, Gibbons et al.'s (1994) *The New Production of Knowledge* that proposed Mode 2 (experiential, practice-based) forms of knowing alongside Mode 1 (abstract analytical forms). Other literatures, including influential management and organisational texts, were used to support the lobby, used by an increasingly vociferous body of practitioner-researchers who wanted to get their personal and workplace studies accredited. This lobby then led to serious consideration by the higher education community about how to respond as well as deal with the challenge to their authority that action research posed and where to place it on university curricula.

One of the main issues in the action research field, often used as a weapon against practitioner-researchers, was how to establish research quality, especially given that action research could not address the challenges of traditionalist criteria such as objectivity, replicability and generalisability. This issue became critical for the field: how would the practitioner research community qualify for research funding if their research were judged in terms of traditionalist social science criteria? A response from established and respected researchers (see for example, Furlong and Oancea, 2005) was that the practitioner research community should itself agree on appropriate criteria and standards of judgement and put those forward for consideration by the wider academic researcher community. This remains an ongoing debate (see Chapters 16 and 17 on issues of validity and legitimation).

But now, given the lobby and the popularity of action research, at least among the practitioner community (who were, of course, potential university customers), the Academy began to see the power of the oppositional challenges of action research. So, given that an effective way of controlling the opposition is to co-opt it, the Academy embraced action research but then proceeded to turn it into a domesticated form that would fit into its own methodological and epistemological frameworks. And this is the situation today, except that it is getting more pronounced.

2. Where is it now?

Consequently, although action research is now widely adopted in higher education institutions, which is good news, the not-so-good news is that it has largely been force-fitted into a form that suits those institutions. This has special implications for some key issues, including:

- the values base of action research;
- implications for you and your action research project;
- the purposes of action research.

The values base of action research

Go back to the Introduction and Sowell's ideas about different kinds of vision. He suggests that visions may be organised into two broad categories, what he calls a constrained (closed) vision and an unconstrained (open) vision. While these are caricatures, he says, with many degrees of difference, they capture reasonably well the idea that some people see processes of enquiry in different ways, including: as (1) working towards definitive answers and closure (a constrained vision), or as (2) resisting closure, other-oriented, innovative and full of possibilities (an unconstrained vision). These ideas can be seen in different domains. An epistemological perspective shows that some people believe in a perfect end state towards which everyone must strive: see Berlin's (1990) critique of the idea (in Chapter 3) that there is an answer to everything, the answer can be found and it will be true for all time. In terms of responding to questions about how we should live, it is assumed that people should conform to a particular social code according to what another person or persons think is the right way. Others believe that there is no definitive answer to big questions; people work out together how they should live, though this implies that they will first agree on the ground rules about listening to the other and not try to impose their own opinions. One of the best examples of these conflicting ideas in action is in the famous debate between Dewey and Russell (Burke, 1994). Dewey saw life as a process of enquiry where we are constantly open to new ideas: his vision was about asking questions and finding new ways of acting (many researchers accept Dewey as one of the major influences on action research). Russell, on the other hand, saw processes of enquiry as about finding answers and aiming for definitive outcomes. Consequently they talked past each other rather than with each other. Further, because Russell's views were accepted by the then mainstream intelligentsia, he was seen as 'right' and Dewey as misguided and something of a crackpot.

This same debate continues today. Universities still value factual knowledge over experiential or practical ways of knowing. It is still assumed that knowledge comes as a final package that is best acquired through listening to an expert. Understandings of what quality in research is may be defined in terms of an existing body of authorised texts. Rorty critiques this view, commenting on what he calls the over-specialisation of traditionalist university-based knowledge with 'highly professional methods [and an] insistence on detail and mechanics' (2006: 23). He promotes instead the idea that knowledge is always produced within a socio-historical context and with an eye towards social hope. To support his argument, he speaks of the differences between philosophers and poets:

> The philosophers pride themselves on skill in argumentation, but the poets suspect that philosophical arguments merely rearrange what is already on the table, whereas the poets themselves put something new on the table. (Rorty, 1999: 70)

He also speaks about the way in which different forms of knowledge are communicated: analytical research is communicated through analytical reports where researchers use the literatures to engage with the literatures, whereas practical research depends more on narrative: 'Narrative means telling a story about something, like the world spirit, or Europe, man [sic], the West, culture, freedom, class struggle. It is the story of some big thing like that, in which you can place your own story' (Rorty, 2006: 43). Further, narrative helps us find ways of transforming realities: 'philosophical reflections did not do much to eliminate slavery, but narratives about the lives the slaves were living contributed a lot' (2006: 67).

Purposes of action research

These ideas are relevant to discussions about the nature and purposes of action research. Some people, including myself, see action research working at multiple levels of experience. At the level of everyday experience it may be seen as an enquiring stance, where we ask, 'How do we make sense of our world? How does engaging with the world give meaning to our lives?' We ask questions and engage with dilemmas while recognising that any conclusions we arrive at are always temporary and open to change. At the more focused level of taking action in personal and social settings, action research becomes a process where we ask, 'How do we make sense of this situation here? How do we improve what we are doing in order to make the situation more meaningful for all?' In both the wider stance and in the more focused situation, action research is seen as a way of being, thinking and acting that enables people to find ways of realising their values in practice, and always in negotiation with others who may hold different values from those of ourselves. Thus doing action research in the personal and social world becomes an ethically informed practice, because it means taking action to critique and develop one's own thinking about how to act while also recognising that we all live and work with others who may choose to think and act differently from us, yet whom we acknowledge as having the right to exercise their choices.

This has significant implications for the reasons for doing action research and its personal and social purposes. There are of course different perceptions among researchers: Kemmis (2006: 464) has an eye mainly to social purposes and how these can be realised structurally. He believes that the aim of action research is to 'create an emancipatory and critical process that has the potential for radical reform, based on social justice' (Meyer et al., 2006: 485). Meyer's own view is that attempts to change practices should take into account personal emotions and relationships as well as the structural ones Kemmis focuses on: caring relationships are core to the conduct of action research whose aims then become to develop deeper understandings among people about how they should be in relation with one another.

Implications for you and your action research project

It then becomes your responsibility to be clear about how you see the reasons for doing your action research and what you hope to achieve. Do you wish to influence structures? If so, be clear about some of the barriers to doing so, including organisational constraints and people's self-interests. Do you wish to influence practices? If so, be clear about potential barriers including people's established ways of practising and their possible reluctance to change.

In terms of this book, which is to alert you to the politics as well as the practices of action research, always be aware of your institutional context. If your main aim is to get your degree, then you will need to abide by institutional regulations and customs. A degree course is not the place to try to influence the reform of degree courses. The aim is to get the degree, after which you can be as activist as you wish. However, if you really wish to influence the reform of institutional processes and practices, go for it but with your eyes wide open, and find allies who, like you, disagree with the dominant orthodoxy, the more powerful the better.

Whatever you decide, it is up to you and your colleagues to influence new directions for action research, which brings us to the question of where action research is going.

3. Where is it going?

Where action research is going depends on you working in collaboration with others. Like everything, action research is a child of its times: it is part of the history of people living in community. At time of writing (2017), the social world appears globally to be in even greater disarray than usual, with a closing down on all sides and across domains: geographical and national borders are closing; there is a universal retrenchment into conservativism; alliances are formed between universities and corporates for the accumulation of economic and intellectual capital; and there is a massive move by many institutions to achieve corporate political power. These structural changes are linked with epistemological changes: a move towards certainty and disciplinary specialisms, especially in STEM (science, technology, engineering and mathematics) subjects; the achievement of instrumental ends; the privatisation of knowledge through the privatisation of universities (a newly developed UK higher education institution can achieve degree awarding powers in a short two years: see the 2016 White Paper *Success as a Knowledge Economy: Teaching Excellence, Social Mobility and Student Choice*; available at www.gov.uk/government/publications). Putnam's (2000) post-apocryphal vision of *Bowling Alone* seems to be coming true and *The Shallows* (Carr, 2010) are perhaps no longer safe for paddling in. War is everywhere, from the wars of international armies to the local wars of lone shooters in shopping malls, and especially to the class warfare of the haves against the have nots.

Yet this is nothing new, though the speed and intensity with which events are reported are new: we have been here before, frequently. There never was a 'Golden Age' when things were better; things have always been problematic. The error is, perhaps, to think that they were never thus, and this returns us to a main theme of this book, namely that there is no Big Book of Answers, no fundamentalist position that tells us which is the right way to live. We must think for ourselves (which is, of course, to take a fundamentalist position), in company with others who are doing the same. This is never easy.

Yet with uncertainty comes hope and opportunities for its realisation: the question becomes how we use the opportunity and who is the quickest off the mark. Stephen Toulmin (1992) explains in *Cosmopolis* how the period of extreme uncertainty following the massive disruption of the Thirty Years War led to a general craving for some element of stability. The post-war vacuum provided a welcome space for the ready acceptance of Descartes' view of certain knowledge. Perhaps the same thing will happen in the time to come: most of us tend, at least sometimes, to crave moments of stability and for someone else to tell us what to do.

This, I think, is what is happening to knowledge at the moment, with implications for action research. There is a closing down of minds and a privatisation of the public psyche, and packages of knowledge are sought by consumers in the same way as are packaged courses such as MOOCs. If caught up in this trajectory, action research will continue to transform into an application for other practices, a one-click way of getting things done.

It does not need to be like this. The vacuums accompanying turmoil can be filled by nimble-thinking entrepreneurial practitioners to create new ways of living in community. It is said in military theory that generals think in terms of strategies whereas foot soldiers think in terms of tactics: de Certeau's (1984) view is that the tactics of everyday life should be seen as of the same status as and oppositional to strategy. Tactically oriented practitioners can work together to create new structures and new practices, geared towards more emancipatory and egalitarian ways of living. They can develop new public spaces that are responsive to local conditions and adapt to local needs. The case studies in this book show how practitioners use intellectual and practical resources to advantage, in the service of others and themselves, working collaboratively.

The most important thing, says Arendt, is to think: to see things from the other's perspective and develop what Bakhtin (1981) saw as a dialogic imagination. Dialogue refers not only to a discursive interchange between people, it is also a discursive interchange between all aspects of life: between thought and action, space and time, and places, spaces and people. Dialogue refers to relationships, and relationships mean energy: the world is made up not of objects, as analytical thinkers would have us believe, but of relationships between the objects, and the nature of those relationships is dynamic and transformational. This is the nature of action research: it is a way of seeing the world as interconnected, where the entire system of reality hangs together in elegant suspension, waiting for the next moment that never arrives.

The future of action research is up to those people who decide to get actively involved in finding new ways to live together in a dynamic reality: those who do research in action. The future of universities lies in their capacity to involve such people in their action plans. Graff (2003) makes the point that a common complaint used to be that students were not ready for universities. The reality today is the reverse: universities are not ready for students. Those universities who insist on prioritising packaged knowledge and hierarchical relationships are simply not in the fast-moving and shape-shifting real world and will disappear. Those who are open to new possibilities, who invest energy into realising the visions of emancipatory potential, will survive.

You and your colleagues are part of this. Take care: become politically savvy and look well before you leap. The future is yours, to create as you please, provided you work together to achieve your hope.

As is my regular practice, I sent this chapter in draft form to colleagues for their critical review, and invited them also to respond to it as they saw appropriate. Four responses appear here: from Margaret Meredith, York St John University, UK; Hilde Hiim, Oslo and Akershus University College, Norway; Joseph Shosh, Moravian College, USA (introduced in Chapter 2); and Josephine Bleach, ELI, Ireland (introduced in Chapter 1).

Margaret Meredith, York St John University, UK writes:

> I read your piece as a call to those who care about such things to take urgent action. Such action, in my opinion, will be both political and personal. Political because I share your concern that what was once public – belonging to all – is becoming privatised and owned by an elite. The privatisation of knowledge to serve mainly private economic ends is a deeper and more worrying phase of this, in my view. And perhaps even critical theory, once the clarion call for emancipation, has also been requisitioned by the university: it is used to analyse policy and practice in academic journals, but where is the actual application of this towards a fairer society? Where is the link between the theory and the practice?
>
> Many times in my life I have felt that a political situation is so untenable that maybe it will have a bright side: that those designated as leaders will feel compelled to seek fresh ideas and take different courses of action. In this respect I have been disappointed many times and have come to the conclusion that if I am not contributing to new ideas of sustainable ways of living, then I can't expect others to do so. And neither can I expect things to change. In the sense of offering something new towards more sustainable ways of living together in communities and on the planet, we all need to be leaders. To me this means working out with others in our own localised spheres of influence what 'better' might look like, how we might get there, and making our insights accessible to others. This may well involve practices that challenge wider political structures and commonly held assumptions. So be it.
>
> It is personal because nothing can really change without the commitment of individuals, a personal responsibility towards our world, assumed without coercion. Many publications about what could be called emancipatory higher education discuss creating transformative experiences for students and generating environments in which previously held assumptions and beliefs will be challenged. A question remains for me: does this mean that teachers in universities have gone through the process of transformation and are waiting for students at this enlightened end point? It seems implausible for me to expect students to transform themselves and challenge their thinking and practices if I am not continuously going through the same process and seeking to transform my own thinking and practices, with personal and social intent.
>
> I believe that many people are attracted to ideas to make their communities and wider society better in some way and will coalesce around values-based commitments to social action. An action research approach would always put values in the forefront and invite discussion and critique around them, seeking to maintain openness and integrity on a personal level and within the self-researching community. Such an approach would seek to frame issues with others, especially the people most affected by them, rather than starting off with a pre-set agenda for action and an already-decided end point. It should constantly seek to work towards making things better for people and planet, perhaps by encouraging new people to participate and to contribute to the dialogical process of thinking together. Like a garden, ideas and practices need nurturing and can never be considered 'done'. In the same way, a democratic community of people researching how to make things better through their actions needs to be nurtured and renewed and so the research and practice of seeking better ways of relating and working

for change continues. Part of the responsibility we need to assume as action researchers is to do our best to let ideas and practices go when they are not serving the purposes of inclusion and fairness, as far as we can tell with our limited understanding.

I can't wait for others to act or for political change before I start this process – the need to find democratic and equitable ways of living together is too urgent, and too many people apparently feel left out, for us to delay.

Joseph Shosh, Moravian College, USA writes:

As a researcher of my own professional practice, I desire to become better than I was, to know more than I did yesterday, and to have the wisdom to take the right action, trusting in the action research process to help me see where I might not be as effective as I wanted to be, to see where I may have forgotten something I thought I had already learned, and to see where my course of action may not have been the best one for all of the stakeholders involved. Of course, as I attempt to articulate my own researcher stance, I can't help but find myself still at odds with a larger society that privileges so-called right answers, scripted protocols, standardization, and certainty. Action research is downright dangerous to the status quo in its insistence upon the examination of a multiplicity of points of view and for its reliance upon dialogue in a world where authentic communication has too often been replaced by sound bites, photo ops, and demagoguery.

New participatory forms of action research are emerging, and these hold tremendous promise in democratizing the research process and engaging members of a community to take new action together, rather than relying on traditional experts to recommend solutions from afar. Where once the action researcher may have sought to improve his or her professional practice in relative isolation, today's local, national, and international networks of action researchers provide support, critical friends, and avenues for sharing research questions, findings, and methods. While local contexts in which action research is conducted are likely to be distinctive, there is much to be learned through dialogue across contexts as democratic change occurs from the ground up and traditionally marginalized communities and even regions of the globe have the opportunity to teach as well as to learn. With the world's action research networks themselves coming together for the first time as part of the Action Research Network of the Americas fifth annual conference and the first Global Assembly for Knowledge Democracy in Cartagena, Colombia in 2017, traditional barriers of language, geography, and economic status will begin to give way to the dialogic enquiry of our shared humanity. These are most exciting and promising times indeed to be joining a newly networked world of action researchers.

Hilde Hiim, Oslo and Akershus University College, Norway writes:

In the 1970s I graduated as a teacher and worked in primary school for some years. Then I took a university degree in pedagogy and stared working in teacher education. Influenced by Lawrence Stenhouse's work I became very interested in teacher research, because it seemed to have the power to strengthen teachers' professional knowledge base and independence. I have worked to make teacher action research an important part of teacher education, and written books about this. I think that from epistemological as well as ethical reasons teacher research is necessary to develop authentic, practice based and professionally relevant knowledge in the teaching profession.

Teacher research and action research have until recently not been so common in Scandinavia. Now that it is becoming more mainstream, we see tendencies for action research projects and processes to be dominated by university researchers. This means that research takes on an instrumental direction, and teachers are reduced to participants in research and development processes controlled by academic researchers: they are also authorised to document the research. The kind of knowledge thus developed is not authentic, professional teacher knowledge. This form of action research does not strengthen teachers' development as independent, ethically committed professionals, as I understood the original philosophy of the teacher research movement.

I think it is important to look at the history of action research and at the epistemological questions that have been raised during its history. If we want pupils and students to become educated as socially independent and responsible individuals, we need independent and socially responsible teachers. This means teachers who are capable of developing their work and profession in democratic collaboration with their pupils and students. To me, practitioner research in the form of democratic collaboration with those involved is what action research is about.

Josephine Bleach, Early Learning Initiative, Ireland writes:

> This chapter really resonates with me, particularly the sentence: 'The future of action research is up to those people who decide to get actively involved in finding new ways to live together in a dynamic reality: those who do research in action.'

> To me, action research is about change and I find the framework of first, second and third person practice (Torbert, 2001) very useful in structuring my reflections, as Director of ELI, on how I negotiate complex personal, political and professional worlds.

> First person practice is about working on and changing myself – challenging my thoughts, values, actions, relationships: my whole way of being. Second person practice is about working with others to change our community – improving our practices, interactions and theories, while making a difference to the lives of others. Third person practice is about networking with others to change the world – supporting, challenging and inspiring each other.

> Key to all of this is reflection and discussion – understanding the past and the present, while you move into the future. Continually questioning what you are doing and why. How will you, your community and the world be a better place because of your action research? Continually learning from others on how you can improve your practice and research.

> Underpinning all three practices are your values, which should act as critical friends as you proceed from one action cycle to the next. All three practices reinforce one another with each practice involving transformation at the personal, community, national and international level respectively (Torbert, 2001).

Summary

This chapter has given brief objective and personal accounts of the history of action research. Many authors in the literatures comment on the idea that action research has been co-opted by traditionalist institutions and turned into a form that suits those institutions' purposes.

These different perspectives may be related to the values base and purposes of different research approaches and the researchers who use them. They also have implications for practitioner-researchers.

EXERCISES

- Do you agree with the views expressed in this chapter? If so, why? If not, why not? Aim to support your opinions through reference to the wider literatures.
- How do you see action research? Do you see it as a life process where people work things out and find justifiable solutions to issues? Do you see it as a way of getting things done in the world? Discuss these matters with your colleagues, and be prepared to defend your views.
- Write out how and whether you see your personal and professional life as a process of enquiry in action. Also write out how you justify your views.

PART II

Why do I need to know?

Part II sets out ideas about why you should do action research and what kind of responsibilities are involved. It contains the following chapters.

At this stage of your enquiry you are asking, 'Why am I concerned?' By asking the question you are showing how you are interrogating established stories about what counts as knowledge and who should be seen as a knower. You are also claiming that your story about what doing research means should be taken as seriously as established stories, which may be different from yours and that you are now challenging. You are showing how you are capable of contributing to new thinking for new practices, grounded in the values of freedom, democracy and account-ability (Chapter 6); your capacity for contributing to new thinking and ideas (Chapter 7); and your capacity for critical engagement with the literatures so that you can show how your ideas make a valuable contribution to new ideas (Chapter 8). You are also showing how you are delib-erately changing your identity and self-perception from being 'just a practitioner' to being a practitioner-researcher and scholar.

Why do action research?

We said earlier that many action researchers undertake their enquiries for two main purposes:

- To learn how to contribute to new practices (this is the action focus of action research).
- To learn how to contribute to new knowledge, ideas and theory (this is the research focus of action research).

Both aspects are intertwined and interdependent.

Many practitioners would probably feel at ease with the idea that they are contributing to new practices, possibly all the more so because this is now the dominant view in the literatures: action research is seen mainly as about improving practices though often without acknowledging that improving practices begins and is embedded in improving knowledge. This view is especially espoused by many organisations, including universities, whose focus is largely on achieving outcomes and position power. However, perhaps fewer practitioners would immediately see their work as contributing to theory or to the history of ideas. In fact, many practitioners are often suspicious of the idea of theory and research, with some having had the experience of being researched on by officially appointed researchers. Practitioners are often heard to say things like, 'Don't ask me to do theory: leave that to the academics'. Such attitudes feed into dominant discourses everywhere, which are that practitioners cannot think for themselves or be in control of their own practices and professions.

Yet this view does not enable practitioners to contribute to thinking about how the world works. It can in fact be disabling, and needs to be changed. This chapter deals with these issues, and is organised as follows:

1. Re-imagining professional identity
2. The importance of seeing yourself as a knowledgeable and competent practitioner
3. The importance of seeing yourself as a knowledgeable and competent theorist

1. Re-imagining professional identity

In Chapter 1 the idea of positioning theory was introduced. 'Positioning' someone is more than allocating them to a role or requiring them to fulfil a job description: it is about how people are positioned and identified, by others and themselves, in a particular social situation, and how they see their relationships with others and themselves. Identities are discursively created: what we say and do leads us to identify others and ourselves in a particular way. Discourses influence what a person becomes as well as who they become. People say 'I'm just a plumber/secretary/housewife' and mentally fit themselves into those stereotypical identities. Sometimes the system of positioning oneself in a particular way becomes a great place to hide. Also, such discourses are generally hierarchically constituted in terms of what counts as social capital: you will seldom hear people say 'I'm just an academic' or 'I'm just a professor' (unless the professor wants to be a vice chancellor, which is a step up the organisational power-ladder).

This view can be perpetuated by both external and internal forces. The external forces include messages communicated through the media, including policy discourses that maintain that, for example, teachers should leave theory to academics (Hattie, 2015). The internal forces may be heard in, for example, practitioners' personal everyday 'I'm just a teacher' stories: they come to believe what they hear, and will frequently maintain that doing higher study or contributing to academic theory is beyond their reach, though this is not the case, as shown via the case studies in this book and many other texts.

From a critically political perspective, this situation has considerable implications for how practitioners should understand and identify themselves. If practitioners wish to be taken seriously, and publicly acknowledged as practice innovators and theory creators, it is vital that they do see themselves as researchers who produce knowledge as well as practitioners who extend it through their work. Only by producing their own knowledge and stories of knowledge creation will they be viewed by the wider public as legitimate participants in debates about what is worth striving for in life, and whose lives count as important. However, public acknowledgement begins with the private acknowledgement of practitioners themselves. It is no good expecting someone else to value your work if you do not value it yourself. You need to appreciate the importance of your work for generating both new practices and new theory, and be clear about how this links with policy formation and implementation. For many people it becomes a matter of re-imagining their professional identities, which can be difficult for those who have adopted a particular way of thinking about themselves.

To assess your own personal and professional positioning, aim to do a personal stock-take. First, consider asking critical questions such as those set out in Tables 5.1 and 5.2 to help you identify possible internal and external constraints.

Thinking about critical questions like this can often be a matter of your frame of mind. In *Mindset*, Carol Dweck (2006) comments on how discourses influence the development of different mindsets: she speaks about a fixed mindset, where a person refuses to believe that things can change, and a growth mindset, where they come to believe that often radical change is possible (see below). These different mindsets represent similar vantage points to the different perceptions of research discussed throughout this book: a constrained vision and a closed society tend to be reproduced largely through the fixed mindsets of its members, whereas an unconstrained vision and an open society tend to be created by people who believe that they have the capacity to recreate their lives as they wish in negotiation with others.

Table 5.1 How do I position myself in my workplace?

In relation to whom?	How do I position myself?	Why do I position myself like this?	How would I like to position myself?	What can I do about it?	Other ideas and comments?
My line manager	I position myself as less professionally knowledgeable.	I have not sufficient self-confidence.	I would like to position myself as equally contributing.	Practise being more self-aware: go on a self-development course.	[Please complete this yourself.]
My colleagues	I am quiet around most people.	I am quite shy.	I would like to be seen as someone whose opinions matter.	Learn to be more self-confident: read some good self-help books.	
My students	Most of my students respect me as their tutor.	I know my subject matter and have good pedagogical skills.	I am confident in my teaching: I would like to be equally confident in my collegial relationships.	I can develop strategies to build up my social skills: I can keep a reflective diary, ask a close colleague for feedback, video and observe myself in a role-play situation.	

Table 5.2 How am I positioned in my workplace?

By whom?	How am I positioned?	Why am I positioned like this?	How would I like to be positioned?	What can I do about it?	Other ideas and comments?
My line manager	Treats me with respect though as less capable.	I am probably not sufficiently pro-active. It could also be the organisational culture.	I would like to be treated as equally capable in my own role.	Develop greater self-confidence; state my own opinion, powerfully and respectfully.	
My colleagues	[Please complete this yourself.]				
My students					

You can develop a growth mindset towards further study by doing preparatory exercises such as in Table 5.3.

The issue of re-imagining one's professional identity is key. Workplace practitioners often have difficulty managing the shift to academic work, especially since the nature of everyday workplace practices is often different from the nature of academic practices. Even the language spoken in those different places is different, depending on one's expectations about the contexts that shape the languages. Gee (2005: 20–1) speaks about discourses with a small 'd' as what we say, while Discourses with a big 'D' refers to practices, including 'language', 'actions', 'interactions', 'ways of thinking', 'believing' and 'valuing': these 'big D' discourses are the kinds of fields where identities are shaped and recreated.

Table 5.3   Developing a growth mindset towards higher education and research

Question	Response
Why do I want to do this course?	I want to get further qualifications.
What do I hope to achieve?	I will use my new qualifications to get a better job.
What external forces might hinder me?	Finances; negotiating leave of absence from work.
What internal forces might hinder me?	Anxieties about HE expectations; will I be up for it? Also, I am a practitioner, not a researcher. I am definitely not an academic.
How do I overcome them?	Think about my strengths; what am I already good at? I can learn how to do research (learning how to do research *is* research). Why should I not see myself as a researcher and a theorist? Give me one good reason.

Engaging with such issues is often problematic and takes self-discipline and a lot of self-understanding and appreciation. Edward Said (born in Mandatory Palestine, American by birth because his father served in the US army, educated in British and American schools) writes about such difficulties: for him, they were the difficulties of reconciling identities and languages as a person growing up between different cultures and with different 'nationalities' (though he speaks in terms of personal history rather than 'nationalities'):

> Everyone lives a life in a given language; everyone's experiences therefore are had, absorbed and recalled in that language. The basic split in my life was the one between Arabic, my native language, and English, the language of my education and subsequent expression as a scholar and teacher, and so trying to produce a narrative of the one in the language of the other – to say nothing of the numerous ways in which the languages were mixed up for me and crossed over from one realm to the other – has been a complicated task. (Said, 1999: xv-xvi)

Wouldn't it be lovely, he yearns, to have a fixed identity, to live in a world where identity was not problematic?

> I have retained this unsettled sense of many identities – mostly in conflict with each other – all my life, together with an acute memory of the despairing feeling that I wish we could have been all-Arab, or all-European and American, or all-Orthodox Christian, or all-Muslim, or all-Egyptian, and so on. (1999: 5)

But this is not the way things are. Most of us have multiple identities, as Said says. He comments that he had two alternatives: 'to state baldly, "I am an American citizen", or to open myself to the deeply disorganized state of my real history and origins as I gleaned them in bits, and then to try to construct them into order' (1999: 6), but as he says, this was impossible. Perhaps Said appreciated only too well that what we see in the world is not necessarily the way the world is: the world is how we choose to see it at any given time. We have to recognise that everything is contingent, as Rorty (1989) points out, that one set of circumstances depends on and is influenced by others. We therefore need to adopt what he calls an 'ironic' attitude, that is, recognising that we are always products of a particular time, place and space, so we need to challenge our own perceptions and hold everything as open to question.

The same issue arises for many workplace and academic practitioners, especially when they work in unfamiliar workplaces and cultural settings. They are expected to identify themselves according to new workplace or cultural norms, which can be quite different from those of their familiar institutional lives or social and cultural settings. This also means learning new languages along with new identities.

Katie Simpson writes:

In my role while working at York St John University as Head of Partnership Development I undertook a Master's in Educational Improvement, Development and Change; this became the catalyst for viewing my practice from a different perspective. I hadn't considered engaging in research before. This opportunity, coupled with encouragement from colleagues has allowed me to develop my skills as a researcher, and this has increasingly become of value to me personally and professionally.

Changing my professional identity has not been without challenges. These include changing how I viewed myself, overcoming a lack of confidence while working with experienced researchers and academics and feeling like an imposter (not a 'proper' researcher).

Prior to my role as Head of Partnership Development I had a background of working in Adult Education but had not considered taking the step from the world of business development into academia. I was given the opportunity by my manager to develop and teach new modules based on the children's workforce and this experience led to a part time secondment as Lecturer in Children, Young People and Education. Following this I have become a Fellow of The Higher Education Academy.

My experience from working in the Academy has also contributed to my developing a new business (www.brightsparkscic.org.uk) which focuses on supporting organisations to source external funding. My business also coordinates research projects so I am able to continue to engage actively in new and exciting research projects. My research interests are based on widening participation, Foster Carers and the Children's Workforce. For me, moving between the two different 'worlds' of business and academia has proved a natural and worthwhile challenge.

Changing one's self-perception/self-identity can be difficult for many practitioners in all contexts, yet there are good reasons why you should make this shift and great benefits to be achieved. I have outlined some of them here.

---

2. The importance of seeing yourself as a knowledgeable and competent practitioner

In Chapter 2 we considered Donald Schön's ideas about the topographies of professional landscapes. Schön was, as I am here, making the point that practitioners should be regarded as competent professionals whose practical professional knowledge is key to developing human capabilities, both their own and other people's.

This idea of developing human capability is core to action research. Sen (1999) describes capabilities as people's ability to think for themselves, and to make their own decisions about how they wish to live their lives. He also makes the point that realising these capabilities requires people to be free, and to exercise that freedom to ensure the continued development of their own capabilities and the capabilities of others. This is done, he says, by 'support in the provision of those facilities (such as basic health care or essential education) that are crucial for the formation and use of human capabilities' (1999: 42). The task for practitioners then becomes how they can learn to think for themselves and make decisions about their own lives, as well as encourage others to do the same. Because practitioners are also professionals, they will not assume that this is just happening, but will carry out careful tests to see whether this is the case: this includes soliciting the feedback of critical others as well as adopting a critical attitude towards their own thinking and perceptions. They will check whether they really are living in the direction of their values of freedom of thinking and the capacity of all to make informed decisions.

You can do the same using strategies such as the personal professional stock-take exercise at Table 5.4.

Table 5.4   Personal professional stock-take

Question – What do I do well? What am I successful at?

Personal qualities	Professional qualities
I have a good sense of humour.	I deal with problems easily and efficiently.
I get on well with people.	I have good relationships with everyone.
I always keep promises.	People can depend on me.
I look after my family.	I work hard and pay attention to other people's needs.

Question – What could I do better?

Personal qualities	Professional qualities
I should not talk so much: I should listen more.	I should listen more: I should consult others more before taking action.
I tend to be a bit lazy: I put off doing jobs I dislike.	I should be more proactive in joining in company life; I should do tasks on time.
I tend not to take problems too seriously.	I should take people's difficulties more seriously; I should take a counselling course.
I often do the opposite of what I should.	I should try to follow company policy more closely, but this can be difficult given that I like to do my own thing.

Enter the idea of action research and how to begin an action enquiry.

Beginning an action enquiry

People have different reasons for starting an action enquiry. You may feel that your current practice is already good, and other people can learn from you, so you will evaluate your work to explain how and why you can show this to be the case. Sometimes you will have a hunch and ask yourself 'I wonder what would happen if … ?' Perhaps something could improve, so you will try out a new style or strategy and evaluate what happens. Is it working? Should you change something? You will then ask 'How do I understand what I am doing? How do I improve this?', and go on to generate evidence to show that you have rigorously tested the validity of any claims that you have improved practice.

Action research becomes part of the practice of your everyday life (de Certeau, 1984), for example when you ask seemingly trivial (but actually highly complex) questions such as 'How do I understand how to use my computer?', as well as much grander questions such as 'How do we self-evaluate our organisation?'

In recent years I have been privileged to work in Cambodia with a group of Norwegian medics and health professionals from the Norway-based Trauma Care Foundation (TCF), working with people in post-conflict zones and mainly in landmine-infested areas, such as Afghanistan and Northern Iraq. Their work has been both to treat landmine injuries and save lives, and to teach local people how to deal with such injuries themselves (see http://traumacare.no where you can also freely download materials). In every setting where they have worked, they have set up a Village University, to help local people develop professional and practical expertise in dealing with trauma and learn to develop appropriate resources for themselves. My work with the team is to help them evaluate and write up their work for wider dissemination.

One of the team is Margit Steinholt, an obstetrician/gynaecologist. Her concern was that countless women died from loss of blood or other complications during childbirth. As part of her work in the Village University in Cambodia she taught local birth attendants – both professional and lay people – basic and extended maternal care practices. The local women also came up with the idea of developing waiting houses for expectant mothers. Margit writes:

'I started working in Cambodia in late 2004, and throughout 2005 other European colleagues, qualified Cambodian midwives and I rolled out training for almost 500 lay health workers in basic obstetrical care. These health workers came from 266 villages in remote areas. We also conducted antenatal classes for women of reproductive age. A main message was to encourage women to give birth at health centres rather than at home. However, after two years of training still very few women opted for the health centre rather than for home delivery. We therefore asked the midwives in our network to interview local midwives and traditional birth attendants to explain why this was the case (see Chan et al., n.d.). The subsequent interview data included:

- that it was too expensive to give birth at the health centre;
- that travel was too expensive;
- that there was no place to stay at the health centre.

'So the problem of insufficient beds at the health centre was quickly identified as one of the major obstacles for many expecting mothers. Also the health centre could not offer lodging, so the mother would have to pay for her stay at a guesthouse, which was prohibitive for most rural Cambodians who live in extreme poverty. So, acting on this advice, we facilitated the building of eight waiting houses in the vicinity of the most remote health centres. The waiting house is a simple building that can accommodate 4–6 women and their companions, with basic facilities and access to a professional midwife on call. Accommodation is free, though women provide their own food and equipment for the baby and themselves.

(Continued)

(Continued)

'Just by strengthening the infrastructure with these eight modest buildings, the number of deliveries increased at all health centres by 50-100%. In 2014 more than 1000 women used them, which means that approximately 1000 women had a safer delivery. Their newborns also got a better start in life because availability of beds meant that mother and baby could be more closely monitored after delivery, and allowed the first doses of essential vaccines to be given to the baby prior to the family's departure for their village.

'The interesting thing was that we - the Western health-workers - were initially quite sceptical about building waiting houses. Studies from other countries had shown that they have little impact on maternal health indicators, and for medically trained personnel, it may be provocative to suggest that material improvements are more important than procedures and medication. But we listened to the locals who were, of course, right this time too.'

Further, according to Sennan Siv, a now-research active local midwife, commenting on interview data gathered from other local midwives whom she and Margit taught:

> Our informants [local midwives] said that the waiting houses make it more convenient to use public health services, especially for delivery assistance, and that they personally use these services more because of the waiting house ... Further, many report an improvement in social relationships and trust between local people and health centre staff. So, based on our findings, we conclude that both rural people and health staff see waiting houses as a valuable service to the rural poor in Cambodia ... [which] is likely to contribute to a reduction in maternal and perinatal mortality rates over time (Siv et al. n.d.).

Let's now think about the problematic issue of living with cognitive and emotional dissonance.

Living with cognitive and emotional dissonance

Many researchers begin their enquiries because they want to improve certain aspects of their work or work situation, so that they can live more fully in the direction of their social and educational values. Sometimes they will find themselves in situations where this is not happening, and they will have to cope with what Festinger (1957) termed 'cognitive dissonance', which can then also lead to emotional dissonance. Ilyenkov (1977) coined the term 'a living contradiction', which may be construed as being in a situation when your values are denied by other people who hold different values, or by yourself. For example, you may believe in freedom of speech but find that this is not allowed in your context. You may find also that your values can conflict with personal and social interests (which are themselves based on values).

Examples of these different sets of values-conflict are as follows:

- You are invited and would like to go to a party to enjoy the company, but you feel you ought to get on with your studies (conflicting values of the importance of sociability and conscientiousness).

- You really don't want to go to the party because you should be studying but you know that you will meet influential people there who will help your career (conflicting values of conscientiousness and self-service).
- As a doctor you wish to spend more time with individual patients but you have to achieve institutional targets for the number of patients you see (conflicting personal values of care and institutional values of efficiency and producing outcomes).

The question then arises: how do we make decisions about which option to choose?

There are no definitive rule books to offer guidance, and perhaps you will have to accept that life is full of irreconcilable dilemmas so you will need to compromise. But as has been pointed out in Chapter 4 and throughout this book, you can develop your own strategies for getting your own way in spite of institutional prohibitions and efforts to stop you. This means first deciding what you really want out of life and what you are prepared to do to achieve it.

Which goals do you wish to achieve?

Perhaps a common-sense response it to try to be clear about your personal and social goals. What is worth fighting for? What are you prepared to suffer for? How do you see your responsibilities as a thinker, a public intellectual who has something to say to others and to the world? Chomsky (1987) speaks about the responsibilities of intellectuals, which are, he says, to tell the truth and expose lies. This can often bring danger as well as considerable dissonance. Said (1994) also emphasises that intellectuals should be critical of their own personal assumptions as well as the external ones to be found, for example, in policy documents: 'The purpose of the intellectual's activity is to advance human freedom and knowledge', he says (1994: 13), and 'An intellectual life is fundamentally about knowledge and freedom' (1994: 44). Positioning yourself as a public intellectual means you will always be an outsider, not part of the bureaucratic machine, yet the loneliness of being an outsider is preferable to selling your soul. Some organisations will want your soul as well as your productive work, so you will then have to make choices about what you are going to keep as your own and what you are prepared to forfeit.

Adopting a critical stance is vital for sustainable organisational development, as shown in the following example.

Margit Steinholt explains how gender issues were always problematic in the Cambodian project, yet were not fully picked up by the male participants until her involvement. She writes:

'In the Cambodian maternity research project we (the European outsiders) initially did not understand the nature of the conflict between local doctors and midwives. In hindsight we perceived that this was a conflict between different professions, a conflict of genders, since most Cambodian doctors are men, and a conflict of wealth and class, since most doctors came from the more affluent urban areas while the rural midwives were poorer and frequently from ethnic minorities ... Interesting also was the revelation that the complexities of these conflicts were not understood fully even by my Norwegian male colleagues who had been working in the Cambodian project for several years before I came on the scene. It was, however, apparent to me from the start because the Cambodian male doctors showed less respect for me whenever I conducted training by myself ... However, now that the problem had been surfaced it could be dealt with.'

3. The importance of seeing yourself as a knowledgeable and competent theorist

In my view, it is the responsibility of practitioners to see and present themselves to others as knowledgeable and competent theorists. Sometimes practitioners are put off by the word 'theory' because both the word and its meanings are often presented in the literatures in dense, difficult-to-understand language. This is when you need to take a critical stance and ask, 'Why do writers deliberately put straightforward ideas into difficult language?' Learn to look behind the smokescreen and see things for what they are: many elites create public images through hyping up their language. Bourdieu, for example, explains how the French Academy of his day expected sentences to be complex and difficult to understand; you could not be accepted as an intellectual unless you did this (see his books *Distinction* [1984] and *Homo Academicus* [1988]). In real life, of course, you can easily communicate complex ideas in everyday language, as is the case, I hope, in this book. Complexity of expression has little to do with quality of thinking.

This is important, as is your responsibility to present yourself to others as a knowledgeable and competent theorist and not apologise for your stance, though not to promote your own self-importance either. When you tell other people about your work, whether orally or in a written report, you are showing two things. First, you are showing how you have learned to develop innovative practices. Second, you are showing how those ideas about practice are your own original contribution, albeit created in company with others. You may have adopted, or incorporated, other people's ideas into your own work, but that work is yours, an original contribution to the body of knowledge. Other people can now learn from you, and adapt or incorporate your ideas if they wish. You need to celebrate this: you are actively showing Arendt's (1958) idea of natality, the idea that you are contributing something new to the world through your research.

You can in fact contribute to the body of knowledge in several ways. Following Noffke (2009), it is possible to see how your thinking can contribute to different dimensions, including the personal (where you show how you have examined your own practice and explain how you hold yourself accountable for what you are doing), the professional (where you show how this can contribute to other people's understandings and encourage them to do the same), and the political (where new practices of self-evaluation and personal accountability become part of everyday organisational practices). In Sharples' (1999) terminology, you show how you are contributing to your own thinking, to others' and to the world's. This happens at the level of practice and of theory: you are contributing to the practical lifeworld by adding your story of practice, and to the intellectual lifeworld by offering your explanations for practice, your theory of practice.

Look at Table 5.5 and consider the different ways you have, or will have, developed useful knowledge and how this can be used.

The idea of contributing to the intellectual lifeworld is important. Edward Said (1994) talks about practitioners as public intellectuals. Perhaps all practitioners should be seen potentially as public intellectuals. Many shopkeepers and pop singers have as worthwhile contributions to make as professional elites. The fact remains that as a professional you are in a privileged position where you can use your voice. Unless you use your voice and profess your status as a public intellectual, you will not be heard. If you are not heard you will continue to be marginalised and not be taken seriously. Freire (1972) argued that it is important to name our world, for in doing so we claim it, and Foucault (2001) speaks about parrhesia, a concept that communicates the need and responsibility of people to speak their truth as they see it.

Yet claiming that you should be seen as a researcher and therefore a theorist brings responsibilities: these ideas are developed further in Chapter 7.

In the meantime, consider now how these ideas about the responsibilities of practitioner-researchers play out further in the fields of practice (Chapter 6) and theory (Chapter 7), and the need for testing your ideas against others in the literatures (Chapter 8).

Table 5.5   What have I learned? How is it useful?

What do I know now that I didn't know before I did my research?	How is it useful for myself?	How might it be useful for other people?	How might it be useful for the world?
I have learned the importance of studying my own practice.	Now I do not take things for granted: I have learned to critique.	I can encourage others not to take things for granted; I can encourage them to learn how to critique.	Through making my research available through a website I can show the importance of practitioners studying their practices and learning how to critique normative assumptions and their own.
I have learned how to write for a reader.	I can use this learning in all my life circumstances.	I can encourage other people to learn how to write for a reader.	I can develop a blog and online conversations to show the importance of learning to write for a reader.
I have learned to identify myself as a researcher as well as a practitioner.	I can use my practice-based research knowledge for all life circumstances.	I can encourage other people also to develop their researcher identities alongside and as part of their practitioner identities.	I can promote the idea of practitioners seeing themselves as researchers too, and of researchers also seeing themselves as practitioners.

Summary

This chapter has addressed the question, 'Why do action research?' It has put forward two main reasons, to do with the importance of seeing yourself as a knowledgeable and competent practitioner and a knowledgeable and competent theorist. For many people this means changing their self-perceptions and self-identification. Currently many practitioners still see themselves as working in a practice context but not in a knowledge context, and action research is often seen as a form of professional development rather than also as a form of practical theorising. To have your work taken seriously as contributing to wider debates, including policy debates, you have to regard yourself as contributing to both practice and theory.

The next chapter considers the responsibility of practitioner-researchers in relation to how they can contribute to new practices.

--- **EXERCISES** ---

- Think about how you position yourself in relation with others in your workplace and in everyday life. Why do you position yourself like this? Could there be another way?
- Think about how you position others in relation to you in your workplace and everyday life. Why do you position them like this? Could there be another way?
- How do you see yourself contributing to new practices? In what way? Why is this important? What are your contributions? Why are they important? Be prepared to defend your position to others and throughout your writing.

The responsibilities of practitioner-researchers: contributing to new practices and new learning

This chapter looks at the responsibilities of practitioners in terms of taking action in the world. 'Action', according to Arendt (1958), is not the same as 'activity'. Activities can take different forms: Arendt identifies three as labour, work and action. 'Labour' is about mundane actions, the basic necessities of life such as washing up and doing the housework. 'Work' is when we live a productive life, during which we produce useful and worthwhile artefacts. 'Action' is when we think and explain our aims and purposes through the way we speak and live our lives: it is a form of meaning-making, a way of giving purpose and direction to life. When you take action you become an actor in the world; this is purposeful, morally committed action. In my view, possibly the most important kind of action is to contribute to new learning that will enable others also to give meaning to their lives; we do this through what we say and do.

There is a big difference between taking action as a practitioner and taking action as a researcher:

- As a practitioner you take practical action to influence what other people do in practice.
- As a researcher you state the reasons and purposes for your actions. You become a thinker: you consider what it means to act; you present your conclusions for others' consideration and think about possible implications. Thinking becomes a main form of action.

When you put practical action and intellectual action together you become a practitioner researcher. Often the two identities of actor and thinker go hand in glove, but often not. Some people act without thinking while others think without acting. Your aim as a thoughtful practitioner is to combine the two: you think as you act and you then take new action informed by that thinking. You act in a way that is in keeping with what you hope to achieve in the world, often in the form of the realisation of your values.

This chapter focuses on the nature and responsibilities of our everyday work as practitioners. My view is that our main responsibility as practitioners, regardless of the setting or professional focus, is to contribute to improving learning, both our own and that of others. Learning acts as the basis for improving practices that we then continually try to improve further. This also carries the conditions of recognising our social and historical situatedness within a dialogical and evolving world.

However, the idea of 'improvement' is problematic, so this point needs addressing first.

The chapter is organised as the following three sections:

1.   The problematic nature of 'improvement'
2.   Understanding influence
3.   Exercising educational influence to improve practices

1. The problematic nature of 'improvement'

In any discussion about improvement tricky questions arise, including:

- Improvement of what?
- Improvement by whom?
- Improvement for what?

Improvement of what?

Consider a permeating theme of this book, about bounded and unbounded visions of how the world works and how you choose to position yourself to achieve those visions. This has implications for how you understand the nature of improvement, because it involves how you identify yourself and others and act towards them. You can choose to see yourself as an outsider, separate from others: your relationship with others becomes that of 'I–It' (Buber, 1937) and you see others as objects in your space. In this case you may believe it is possible to improve them: perhaps you would think you know best and have the right and responsibility to put them straight. However, if you see yourself in a spiritual dialogue with others, sharing the same world with equal entitlement (in Buber's terms, you develop an 'I–Thou' relationship), you would probably see your responsibility more as helping them to act for themselves, or if necessary to act in their interests if they are not able to take action themselves. This has implications for how, as a collective, you negotiate your understanding of what counts as 'good'.

Odd Edvardsen is a member of the team that includes Margit Steinholt, introduced in Chapter 5. Odd is a nurse and a nurse educator at the UiT, the Arctic University in Tromsø; he and I worked together there as participants in an action research group. In 1999 a small group of health workers, including Odd and Hans Husum, a surgeon, established the Tromsø Mine Victim Resource Centre (TMC) in the University Hospital in cooperation with the Faculty of Health Sciences (see Edvardsen, 2006; Husum et al., 2000). Odd and Hans worked together, and with others who wished to share their work, in a range of war zones, including Burma, Northern Iraq and Angola. The initial focus was on treating landmine victims, but later, in what then became post-conflict zones, this developed into helping communities learn the necessary medical and practical knowledge to help themselves. Odd and I spoke frequently about the politics of knowledge in relation to who owned professional knowledge: whether organisational elites (which is the view in the dominant literatures) or locals. Reflecting on his work with others in Cambodia, he says:

'When I think about the politics of knowledge, the priority seems to be the need to build local competence. People can acquire knowledge and adapt it to their local context. This has been done in many places: it was a core theme in the work of Paulo Freire, and is an important political concept for influencing development projects. This was our experience too. Seen from an action research perspective, it is obvious that the local people we worked with were able to assess their own practices and identify which fields they wanted to improve. Our approach was to teach directly in the villages – hence the Village University. We needed to challenge the hegemony of the knowledge tradition imposed by the dominant Western NGOs. Our aim was to develop a chain of survival in the rural areas in order to get the injured to the surgical hospital alive. We trained locals in basic and advanced life support and they in turn educated a lot of first helpers as assistants. They also took on the training we delivered to the medics and modified it according to their needs. It was a chain of survival but it also became a chain of new knowledge and practices. The death rate went down from about 40% for mine victims to about 10% in the areas we were working in.

'But other considerations began to emerge: what about the living conditions for the survivors? Also, more women were dying in childbirth than people dying from mine injuries, so what about them? Malaria was also a big problem for the injured when the trauma attacked their immune system. The local chain of survival needed to broaden its scope. Also local people need sturdy prostheses but to avail of prostheses from the World Health Organisation, which was the recognised supplier, people had to leave their homes and jobs on their farms and go to the city, which was difficult for them. So we had to change our focus again, from saving limbs and lives to helping people learn how to save themselves. This shift happened over time and is probably now the main focus of our work.

'We set up a research school in Cambodia, and ran professional education courses for doctors, nurses, midwives and other health professionals, to teach them basic subject knowledge about medical care and how to research these matters for themselves. Twenty participants from urban and rural areas became participants: the course lasted for four years, and at the end all twenty graduated with distinction.'

Improvement by whom?

Questions arise: is 'improvement' something done by one person to another? Or is it something that people do for themselves, perhaps supported by others? From this second perspective, taking action becomes a matter of how you can help people to find ways to improve themselves.

The idea of improvement is everywhere in the literatures, including in action research literatures. The dominant view is that 'experts' provide others with answers to problems, that it is the responsibility of experts to improve others. It is also assumed that something has to be wrong for that improvement to happen, though this is not the case. As Hopkins stated 'You don't have to be ill to get better' (cited in Ainscow, 1999: 84): even Olympic champions, the best in the world, strive to improve their performance.

The view adopted by Odd and colleagues is different. They believe, like other critical researchers including Chambers (1993), Easterly (2013), Sen (1999) and Stiglitz (2002), that:

- all development work, whether this focuses on organisations-based professional development or community-based rural development, should be person-centred and learner-centred; any knowledge generated must be relevant and useful for the people whose needs it serves within their own cultures and traditions;
- mental and spiritual growth emerges through learning, and this implies that people must be free to learn and imagine what works best for them in their own situations;
- all people are capable of thinking for themselves and able to decide what is right for their particular circumstances, and all people have the right to research (Appadurai, 1996) and come to their own conclusions;
- so-called 'indigenous or local knowledge' is as valuable, and should be as valued, as the 'authorised knowledge' of higher education and corporate settings;
- all individuals and collectives are capable of self-organising and adapting to changing circumstances, and all are capable of imagining new futures and producing action plans for how to achieve these;
- ideas are created through dialogue, which itself involves interpretation and negotiation, and the growth of knowledge may be seen as a process of unbounded potential where ideas change their form through negotiation to form self-renewing ideas.

These assumptions are also those of action research: development work then becomes a form of educational enquiry in action. The assumptions are also informed by the key principles of natality (that all citizens are seen as actors who contribute to the renewal of the social world) and plurality, with the implication that it becomes the responsibility of those with position power to help less powerful others realise their capacity for action and the creation of new possibilities. It becomes the responsibility of legitimised institutional researchers to encourage everyday citizens to do research, develop appropriate meta-cognition in order to explain their own learning and social practices, and publish their work through spoken and written texts so that still others may learn from them. Practitioners' work therefore takes the form of ever-widening circles of influence, with the exponential potential for unlimited acts of influence, where knowledge is in a constant state of being passed on, developing through the process.

Odd continues:

'Through working with our research group in Tromsø, I also began to appreciate more deeply the potentials of action research, and this in turn helped me to understand what I was doing in Cambodia. The politics of knowledge were evident in the end-of-project research conference, held to celebrate the achievements of the locals who had taken part in our professional education programmes, when an academic from a local university challenged what participants were doing. He came from a position of institutional power. This was symptomatic of the kind of opposition we faced. Even from the beginning of the project we came up against the opposition of central health authorities and also from organisations like UNICEF or Médicins Sans Frontières: these kinds of organisations tend to be against sharing their knowledge of pre-hospital procedures. They told us, "You cannot teach people; besides, it is unethical to teach people procedures for which you need to be a qualified doctor in Europe." Well, perhaps it is the case that people in Cambodia have less competence than in Europe, but there are very few doctors in Cambodia, especially in rural areas, so you have choices: you can let them die or you can give knowledge to the people. But this means you have to believe that people are able to learn. And we did: right from the start of our project. It was clear that people could learn very well. We developed these kinds of initiatives in collaboration with the local health authorities; however, we did not introduce parallel structures but always included whatever local resources were available in the health system.

'They also learned how to be teachers so that they could teach the next generation, and they also knew what was good for local conditions too. The contribution of us Europeans was to teach them anything they did not already know, and introduce them to some pedagogical strategies such as systematically reflecting on their experiences and developing new understandings. You also need to ask people, "How do you communicate your learning to others? What methodology do you use?" They decided to hold regular meetings to discuss their experiences and learning, and they also made systematic time for reflection. This was a pedagogical experience the likes of which they had never had before. They regularly reflected on their experiences and contributed to one another's learning.'

Improvement for what?

However, if you adopt an unconstrained or unbounded stance, you do not set out to impose change on others. Change imposed by an external agency does little for sustainable renewal. Change that comes from within, and according to people's own wishes, does. Polanyi speaks about the capacity of all systems to self-organise: he says that if you try to fit ten potatoes together perfectly you will not succeed: but if you put them into a sack and give them a good shake, they will self-organise (cited in Mitchell, 2006: 22–3). The idea of self-organisation is core to complexity theory and action research: systems and sub-systems have the capacity for spontaneous self-organisation. Nature manages itself (perhaps 'management' on this view means 'managing to stay out of the way'). Your work is therefore to contribute to your own and other people's capacity for independent thinking: they decide how they wish to live, and you support them while they work things out for themselves.

Odd continues:

'But part of doing a development project is to ask, "So what? What are the consequences of your contribution?" We were also aware that we Europeans had so far only delivered professional education programmes, with a strong medical and healthcare focus. We now had to think about how we could help people to evaluate their own work. This would be the last step in making them independent of us foreigners, the last stage of dependency. So we ran a pilot that opened up new perspectives, about how to do basic science and what kind of research methods to use. We decided to offer courses in qualitative and quantitative studies; people could choose. I was involved in the qualitative group and we talked a lot about what action research involved. This was not straightforward because there were different opinions

(Continued)

(Continued)

about this among our Norwegian team of teachers. My own views were about how you can improve things and evaluate them. So we developed projects that looked more or less like action research projects.

'What about writing? This was a big challenge for everyone. Doctors had some academic training as did midwives, but generally speaking they were very practically oriented, not theoretically. Also, except for one of the doctors their English language skills were zero. The problem in Cambodia is that the whole international literature is unavailable as there are no translations. So we spent a lot of time translating important articles, but when they started to do research they couldn't access what had been done in the field internationally. A further difficulty was that all our teaching was in English so needed to be translated at every step. And they needed a lot of help when writing up their project plan. And when it came to writing up their experiences, well, we might as well have been on Mars. Reflecting on their experiences was challenge enough but to do it in writing was - Wow! However, the results showed that it is possible but it was tough: so many things were alien to their experience.'

Let's now consider the nature of influence.

2. Understanding influence

People sometimes think influence is sinister and negative. This is not so. We are all influenced all the time, and we have the capacity to exercise influence. We learn how to think and act and make choices. This does not just happen. We learn from our books, families, friends and colleagues, according to the specific traditions of our particular culture. Some people choose not to be influenced by social norms, and therefore to do their own thing, but this choice is itself influenced by other voices. Our relationships of influence are multidimensional. They are horizontal across space and time, in terms of who we are currently interacting with, and vertical, existing through space and time. Most of us are influenced by what went before and by visions of the future. These ideas may be found in different bodies of literature, including that of dialogue, drawing on the work of Bakhtin (1986), Buber (1937), Macmurray (1961), and complexity theory (Mason, 2008; Waldrop, 1992).

As well as being influenced by others, each person has the capacity to exercise influence. What we say and do potentially influences others, whether we realise it or not. This then has enormous implications for all of us. How can you ensure that your influence contributes in a life-affirming way? How can you help yourself and others to grow? And in which direction do you want to grow: towards critical self-reflection or towards reinforcing prejudices?

Odd says:

'But the Cambodians managed to make their way in very small steps. Many of them held interviews with other local people and reflected on their experiences and then they did it again and began to understand why the interviews were successful. We talked about how the interviews we held were quite artificial, possibly because the people being interviewed had never been interviewed before. We asked, why interview? They said they wanted to find out different things, what the situation was like in the villages for example, and assess the level of knowledge and competence of local people. From participants we Europeans learned about the everyday life of families, and what it meant to do different kinds of fieldwork. When participants decided what kind of projects they would do, one group focused on pregnancy classes and interviewed pregnant women: this helped them to check whether their own work was useful. In traditional local contexts there are a lot of superstitious beliefs about pregnancy which people tend to observe. Our participants interviewed first helpers who had attended our courses to evaluate how they perceived the importance of the course and the extent to which were they able to develop their practice. But interviews are Western ways of getting knowledge and Cambodians have an oral culture, so if you have never been interviewed before, how do you respond to the word "interview"? They initially asked, "Why should we hold interviews? What is an interview?" But we practised in the classroom and they interviewed each other and reflected on the experience, which was very useful, though it was usually a one-way interview. I recall one participant who imposed his views on some poor woman who was acting as his informant: they had very short "yes-no" interviews. Over time, participants began to learn the importance of a conversational approach, but this happens only when and if you are you interested in other people's experiences; it will not happen if you are not.'

Related concepts in the literatures

Working with the literatures can help: other writers can give you strong conceptual frameworks for sorting out your own ideas. A conceptual framework may be seen as a picture frame that contains existing ideas within itself or as a sculptor's armature around which you build new ideas (McNiff, 2017). Both perspectives can be useful for different contexts.

Some theorists, such as Rousseau and Hume, believed that a child is born as a 'blank slate' or 'empty vessel' into which learning, usually information, is poured. They seemed to believe that people have to learn to become human. Conversely, Chomsky (1986) says that people have an infinite capacity for knowledge generation as part of their genetic make-up. On this view, we have unlimited potentials to learn an infinite amount of new knowledge. Polanyi (1958) says much the same, also maintaining that we know more than we can say. We know how things are, but cannot always explain why, and we know how to do some things without knowing how we do these (riding a bike, for example, or recognising the face of someone you know out of a million other faces). Polanyi calls this personal, or tacit, knowledge. We all know more than we can say.

These ideas link well with an idea by Valéry, elaborated on by Said (1997: 14). Like Polanyi and Chomsky, Said speaks about the idea that each individual is born with originality of mind, the capacity for independent, original thinking. They use this capacity to filter, or mediate, whatever they hear and experience. Consequently, when you say something to another person, that person does not necessarily immediately agree with everything you say, but filters it to decide which pieces to accept or reject: they exercise their capacity for critique. We all tend to do this, when, say, we listen to a news broadcast and decide whether or not we agree with what is being said. You are doing the same as you read this book. This idea is important when it is a matter of understanding how learning happens. A major responsibility for practitioners is to learn to critique the Discourses (what is said and done) in which they live, and not accept everything they hear.

Processes of coming to know (learning) are complex. One view is that we raise our deep tacit knowledge to an explicit level. This idea can be linked with Chomsky's (1965) and Goethe's (1988[1790]) ideas about generative transformational capacity, a developmental process that enables a present form to emerge as a new form. These ideas give rise to a theory of learning that accepts the infinite capacity of humans to create an infinite number of new forms of knowledge, and to transform their existing knowledge into new improved forms. This means that each person should be recognised as having the capacity for creative choice and for making original contributions.

Now link this with an idea from Habermas (1975): in the processes of social evolution, he says, people are not capable of not learning, that is, we automatically learn as part of our genetic make-up. The question arises, how do people decide what to learn? This has implications for practitioners with agency. Do we exercise our influence in ways that respect each person's uniqueness of mind and unlimited capacity for unlimited acts of creation, or do we aim to influence so that we deny those opportunities? Do we give others the choice to exercise their capacity for choice?

Odd says:

'We aimed generally for empowerment at different levels: if you are introducing knowledge that is useful to people they will develop. In the graduation ceremony there were midwives who had previously been shy and not able to look at you, now they blossomed and developed great confidence: boy, were they strong! They were proud, and rightly so. You could see this in the group: initially it was the doctors who took a leading role but after a while the girls and nurses began to join in the discussions too. The doctors learned important lessons about the need to listen and learn. We put doctors into placements outside the city and they came back shocked and said they had learned how bad the living conditions were. It was a real eye opener for them. Some of the others were close to the villagers. Others were aware of their superior social position so felt they were able to look down on someone else. The idea of action research, however, is "How can I go into my own practice and see what I can improve?" This was an important motivation and they were all committed to that.'

Influence does not 'just happen', as Marlin (2002) and Chomsky (1991) emphasise. Accepting or rejecting influence is a matter of discernment. We hear voices everywhere, through advertisements, films and comedy shows. Which ones we attend to is up to us. We are all able to exercise our originality of mind and critical judgement when deciding what to think and how to think. Having said this, it has to be recognised that some people choose not to think for themselves, and other people are persuaded to believe certain things. This is often a case of insidious influence.

It is not only a matter of you influencing others, but also of how you are influenced. What you do and how you do it is your choice. Choosing is one of your freedoms. While imprisoned in a concentration camp, Victor Frankl (1963) chose to adopt life-affirming attitudes, and Etty Hillesum (1983, quoted in Todorov, 1999) chose to forgive her persecutors. Most of us are able to choose, even though we may live in prisons of one kind or another. Retaining this capacity is sometimes impossible when a direct assault is made on controlling our minds.

Choices frequently involve tension, which can be both creative and obstructive. Choices are seldom simply a matter of right and wrong, but often a question of choosing between competing rights. Who was 'right' in the civil war? The project in Cambodia became as much about post-war peace-building as about learning subject knowledge; people learned how to care again about others who held different views. Perhaps we all have to learn how to negotiate a way through so that we can live as we wish in company with others who want to do the same.

3. Exercising educational influence to improve practices

You can show how you are improving practice through improving learning by exercising your educational influence in your own and other people's learning. Does your dissertation show you thinking for yourself and encouraging others to think for themselves? Do you create the kinds of relationships that will encourage people to feel safe enough to critique? This means they can also critique you. How do you show that you are influencing in an educational way and not cleverly manipulating?

In an interview, a senior surgeon recounted his experiences of participating in the professional education course. Reflecting on his experience of the civil war he says:

'I was on a mobile team at the front line combat zone for three years, along the Cambodia-Thailand border. We had a lot of casualties, about 60% from landmine injuries, the rest from bullets and other weapons. Difficulties were compounded because of general disease such as malaria, affecting more than 50%. I performed more surgery on the front line than in hospital ... There was a lack of everything: lack of medicine, lack of transportation. Cambodia is a poor country. Some died because of the lack of medicine. Some died of complications including post-operative wound infection. The experience of field surgery is awful.'

Speaking of the knowledge gained through the research training course, he says:

'The course helped me learn how to stop or reduce post-operative wound infection. I now have that knowledge. During the research and afterwards, I also spread the knowledge around the hospital. I will use this knowledge and share it with young physicians who can learn to do the same. Without the course it would be just like during the war. I would not have this knowledge; I would not know what to do.'

Similarly, a senior administrator, speaking of the experience of the Village University, says:

'Prior to doing this course I had limited knowledge of research and saw no need to do it. As a senior leader all I had to do was point my finger and people would do what I told them to. I had no knowledge of technology: I could not even send an email. I also had no understanding of what went on in rural communities, the difficulties they faced, or the work of, for example, traditional birth attendants. Now, after the four years of the course I can send emails. I also have deep knowledge of the conditions of people in rural communities, and I am anxious to pass on my knowledge institutionally. Getting to this point has meant I have had to get rid of previous thinking and see others and myself as equal. I now want to influence systems so that this equality can continue.'

Demonstrating educational influence involves certain conditions, including:

- you make a commitment to your own capacity for knowing;
- you can produce evidence to support what you are saying.

You make a commitment to your own capacity for knowing

Polanyi (see above) says that any act of knowing involves commitment, a personal faith that the knowledge we create is potentially right. It can be difficult, he says, to make such a commitment while also accepting the possibility that one might be mistaken. Nevertheless, this should not prevent each one of us from making our claims to knowledge with universal intent (Polanyi, 1958: 327), that is, saying that we have learned something, with the intent of helping others to learn from our learning. We must also be open to ongoing critique, so that we can refine our learning in light of the critique.

You can produce evidence to support what you are saying

The idea of evidence is crucial in all research, including in action research. Research is a process of finding out in order to create new knowledge. If you say you now know something that you did not know before, you can be reasonably confident that someone will say, 'Prove it'. While you cannot 'prove it', and nor should you even get into using such language, you can produce reasonable evidence to support your claim to knowledge.

At this point think about how you can demonstrate how you are exercising your influence to improve learning for improving practices, both your own and other people's.

Evidence is generated from data (see Chapter 15), so to produce evidence of your influence, you would need to provide data that showed how learning influenced your own and other people's actions. In *You and Your Action Research Project* (McNiff, 2016b: 163) I made the point that in any learning episode the influence of learning can happen at multiple interrelated levels, including the following:

- How you are developing your learning to inform your actions.
- How your learning (and actions) contribute to other people's learning and, in turn, their actions.
- How their learning and actions influence your own.
- How these mutually reciprocal processes amount to the transformation of existing knowledge into new knowledge with potential for ongoing influence in the world.

This set of relationships can be summarised as in Figure 6.1.

When you produce your research report you will make the claim that you have improved your practice by improving your learning, and you have encouraged others to do the same. The others in question would be people such as your students, colleagues, peers and those in senior positions.

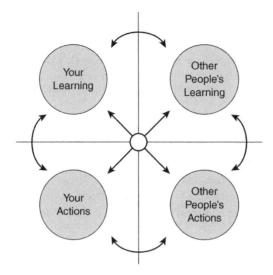

Figure 6.1   Transformational relationships of mutually reciprocal influence

Credit: McNiff, 2016b: 164

Your claim to improved learning would be supported by validated evidence (see Chapter 15 for advice on generating evidence). This can be problematic. It is straightforward enough to produce illustrative material to show people in action, but it is a far more rigorous process to produce evidence, which is about extracting from your data those instances that you believe are manifestations of your values in practice, which in turn have acted as your criteria for making judgements about quality. For you, your commitment to learning is a value that inspires your work. How to produce evidence of learning?

Producing evidence of your own learning

Producing evidence of your own learning is not difficult. You can, for example, find data in your learning journal, and point to instances when you learned something new and articulated what you had learned. You can explain the significance of that learning for you. You can produce memos, tweets and emails when you seemed to be saying new things, influenced by new learning.

Producing evidence of other people's learning

Producing evidence of other people's learning is more problematic as it means producing instances of them saying that they have influenced their own learning or that someone else, including you, have influenced their learning: your evidence would be more robust if you could get their testimony that this actually was the case. This means asking the people themselves to say what they have learned and the significance of their learning. Their responses would stand as evidence of their learning. In this way, it is possible to show how learning enters into action, so action is shown to be purposeful and committed and not just a spur of the moment reaction.

Reflecting on the consequences of his learning, the senior administrator continues:

'The [European] tutors emphasised that there would be no pointy noses in the air, chest up and shiny shoes. My feet became dusty equal to midwives and traditional birth attendants (TBAs), and they accepted me. The relationship became equal and we could respect each other.'

A health centre manager commented:

'We became like brother and sister, though it depends on the person. When you come here you expect a picnic, not a tablecloth. You come here with an open mind, no plans – you simply get on with it. We staff are free to make decisions, and ordinary people can learn with and from us. This was the process. You cannot change people but you can do something to change systems. People change themselves and you can exercise your influence.'

A further step is needed, however, if you want to produce evidence of your influence in other people's learning. Again, this means asking them questions such as, 'Have I influenced your learning? How?' The fact that they may learn to copy what you say, or use your language, is no evidence that they have learned to think for themselves. You can produce, say, video clips of people debating and using their capacity for creativity, but to claim that they are doing that because of your influence means getting their testimony that this is the case.

Producing evidence of your educational influence can be difficult, but it can be done. More advice and ideas are presented in Chapter 15.

Summary

This chapter has considered issues of what it means to improve learning in order to improve practice. It has especially considered ideas to do with the nature of influence, and how you can exercise your own educational influence to improve practices. Doing action research emphasises the need to exercise influence in ways that are educational. This becomes one of the responsibilities of practitioner-researchers.

This chapter has considered ideas about contributing to new practices through improving learning. The next chapter looks at ideas about improving theory through improving learning.

─────────────────────────── EXERCISES ───────────────────────────

- How do you understand the idea of improvement? Do you see yourself improving others or helping them to improve themselves?
- Similarly, how do you understand the idea of influence? How do you exercise your influence, and in relation to what?
- Do you set out to persuade others to see things your way or to make up their own minds about what is the right way for them? How do you manage the dilemma when you are convinced that they are on the wrong path and should follow your way?
- Write about any workplace or everyday life episode when you had to confront this dilemma. Say what you did and why you did it.

The responsibilities of practitioner-researchers: contributing to new thinking and ideas

In Chapter 6 we considered the responsibility of practitioners to act, and said that perhaps the most important form of acting was to think and, based on that thinking, to act practically in the world. A core aim of this process is to contribute to new learning for new actions: action should always be informed, which means using one's judgement and ethical imagination. In this chapter we switch the focus to the responsibility of practitioners as researchers and the potentials of contributing to new ideas and new thinking. Appadurai (1996) said that it is the right of all people to research. I agree with this and would also maintain that it is the responsibility of all people to research: we all need to do research if we wish to challenge misleading and outmoded ideas, contribute to new thinking and suggest better options for living. I would also re-emphasise the need to appreciate research for what it does in helping us to make sense of and interpret how we understand our place in the world and in our using it to promote improved understanding and justice through sharing ideas. The new learning in question therefore becomes learning for self, for others and for the world. These ideas provide the contents of the chapter:

1. Responsibilities of doing research for oneself
2. Responsibilities of doing research for others
3. Responsibilities of doing research for the world

1. Responsibilities of doing research for oneself

We are constantly bombarded with information, much of it untrue. It is the responsibility of all thoughtful persons to find out for themselves what is going on so that they can decide whether or not to believe what they are told and act accordingly; it is a matter of self-education. In the same way as you are responsible for your practical actions so you are also responsible for your intellectual actions (that is, your thinking and decisions). This means being alert to the news as communicated through the media, and constantly using your capacity for critique to under-standing the wider contexts in which issues are located and the form of discourses used to present these. You need this kind of critically-filtered information in order to take part in debates about the kind of social order you wish your children to live in.

> The action moves from Cambodia back to Ireland and Northern Ireland, in the 1990s. I tell about my learning about discrimination, prejudice and conflicting stories.
>
> A child of Scottish-Irish descent, I grew up in England and won a scholarship to what was then a direct grant secondary school: this was a school for girls from privileged families, though the school had to take a quota of scholarship girls, usually from working-class back-grounds, in order to receive its government funding. I hated my schooldays because students and teachers were snobbish and laughed at my Scottish accent, though I will always be grateful for the first-class education I received. I will also always be grateful to my parents for working as they did in order to send me there.
>
> As part of our history lessons, we learned the orthodox stories. These included stories about the Irish rebellion. I grew up thinking in terms of the Irish as rebels. Also my father had joined the British Army as a boy soldier and told proud stories of going to Ireland as his first posting to fight those Irish rebels. This was the standard story in those days, the story I grew up with.

Developing the capacity for critical thinking means constantly being alert to efforts to mis-lead you, as outlined in Chomsky's (1991) *Media Control: The Spectacular Achievements of Propaganda*. There he explains how ordinary people are persuaded via a sophisticated propa-ganda system to believe that they are not capable of thinking for themselves. This practice comes largely out of the desire of small groups of privileged elites, mainly within the corporate business community (including the now corporate academic community), to keep ordinary people from questioning the messages they are given, and also from aspiring to get involved in debates about how countries should be run or what kinds of societies are worth living in. It is a form of fundamentalism where it is forbidden to question the truth of what you are told. Traditionalist views of history work in this way: history is supposed to stand as a record of the achievements of great people (usually men). However, critical historians such as Howard Zinn (2005) explain how this is not the case: Columbus did not 'discover' America – it was already there, populated by thriving communities, whose cultures he aimed systematically to destroy in order to appropriate the land and extract whatever mineral wealth was available. Similarly, media moguls aim to appropriate the public intellectual landscape in order to impose their own version of reality: witness the power of Sky Television that decides who gets to watch the cricket, and who decides what is newsworthy. As Edwards (1998: 133) comments, 'We are trained to be passive consumers, not active thinkers, citizens and moral agents'. Referring to the Herman–Chomsky critique reported in *Manufacturing Consent* (Achbar, 1994), he cites Chomsky as saying:

> In order to progress you have to say certain things, what the copy editor wants, what the top editor is giving back to you. You can try saying it and not believing it, but that's not going to work, people just aren't that dishonest, you can't live with that, it's a very rare person who can do that. So you start saying it and pretty soon you're believing it because you're saying it, and pretty soon you're inside the system. (Chomsky, 1992: 69, cited in Edwards, 1998: 175)

In your case as a participant on a higher education programme, replace 'copy editor' with 'supervisor', and replace 'top editor' with 'dean' or 'vice chancellor'. But again a word of warning: get your degree first and then become actively activist.

In the meantime, you can combat these efforts at closing down your thinking using a range of strategies, including the following.

Acknowledging yourself as an intellectual: An intellectual is not necessarily an academic practitioner. An intellectual is anyone who has a natural inclination to question things, thinks through issues and comes to their own conclusions, from a desire to self-educate and use their ideas. This applies to people everywhere: people talking in supermarkets and across the garden fence are as much intellectuals as those in universities. Further, being an intellectual does not mean thinking from nine to five as part of a day job: this, for Said, is to be a 'professional intellectual' rather than an 'amateur', who, he says, is someone who has a 'love for and an unquenchable interest in the larger picture, in making connections across lines and barriers … in caring for ideas and values despite the restrictions of the profession' (Said, 1994: 76). Thinking for yourself is a life commitment to question and enquire into different stories beyond your specialism. Bayat (2009) talks about 'life as politics': by identifying yourself as an intellectual you insert yourself into the public sphere and use your intellectual acuity for others' benefit.

> In 1992 I was invited to go to Dublin to support the development of what became known as the Schools-Based Action Research Project. This was a highly successful project, run by a private education institution, involving close to a hundred teachers from across Ireland (it is written up as McNiff and Collins, 1994). Out of that project developed a three-year master's degree project: working later directly with the accrediting University of the West of England, I supported groups of teachers around Ireland so that 75 were awarded their master's degrees (this also has been written up, as McNiff, 2000). One of the most striking features of my experience was that, when I first went to Dublin, I looked for the Irish rebels the history books had spoken about but could not find any. What I did find was charming, friendly people who loved the fact that I was Scottish (which was how I identified myself at that time) and related well to my accent.
>
> I could not understand what was going on, so made it a point of business to explore the history of Ireland, and spent hours and hours reading and talking with people. I began to understand that Ireland was not full of nasty rebels but of people who had suffered egregious forms of injustice at the hands of British imperialists, among whose number I was now positioned. I recall being told, 'Our situation is because of your British ancestors.' Not my ancestors: but this was the irony of how I was positioned.

Understanding your own field thoroughly: In order to comment on your subject area you need to know your field well. This means engaging with the literatures, both of your own specialism and of related fields. Rorty (2006: 79) speaks about the importance of reading all books, including old ones: 'The more influential old books one reads, the more prudent one becomes, because the sources and histories of contemporary ideas become clearer'. To be taken seriously as a professional and a person who thinks about their profession and its usefulness to society, you will need to demonstrate your understanding of the wider historical and social issues in which your understanding of local professional issues is embedded. Take care, however, not to focus on an increase in 'know-that', as recommended in the UK (2015) White Paper Report, at the expense of developing deeper understanding of practices.

In August 2016 I visited the commemorative exhibition 'Revolution 1916', an exhibition of the 1916 Easter Uprising, at the Ambassador Theatre, O'Connell Street. It was a heartbreaking experience. What was particularly heartbreaking for me was to think that my beloved father may have been there: that may have been the first posting he was so proud of. But he was a soldier and did what soldiers do.

In the commemorative booklet are recorded Pádraig Pearse's words, prior to his execution:

If you strike us down now, we shall rise again and renew the fight. You cannot conquer Ireland; you cannot extinguish the Irish passion for freedom. If our deed has not been sufficient to win freedom then our children will win it by a better deed.

Perhaps action research is about winning by a better deed.

Making your own theories of practice public: Through questioning the way the world works and taking action based on any new understandings you can say that you have generated your own theory of practice. However, this involves demonstrating a responsibility to the research process in terms of testing the validity of knowledge claims, explaining how you position yourself in the research, which methods you have used to gather data and why, and all other issues of methodological rigour, as explained in Chapter 15. Unless you show yourself to be a rigorous researcher people will not take you seriously as a theorist. This would be a tragedy because your theories of practice can contribute much to wider understandings and to moving your field forward.

The above refers to your ontological responsibilities and commitments. Now let's consider your responsibilities towards others, including your ethical commitments.

2. Responsibilities of doing research for others

Doing research for others may be defined as researching with social intent: you intend your research to be used by others for their purposes. This has implications for you, including the following.

Demonstrating your commitment to social justice: Your research needs to demonstrate a commitment to social justice and a willingness to challenge discrimination and unthinking prejudice in all its forms. This means challenging your own thinking, as well as that of others. Your dissertation needs to show the process of you reflecting in action and rethinking as appropriate, coming to new conclusions and being alert to stereotypical forms of language or assumptions. Many research methods books are written from the perspective that research is conducted only in universities and not also by shoppers in supermarkets. In the action research literatures it is commonplace to read accounts by professional researchers who position others as participants, not researchers in their own right. Eikeland (2006) takes the research community to task, saying that acknowledging others only as 'participants' demonstrates a condescending form of ethics, yet he still writes as if research is done only in universities.

I became highly active and activist in Ireland, promoting action research through organisational professional education programmes, and eventually getting invited to teach and develop programmes for government-sponsored agencies and even at universities. I worked for about five years on a part-time basis for the National Centre for Guidance in Education (NCGE), a programme specifically designed to support guidance counsellors in schools and colleges (further publications came out of this project, including Darbey et al., 2013). I also organised conferences, including one at the University of Limerick, and arranged for the publication of proceedings (McNiff et al., 2000); this initiative was supported by the Educational Studies Association of Ireland and the School of Education, Trinity College, Dublin – a most significant demonstration of approval. The final initiative in Ireland was to negotiate the delivery of a doctoral programme, hosted by the University of Limerick, and supported by the University of Glamorgan and the University of the West of England. Eight teachers achieved their doctoral degrees (their doctoral theses may be accessed from my website at www.jeanmcniff.com/theses.asp).

What was significant through all these projects was that practitioners' knowledge was being celebrated, challenging the traditional orthodoxy of the elitist university. For me, working in Ireland was a long-term action research project, comprising multiple embedded projects, rooted in critical thinking, during which I realised my dream of enabling 'ordinary' practitioners to achieve their dreams too. As a direct result of these initiatives, systems have changed: prior learning is now recognised as credit for higher degree programmes; structured doctoral programmes are widely delivered (one of the successful doctor-graduates I supported was told, on applying for a job on the strength that she had been awarded a PhD, 'Yes, but yours is not really a proper PhD'); and practice-based research is a standard feature on university programmes. I was not the only person working in this way at the time or who influenced the development of new attitudes and practices, but I was definitely in there somewhere.

Treat others as ends, not means: Eikeland is right to challenge the hidden assumptions in much social science research, where participants are often seen as data or statistics, a dehumanising practice that demonstrates hubris and disrespect towards others. Participants become what Arendt calls 'superfluous': they become means towards an official researcher's ends. Alarmingly this is happening in much worldwide university-based action research, which has of course been quietly turned into a version of established forms of traditionalist social science. Challenging this view can be dangerous for practitioners. If you choose to do so, and you should, you should also ground your arguments in established texts to show that a strong body of literature exists that has informed your thinking, and that yours possibly now contributes to a new strand of thinking. You can justify your ideas by appealing to the wider research community and showing that strong precedents exist in the established literatures.

However, this can lead to considerable soul-searching because it means actively engaging in dissent, though you can do this quietly. Crawshaw and Jackson (2010) say that small acts of resistance can lead to massive social change: they tell the lovely story of the rise of Solidarity, a popular movement created by striking workers in Poland. The authorities put tanks on the street to stop the uprising. Poles organised protest activities, including a boycott of the official television news, and many agreed to go for a walk when the news was on television. Some even went so far as to disconnect their television sets and take them for a walk in a wheelbarrow or perambulator. '... if you see your neighbour taking their TV for a walk,' said one Solidarity supporter, 'it makes you feel part of something' (Crawshaw and Jackson, 2010: 5).

You don't have to do what you are told. You have the right to dissent: you have the responsibility to research. Crawshaw and Jackson (2010: 3) quote from Monty Python's *The Life of Brian* as follows:

> Brian: You're all individuals!
>
> Crowd: Yes, we're all individuals!
>
> Man in crowd: I'm not.

Doing action research becomes a politics of resistance, which then turns into a politics of activism: you refuse to be fobbed off and silenced, and you insist on thinking for yourself to inform your own action.

Showing how you are contributing to the community of scholars and professionals: Especially important here is to show how you are contributing to what has become known as 'the new scholarship'. This idea began in 1990, when Ernest Boyer, then President of the Carnegie Foundation for the Advancement of Teaching, spoke about the need to develop a scholarship of teaching, that is, the systematic, high-level study of teaching practices. This would not simply be study of the actions of teaching, which could be understood by asking questions of the kind 'What skills and techniques is the teacher demonstrating?', but study of practice from within the practice that could be understood by asking questions of the kind 'What am I doing to encourage learning?', 'How do I evaluate my work?' This form of enquiry-based teaching would be undertaken by those who regarded themselves as research-active teachers as well as teaching-active researchers. Professional education would no longer be in the form of 'tips for teachers' or 'notes for nurses', offered on one-off professional education days and only in practice settings, but an ongoing discussion across sectors, phases and disciplines about how practitioners could study and theorise their practices.

This idea has profound implications for all practitioners in terms of how they understand their work and their professional identities, and what they see as the object of their research. As noted earlier, many practitioners usually have no difficulty in seeing themselves as practitioners but are often reluctant to view themselves as scholars, whereas many higher education people tend to see themselves as scholars rather than practitioners. For all parties, the issue of what is studied is of key significance: whether to be proficient in one's subject matter only and demonstrate understanding of its theoretical base, or to extend one's professionalism to being proficient in practices and able to demonstrate how this practice itself becomes a form of practical theorising. Boyer's (1990) idea of a scholarship of practice (he was speaking about teaching) was grounded in the idea that teaching (and by extension, practice) itself is a form of enquiry, whose findings need to be made public so that other people can learn from these. The findings that practitioners generate from studying their practice can contribute to a knowledge base that is created by practitioners for practitioners, across domains and disciplines. Achieving this calls for considerable honesty because it is possible to manipulate others into believing that you are acting for their interests whereas you may actually be acting for your own.

3. Responsibilities of doing research for the world

In his *How We Write*, Sharples (1999) says that writing is done in the world and for the world. Similarly, Hannah Arendt considered giving the title 'Amor Mundi: For Love of the World' to the book that was eventually published as *The Human Condition* (1958). She said she loved life and the world though often terrible things happened that made her and others despair. It was important not to get dragged down by such things but to accept them for what they were: in my view, they are aspects of what Berlin (1990) calls *The Crooked Timber of Humanity*. He says that trees do not grow straight: humans are not perfect, and can often be downright dreadful. But we have to accept that this is the nature of our humanity and each of us as individuals is complicit in it. It is the responsibility of all to find ways to combat it and to try to influence the thinking of those who do not care.

It is the same with action research: you do research in the world for the world. It is a way of forging understanding with others and explaining what the process involves. We can also acknowledge that we sometimes make mistakes. Action research is not about working towards a perfect outcome: it is about finding ways to make sense of what is going on here and now and deciding as wisely as possible what to do next. This is a core difference between the constrained vision of traditionalist research and the more unconstrained vision of action research. In traditionalist research it is understood that there will be an outcome and that this is predictable. This was the nature of Marx's view of history: he believed that the future could be predicted because human progress happened according to certain laws. This view of history was grounded in a view of knowledge as predictable and controllable through following specific rules of enquiry. Yet it was demonstrated again and again to be flawed: Popper (2002) says that it is impossible to know what you are going to know until you know it, and Rorty comments (2006: 110) that 'Marx made himself look silly when he claimed to know what was going to happen next, as opposed to making suggestions about what ought to happen next'. However, Marx's overall aim was to influence other people's thinking so that they would act differently than they had in the past, and so change the future. This is also the aim of action researchers.

In the mid-1990s I began working in Northern Ireland, on the programme 'Education for Mutual Understanding', which at the time was the Northern Ireland counterpart to Personal and Social Education. It was here that I encountered the full force of prejudice, where religion and politics are welded together, and one side blames the other for the evils of the world. It is difficult to be neutral: you are usually expected to position yourself for or against one or the other. The long peace process continues today but you can walk around the streets of Belfast in safety and admire the beautiful city. The final report of the project (McNiff et al., 2001) may be accessed from www.jeanmcniff.com/items.asp?id=76; it tells the story of teachers

(Continued)

(Continued)

working in difficult workplace circumstances while combating the stories they have learned, as I did right through my time on the island of Ireland, and still do today. As a direct result of the work in Ireland, I was invited to work in Palestine in 2001 and in 2002 in Israel; this became an ongoing project for the next three years. Throughout it meant combating the entrenchment of hostilities, based on long histories of oppression and festering prejudice. In Belfast I asked a young man 'Why do you continue parading to celebrate an historical event that most people seem to have forgotten about?' His response was 'Because it's our culture.' Cultures are not written in stone: cultures are people, and people can change who they are if they have the political will.

This view is also echoed by other philosophers and is one of the most important issues in action research and in contemporary civic life: to resist messages that there is 'one right way'. Believing that there is 'one right way' is to slip into fundamentalism. This has happened throughout history: philosophers and other thought workers have promoted specific views of how the world should work. Their ideas become known, among other terms, as social theories, and many people promote those theories as the best possible way of doing things. This idea permeates politics, education and the professions. Yet it is perhaps the most dangerous ideology of all. Take the idea of freedom: Berlin (2002) says that freedom is something to be desired and fought for, but when it is imposed it stops being freedom and becomes slavery. Traditionalist views of freedom as a set of mandated ideas become violence (see McNiff, 2001, 'Peace education and other stories of violence', available at www.jeanmcniff.com/items.asp?id=82&term=peace+education). Currently the action research community has produced many separate groups who maintain that action research must be done in a particular way: so many cycles of action enquiry, or the need to have so many participants in a research group or validation meeting. A colleague of mine nearly failed his master's degree because he had not made an 'intervention'. He protested, saying that an intervention looked more like interference: besides, there were good reasons not to 'intervene' in the particular situation he was working in. He managed to persuade the programme managers that his view was justified, though they did not change their programmes or criteria for judging quality. I regularly receive email enquiries about doing action research, and I am appalled by some of the issues raised – and on a regular basis (see Chapter 10). These kinds of arbitrary rules are springing up all over the place, and you need to be aware of the situation so that you can defend against it. Rules are established through the agreement of communities who themselves come from and live in a certain tradition. I was once on a panel of four at the American Educational Research Association annual meeting, where we were asked 'Must an action research project produce a definite outcome for it to be judged as good quality?' Two of the panel said yes while another panel member and I said no: the only outcome of action research, as Dewey maintained, is more and better learning. As outlined in Chapter 1, there are multiple traditions in the action research community, though most would share a common set of personal and social values and ethical commitments. But there is no law that says an enquiry must complete two cycles of action reflection or that you must involve a critical friend. Yes, it does make sense to involve others who can give you critical feedback, and this will probably make for a better dissertation, but it is not compulsory; saying that it is constitutes a form of everyday fundamentalism. However, caution as always is advisable here: as a course member of an accredited programme be aware, and if you appear to be going outside the established 'rules', put an explanatory note into your dissertation to show that you are aware of the debates and can argue your own case. After you get your degree, go for it.

So, how does your research qualify as research for the world? How do you contribute to new ideas and new thinking? Here are some ideas.

How to contribute to new ideas and new theory

1. First, consider what inspires your life. Different people have different views: Fromm (1956) says that what gives our lives meaning is our ability to enjoy loving relationships and productive work; Al Capone saw his productive work as crushing the opposition. What are the values that give your life meaning? Articulating values can be difficult, but it is important to do so.
2. Second, consider whether you are living in a way that is consistent with your values. If you are, how can you show it? If you are not, what can you do about it and then show what you have done? Again, articulate this in some way so that people can access your descriptions of and explanations for practices.
3. Now show how you have addressed this issue, again offering descriptions of and explanations for practices. This will involve gathering data and generating evidence from those data to ground your claim that you have addressed the issue. You will also have to test the validity of your evidence by testing it against other people's critical feedback.
4. Finally, write a research report and give it to someone to read. Or produce a multimedia presentation and show it to workplace colleagues.

This process has been disciplined and systematic; it has been achievable and not too difficult. It has in fact been a process of generating theory. Your descriptions of and explanations for your learning are your personal/collective theories of practice. There is nothing esoteric about this. It is a systematic procedure for accounting for your practice, why you do what you do: you explicate (explain explicitly) the processes you have gone through. It also shows that you are not just doing it in a haphazard way, but are thinking carefully and responsibly about your actions and their influence in other people's lives.

Link this idea with ideas about the need for you to believe in yourself, and not be persuaded that generating theory is difficult or that you are incapable of doing it.

*   Be aware of what is going on. Be aware of the messages you are hearing. Which ones do you believe?
*   Be aware that you are more likely to retain existing biases when you are on your own. Access some of the available work on websites and read widely and you will soon see that other people also want to think for themselves. Plenty of practitioners are putting their theories of practice into the public domain, and other people are learning from them.
*   Be aware that other people need to hear that they are not alone either, and should take courage, perhaps from accessing your work. You have something important to say.

So how are you contributing to new theory? You are contributing in the following ways:

- You are reconceptualising yourself as a researcher, not only as a shopkeeper, steelworker or secretary. Your practice is a form of research, and your research is a form of practice. Other people can learn from your example. You are constantly generating valuable theories, and modifying these to keep up to date with your developing practices.
- You are refusing to be identified as 'just a shopkeeper' or 'just a secretary'. You are moving across and through open spaces, created by you and colleagues, to form a new professional identity as a practitioner-researcher. You are developing new professional discourses with others who also regard themselves as practitioner-researchers.
- You are getting involved in debates about the nature of practice and its uses. You are not prepared to accept other messages that your work is to deliver a service or a curriculum. Your work is to influence learning for improving practices.
- You are contributing to the wider body of knowledge through making your work public. You are also helping others to speak for themselves and regard themselves as actors in the social world, not bystanders.

The responsibilities of researchers: some implications

However there are implications of presenting yourself as a researcher and theorist: here are some.

You need to decide whether to be what Said (1994) calls a 'professional' or an 'amateur' intellectual. A professional intellectual is someone who does a job of work that fits in with the status quo; they produce results as required by those who commission the research. There is nothing wrong in this stance, but it is not what Said means by being an 'intellectual', namely someone who considers that to be a thinking and concerned member of a society entitles one to interrogate what is going on behind the scenes. A 'professional' view, he says, encourages researchers to adopt a nine-to-five mentality and not to look beyond their four walls. He also refers more approvingly to an 'amateur' intellectual as someone who is not moved by profit or reward and is concerned about issues outside of their own context. Similarly Chomsky (1969) speaks about the 'specific' intellectual who is hired to sell their knowledge and does not question the ethics or wider purposes of doing so, and the 'organic' intellectual who engages in political struggles, mainly on behalf of those who are subjugated and silenced or cannot speak for themselves. Arendt (1958) uses the language of 'theorist' instead of 'intellectual': she says that theorists are vital to stabilising a social order, especially when under attack by ideological regimes.

All these theorists emphasise the importance of engaging in the public realm with a view to influencing thinking and actions. They consistently make the point that we are always in association with others and that thinking and acting always need to be done with others in mind. It is vital never to be cut off from others in order to safeguard against dogma and the silencing of others. When she reported on the trial of Eichmann in Jerusalem, Arendt (2006) explained how his main crime was not being able to see things from another's point of view: he was cut off from the world through his own self-absorption.

It is crucial that practitioners see themselves as having much to contribute to public thinking. By representing ourselves to the world, says Said, we also represent ourselves to ourselves:

Whether you are an academic, or a bohemian essayist, or a consultant to the Defense Department, you do what you do according to an idea or representation you have of yourself as doing that thing: do you think of yourself as providing 'objective' advice for pay, or do you believe that what you teach your students has truth value, or do you think of yourself as a personality advocating an eccentric but consistent perspective? (Said, 1994: xiii)

An intellectual, says Said, has to rely on themselves: 'There are no rules by which intellectuals can know what to say or do; nor for the true secular intellectual are there any gods to be worshiped and looked to for unwavering guidance' (1994: xii). You are on your own, though also always in company with others who are also on their own in company with you. Perhaps this is where your strength lies: you, individually, are a formidable figure within a corporate world of yes-sayers and someone to be reckoned with; and you, collectively, form a fabulously powerful group of people who insist on using their knowledge for the benefit of other humans, non-humans and the planet.

It does not matter if you are working in a small context. Look at the conversation between Sir Thomas More and Richard Rich, in Robert Bolt's play *A Man for All Seasons*:

Sir Thomas More: Why not be a teacher? You'd be a fine teacher: perhaps a great one.

Richard Rich: If I was who would know it?

Sir Thomas More: You, your pupils, your friends, God. Not a bad public, that ... (1960: 4)

Whatever your profession you are also a teacher: you teach by explaining and you teach through doing: your form of life becomes a living pedagogy. You are also a writer: you disseminate ideas in the hopes of influencing other people's thinking and therefore their actions. You show how you have set and are living up to your own high standards.

Like Berlin (1990), you don't have to believe there is a 'right way'. You need to choose your own way and then justify it. Thinking involves making judgements that have to be justified.

You have the capacity for influence: for self, others and the world. If we live on in the legacies we leave to the world, our responsibility is to use our influence well and in the service of others.

Summary

This chapter has considered the responsibilities of practitioner-researchers in relation to contributing to new ideas and new theory. These responsibilities are towards yourself, towards others and towards the world. The chapter emphasises that a main responsibility is to think for oneself and to see one's knowledge always as contextualised. While it is argued that there is no universal 'right way', the case is also made for why you need to take a stand, which you should be prepared to justify.

The next chapter speaks about another important responsibility, that of showing how you are engaging critically with the literatures in order to improve the quality of your own thinking.

EXERCISES

- How do you see yourself contributing to your own learning? Do you do this through reading and talking with others, or by another means?
- Are you clear about what 'critical thinking' means? Tell your colleagues about episodes when you have had to challenge your thinking. What happened? Also comment on the experience, and whether it meant short- or longer-term changes in perspectives.
- What is the difference between treating others as means to an end and as ends in themselves? Do you see these practices in your workplace and in your everyday life?
- Write about how you believe you are living your values in your practices. Explain how you are contributing to new theories. Explain also why you should see yourself as a public intellectual, or why you choose not to.

The responsibilities of practitioner-researchers: engaging with the literatures

Doing your action research project involves reading as widely as possible and engaging critically with what you read. Showing that you have done so is a core expectation in writing up your action research project: you need to show your familiarity with what other authors are saying, acknowledge their influence in your thinking, and show how you are building on their ideas in order to develop your own.

When they read your dissertation, examiners will look mainly for two things:

- That you are making a contribution to knowledge of the field. At undergraduate or master's level this contribution need not be original: you can report on existing work such as your interpretation of a topic or text, or say that you understand something better through studying a particular topic. At doctoral level your contribution must be original: you must explain how your research moves the field forward, practically or intellectually.
- That you are demonstrating critical engagement. This should be engagement with the literatures and also with your own thinking as you read what those literatures say. 'Critical' must be critical: it should not be simply reporting on established knowledge but your own imaginative interpretation of what an author says. You can agree or disagree with what you read but you must show that you have read a text in order to critique it. To achieve this, you will need to read as widely as is appropriate for your academic level: at undergraduate level this may mean reading perhaps twenty texts; at doctoral level it can mean reading hundreds. Your reading should cover a range of fields including your subject area, methodological issues and key debates in the subject or profession. The texts you cite should include up-to-date texts that record the latest developments in the field, as well as foundational texts that show the origins of the field and its ongoing development. The texts themselves should include books, journal articles, newspaper and other media reports, book reviews and opinion pieces.

These become the main criteria by which your work is judged. Other criteria are spelled out in Chapter 18, but these two are the most important. Most higher education institutions publish these in their handbooks for students and examiners.

Making a contribution to knowledge of the field means putting ideas into the already existing body of knowledge. The 'body of knowledge' refers to all the knowledge available about the topic as contained in the literatures, that is, all the written or spoken texts about the topic (as above). The 'field' is the subject area: this could be a discipline such as teaching or nursing, a particular topic such as collaborative learning, or a particular theme in an author's work.

This chapter considers what it means for you to engage critically with the literatures. It is organised as follows:

1.   What does critical engagement involve?
2.   Doing a literature review
3.   Using the literatures in your own work
4.   Working with texts

1. What does critical engagement involve?

Critical engagement starts with your understanding that critique is vital for considering assumptions and claims and checking that these are justified. It applies to critiquing your own thinking as well as that of others. At a personal level it means producing evidence to support any knowledge claims: if you say 'I have improved my practice', readers will expect you to explain in what way you have improved your practice and which aspect you are claiming to have improved. Any claims must be supported by authenticated evidence, otherwise they will stand simply as your opinion. An experienced examiner will see through unsupported claims and will ask 'Where is your evidence? How do you justify these claims?' At a public level this means challenging assertions heard in private and public discourses, often as communicated through the media. When you hear claims such as 'foreigners are taking our jobs', it is your responsibility as a researcher to investigate whether this claim should be believed, and if it turns out to be false, to expose it for what it is.

So how can you demonstrate your critical engagement with the literatures? Some of the steps involved are as follows:

• Reading carefully and imaginatively.
• Reading actively.
• Reading original works.

Reading carefully and imaginatively

Critical engagement means reading a text carefully and imaginatively, asking yourself critical questions throughout, and being open to new ideas that emerge through reflection on your reading, and through reflection on your reflection. This means asking focused and extended critical questions, such as in Table 8.1.

Table 8.1 Focused and extended questions

Focused questions	Extended critical questions
What is this person saying?	Are they stating a position about a topic? Are they reviewing what has already been said or are they saying something new? What am I learning from them?
How are they saying it?	Are they agreeing with existing opinions? If not, in what way are they disagreeing? What are the main areas of disagreement?
Why are they saying it?	Do they want to strengthen existing arguments? If so, how do they do this? Do they want to challenge received wisdom? If so, what new perspectives do they offer?
Do I agree with them?	If so, why? If not, why not? Which issues and arguments do I agree or disagree with? What different interpretations would I have for the points being discussed and the arguments being made?

Reading actively

Reading actively means keeping notes as you read, identifying key ideas in the text, and writing your own responses to the ideas. Always note the page number if you refer to an idea or write down a quotation. Some people choose to highlight ideas in physical and electronic texts or write notes and responses in the margin. Remember to make a note of anything important and also say why it is important (that is, keep a record of your learning as you read, as in the notebook entries in Figure 8.1).

I am reading *Uncle Al Capone* by Deidre Capone (Racaplodge LLC, 2010). The text says:	My response to my reading
Page 1: I am a Capone … For much of my life, this was not information that I readily volunteered. In fact, I made every effort to hide the fact that I was a Capone, a name that had brought endless heartache to so many members of my family.	Why is the author writing about this now? What is so special about the idea that she is a Capone? Why didn't she write about it before?
Page 7: [when I went for a job the boss asked me my name.] 'Are you any relation to Al Capone?' he asked. 'Yes,' I admitted, 'he was my uncle.' … 'I'm sorry,' he said, 'but we can't have you working here. I'm going to have to let you go. You're fired.'	What was going on culturally and politically that the boss took immediate action like this? When was this written? Were there no rules of employment at the time?
Page 115: The historians have it all wrong. My uncle Al did not die on Saturday evening, January 25, 1947 with his family at his bedside; and his funeral was not the sorry, lonely affair it's been made out to be. He didn't even die of complications of syphilis, as is commonly accepted.	Who do you believe – this author, who is Al Capone's niece, or established historians who have done a lot of background research? What are your reasons for choosing to believe one or the other?
Page 167: This page shows a photograph of Al and two friends, one with his hands up, while Al is holding a gun to his head. The caption, written by Deidre Capone, reads: 'This is the only photograph in existence where Al Capone has a pistol in his hand. On the back of the picture my grandmother wrote "Al plays cops and robbers while hiding out in Wisconsin. 1925"'	Do you believe this? If so, why? If not, why not?

Figure 8.1 Example of a reading notebook, with critical reflections

Reading actively means reading for information and also for ideas. When you get stuck into a text you can explore how the ideas expand your own thinking and generate ideas. Reading can contribute both to what you know and how you come to know it; it becomes an exchange of ideas between you and the author.

Reading original works

To engage critically you should read the original work; this is called 'a primary text' or 'primary source', not a secondary one, which is someone else's interpretation of the original. Secondary texts can be helpful if the author's ideas are complex or if the original text is written in a dense style; a secondary text can help you identify key points and themes from an original text, but should not be seen as a substitute for the original: much better would be to offer your own interpretations. In principle you should read an entire text but this is not always possible because of time or other constraints, so ask your supervisor or other course members about which chapters may be most useful for you, or for other helpful articles by the author. You can find a lot of original articles online or ask for help from your library or resource centre.

Remember that your work is assessed in terms of showing what you have read (namely whether you have engaged in appropriate depth with subject knowledge), as well as demonstrating your critical engagement. In academic work the quality of your text will tend to be judged largely in terms of your knowledge of the literatures: this involves comparing key themes among authors, how you assess arguments and what contribution you make to those arguments. This is a key point for action research: when you submit your dissertation for academic accreditation it will be judged both in terms of what you have done and also in terms of how well you can relate what you have done to arguments in the literatures.

Jessica Martin is a Portage Home Visitor; she achieved her BA (Hons) degree, working with children and families in the early years, at Pen Green Research Base, UK. She hopes to begin her master's studies in 2016. She writes:

'The process of first-hand experience while also doing my research enabled me to learn both about my chosen topic and also about what it means to be an effective reader. I chose a topic of particular interest to me in order to maintain my enthusiasm for what I was reading in the literatures. I found, to my surprise, that the greatest challenge of doing a literature review was the struggle to keep it concise and relevant. I often found myself wandering down a long trail of peer-reviewed journals and government legislative documents, only to realise that none of the information, regardless of how interesting it was, could be used in my study. This meant I had to learn to narrow my focus. I also found that analysing what authors were saying left me fluctuating between panic and epiphany on a much too regular basis. I came to appreciate that, difficult though it was, it was essential to look deeper and analyse the underlying values expressed by authors; I later brought the same understanding to working with participants and analysing the data. By engaging in this kind of critical study I was able to identify just two themes – participation and patience – which enabled me to focus in my writing and pursue an integrated research study.'

Now consider what this means in terms of doing a literature review

2. Doing a literature review

Doing a literature review is generally compulsory in traditionalist research, though it may not be in action research. Ask your supervisor's advice about your institution's policy on doing a literature review. If you undertake one, it involves finding out what other people have already said about any particular areas or contexts you are studying, and the possible relevance to your enquiry. It also means being aware of how to engage with others' ideas and reference these, and ensuring that your work is seen as linking with or making its original contribution to those same literatures. This means engaging with questions such as the following:

- Why do a literature review?
- Which literatures to engage with?
- How to engage?

Why do a literature review?

The reasons why you should do a literature review include:

- to find out what other people have said about your topic;
- to test your thinking and research findings against the views of key authors;
- to demonstrate critical engagement in research and scholarship;
- to develop your conceptual and theoretical frameworks;
- to demonstrate the originality of your contribution to knowledge of the field, and its potential significance for other people's learning.

Finding out what other people have already said about your topic

The aim of your action research is to generate a knowledge claim about how you have improved your practice in a particular area or context. Remember that making a knowledge claim does not mean simply stating your opinion, but showing that what you are claiming is grounded in authenticated evidence and tested against the critical scrutiny of peers (remember, too, that many of your contemporaries are your peers). Your peers will wish to see, therefore, that you can demonstrate your understanding of what other people have said: this shows the exercise of your scholarly responsibility as you are showing your working knowledge of progress in the field and how that progress might be assessed. You can find plenty of advice on how to do a literature review on the Internet (see for example, http://library.bcu.ac.uk/learner/writingguides/1.04.htm and www.rlf.org.uk/resources/what-is-a-literature-review/). Your own institution will publish its own guidelines, too. Many institutions also offer special courses on how to do a review.

Testing your research findings against the views of key authors

By demonstrating that you have engaged with the ideas of other authors in the field, you can show that your knowledge is up to date, that you have drawn on others' insights and developed them, and are now offering your original interpretation or creation. You can also use others' ideas to justify and support your own knowledge claim (but not to reinforce prejudices; see below). Showing that you have read widely is evidence of your capacity for scholarship (you have engaged with literatures already in the public domain) and for research (you can contribute to new literatures and influence new directions in the public domain).

Demonstrating critical scholarly engagement

Do not use others' ideas to reinforce your own prejudices: use your capacity for critique. The quality of your work and the dissertation you write will be judged largely in terms of whether you do this. This works at two levels: (1) critiquing what other people think, and (2) critiquing what you think. It involves reflecting on whether you are justified in taking a particular stance or whether you may be mistaken. It also means checking that you have produced authenticated evidence to support or challenge your own knowledge claims.

Developing your conceptual and theoretical frameworks

Broadly speaking, a concept is an idea, and a theory is an explanation for that idea. A conceptual or theoretical framework is a set of ideas within which you will locate your thinking and writing. Examples of conceptual frameworks are freedom, gender and colonisation. Examples of theoretical frameworks are liberation theory, feminism and post-colonial theory. Concepts and theories are informed by values. As you read consider which values have informed the text you are reading. Do you share the same values or hold different ones? Your own values will therefore transform into new frames of reference that you can draw on for future thinking.

Demonstrating the originality of your contribution to knowledge of the field, and its potential significance for other people's learning

Knowledge can be discovered as well as created. Through discovering and engaging with other people's ideas you will show how you have possibly reconfigured and recreated these as new ideas. You will make those reconfigurations your own and also make them public, so other people can learn from you and reconfigure those ideas in turn. Thus knowledge is mobilised and transforms into new forms. This is a powerful idea with major significance. It means you are contributing to an ever-growing body of knowledge about a particular field. That field will never be bounded because of the addition of new knowledge that is appropriate to ever-changing contexts. Knowledge and knowledge production are ongoing unbounded transformational processes with the potential for contributing to human, non-human and planetary wellbeing.

Changing perceptions of what counts as cultural value

Remember, also, that social and cultural contexts are changing and that what counts as 'literature', as part of those contexts, is changing too. In *Bring on the Books for Everybody* (2010), Jim Collins challenges the power of the traditionalist Academy that specifies what counts as 'good literary taste' and consequently which books should count in a literature review. He writes about how digital technologies have enabled easy access to otherwise inaccessible literatures and how this now influences what counts as cultural value:

> Trollope and Flaubert at the beach? ... Trollope on Masterpiece Theatre, of course, but never at the beach, the most notoriously nonintellectual location within American culture, where one is supposed to read only for pleasure. (Collins, 2010: 5)

He also makes the point that access to reading has (in his words) empowered readers:

> This desire to take books to the people of the world on a grand scale is not restricted to Google, since it is also the principal goal of Barnes & Noble ... and Oprah Winfrey's Book Club – a project epitomized by the charge she gave her 'book elves' as they hand out hundreds of copies of The Good Earth to her studio audience at the end of her Anna Karenina show: 'Bring on the books for everybody!' (2010: 9)

He cites Bloom in *How to Read and Why* (2000: 19) as saying:

> Reading well is best pursued as an implicit discipline; finally there is no method but yourself, when your self has been fully molded. Literary criticism, as I have learned to understand it, ought to be experiential and pragmatic, rather than theoretical.

This also reminds me of the time, at an exam board meeting, when I defended a master's student's citation of a comic as part of her literature review. Citing the comic was her choice, which she defended with gusto. I think the university needs to broaden its perspectives about what counts as 'literature', and 'good literature' at that.

Anonymous contributor writes:
   'I dropped out of school at the age of thirteen because I could not stand the regimentation. I simply refused to go. It was a shame, really, because I loved reading and history so I did miss the opportunities for access to books that school provided. However, I remember the first time I walked into a public library. There were all these books, and they were all free! I couldn't believe it. So I spent all day every day at the library, devouring book after book. It was just a magical experience.'

3. Using the literatures in your own work

Aim to use the literatures at every point of your research. The key points here are as follows:

* Identification of a research issue.
* Contexts.

- Methodological issues: monitoring practices and data gathering; identification of participants; ethical issues; processes involved in the research; testing the validity of knowledge claims.
- Taking action.
- Interpretation and analysis of data for the production of evidence.
- Making provisional knowledge claims.
- Explaining the significance of the research.

These are set out in Table 8.2.

Table 8.2   Using the literatures at key points of your research

Research point	Using the literatures
Identification of research issue; reasons for choice of research issue	Draw on contemporary and foundational texts to explain what your research issue is and why it is important and relevant to everyday living: e.g. draw on texts to show why professionalism is a key issue for practitioners; why nursing is in crisis; why environmental issues should be mandatory on schools curricula. Show that other authors share your concerns, or if not, why they should.
Contexts	Draw on the literatures to show what is going on in the current context that inspires you to do your research. Refer to Ball's (2003) ideas about how teachers are being turned into servants of the state; Bernstein's (2000) classic ideas about the pedagogisation of knowledge.
Methodological issues	Draw on established texts such as Denzin and Lincoln (1998) for how to gather, interpret and analyse data; and texts such as Jørgensen and Phillips (2002) who speak about contemporary issues such as discourse analysis as theory and method, or Brinkmann (2012) who speaks about qualitative enquiry in everyday life. Draw on the literatures to justify every methodological point you make.
Taking action	Justify your actions by appeal to authors such as Arendt (1958) and the need for focused action; to Elliott (1991) and action research as praxis; to Carr (1995) who sees research as for education, not only about education. Appeal to the more critical texts such as Apple (1993) and Giroux (2003) to show how and why you did your action research in order to try to influence unsatisfactory situations.
Interpretation and analysis of data for the production of evidence	Explain how respected literatures speak about the need for careful interpretation of data in the production of evidence (Gadamer, 2004; Nixon et al., 2016). Show that you know how to analyse data by explaining what content analysis is and how this has enabled you to come to important findings. Show that you have read about justifying why you have tested the validity of knowledge claims (Habermas, 1987; Lather 1991); and how those findings may inform new practices (Rorty, 1999).
Making provisional knowledge claims	Explain how the scholarly literatures insist that knowledge claims should be held lightly – Feynman (2001) and Polanyi (1958) in scientific enquiry; Sterling (2001) in environmental enquiry. Show your own commitment to the capacity to change your thinking in light of a better argument or evidence (Habermas, 1987; Said, 1994).
Explaining the significance of the research	The significance of your research means responding to the question 'So what?' Many texts maintain this attitude, including most of the ones cited in this book.

Use the above as an exercise for appreciating the significance of your own research: identify each critical action point and write out ideas about how you will use the literatures in support of that point.

Now think about how you can actively work with texts.

4. Working with texts

Appreciating how to work with texts means thinking about what you do when you read and write. Think about what is involved when you read: think also about the heuristic devices here in the form of 'Wh–?' questions, for use when you read.

'Wh-' questions

'Wh–?' questions tend to take the form 'What? When? Where? Who? Which? Why?' as follows. (For our purposes we can include 'How?' here also.)

What do you do when you read?

Think about the ideas you are reading. Read with critical appreciation and judgement, and decide whether you agree or not with what an author is saying. Keep a record of what you read on your computer, or perhaps on index cards or in a dedicated notebook.

When do you read?

Aim to read about key issues prior to doing your research and keep at your reading all the time. Ideas may change and so your reading will need to change also. Make time for reading, and do at least a small amount each day to keep in touch with your thinking. Negotiate with family and friends for time out to read. Reading is a major part of doing research so try your best not to skip it.

Where do you read?

Use every opportunity to read, whether on the bus or just waiting for the kettle to boil. Use library resources to find books and journals. Access websites. Start a blog. Exchange text messages with friends about key books and articles. Set up discussion seminars using an online forum around your research topic.

Who do you read?

Everyone has their favourite authors. Find yours, and treat them as good friends. Try communicating with them by email if they are alive and available. Write out relevant quotations ('quotations', not 'quotes') in your quotations book and use these, and remember always to reference them properly (see below). Also read other authors, including those you disagree with. You will need these too to justify your own opinions (although you may come to see that they were right).

Which works do you read?

Aim to read relevant literatures, but anything that takes your interest can be useful for your study. Books on architecture or landscape gardening can be relevant to organisational studies: you can explain how to organise and structure aspects of social exchange. Rowlands (2005) has stated that everything he has learned about philosophy has come from watching television. This can be the basis for cultural studies too.

How do you read?

We are all different and have our own ways of doing things. Whatever works for you is right but be sure to focus on what you are reading so that you do so actively and don't daydream.

Why do you read?

You read both for pleasure and information. Look on reading as a complementary aspect of writing.

Let's now consider what you do when you write in relation to engaging with the literatures.

What do you do when you write?

Here are some things to look out for in academic writing in relation to engaging with the literatures: some take the form of 'dos and don'ts'.

Writing a literature review

As already noted, it is not always compulsory to do a literature review in an action research text though it can be useful. If you are critiquing current policy in early years education, you may need to write a dedicated chapter to show what is going on in that policy domain. If you choose not to do a formal review chapter, make sure that you engage with the literatures throughout your dissertation.

Also remember that a review is not simply a list of books and other texts. You will need to know what those texts say and give some kind of informed commentary about them. This is hugely important: do not cite Foucault in your dissertation unless you have read at least some of his relevant works. Your examiner may be an authority on Foucault and want to involve you in a discussion, so you really do need to know what you are writing about. You do not need to read Foucault's entire output but you do need to read those texts you wish to reference.

Name dropping

Do not drop names as the fictional author does in this sentence (citing fictional sources): 'Many writers comment on the need for fairness in football refereeing (Beckham, 2010; Capello, 2007;

Ferdinand, 2009)'. You should at least summarise the views of the authors you mention. Bassey (1999) critiques practices that he calls 'kingmaking' and 'sandbagging': this is when a writer tries to impress readers without solid justification or to shore up a weak argument. Readers (especially examiners) are experienced and know what they are reading, and they will quickly see through ploys like this.

Do not plagiarise: learn to reference properly

Plagiarism is one of the most serious issues in academic or any writing. It is easy to plagiarise without it being seen precisely as plagiarism: you move an author's ideas or words around slightly, or put an idea into your own words without acknowledgement. Be aware that really sophisticated anti-plagiarism programs are now available, and some institutions run these checks on all submitted dissertations. However, some people will still get away with this but then there is no integrity. Remember that someone may do the same to you one day. Always reference ideas and words you get from other people meticulously. It will be honourable for you and respectful to them. Plagiarism is illegal, and being found out can mean dismissal from a job or, in the case of accredited courses, dismissal from a course.

Do not make sweeping statements: do not say what is not the case

Avoid making sweeping, unfounded or absolutist statements, such as 'It is always the case that ...'. It may not always be the case. Do not say 'Research shows that ...' without concrete references to published research.

Use 'I'

There are hundreds of 'dos' and 'don'ts' for engaging with the literatures. A main 'do' is to write in the first person: use 'I' with conviction, and celebrate your capacity to write high quality texts that will withstand the most rigorous critique. Previously, the use of 'I' was avoided; today, in action research and much case study research, the use of 'I' is expected (but not for purposes of self-promotion). This is your research, and your original claim to knowledge, so go ahead and celebrate it with honour. You have earned your place in the world of research.

Keeping references

Compile a systematic record of references and keep this active. Keep your 'References' workbook with you and maintain a record of your reading: wherever possible note the full reference as you read. Check with your supervisor which system of referencing your institution uses: many word-processing programs offer a choice of referencing systems. If you like a particular phrase or sentence write it down accurately, word for word, and note the page number. When you use quotations in your reports, you must give a page reference. Do not ignore this advice. It can take hours to track down a missing page reference, and is virtually impossible if the book is back in the library. Do not forget to record the page numbers of the chapter in your references when you quote from any text: look at how the references are laid out in this book and compare it with other systems in other books.

Note also that when you put a reference to a journal article into your references list you must record the pages of the article: study how this is done from the references list in this book.

Conclusion

Showing that you have read widely and can engage with your reading is a sign of good quality professional and academic practice. Take care with your reading and make sure that you do it justice in your dissertation. Effort always pays off in the long run. Make sure you enjoy it too, and decide, here and now, that one day you will contribute to those literatures and scholars of the future will reference your works.

Summary

This chapter is to do with what it means to engage critically with the literatures. It considers what is involved in doing a literature review, and how to use those literatures at every point of your own work. Advice is given about working with texts and developing good reading habits.

The next chapter moves into the practical, and considers how to use the advice offered so far in planning and doing an action research project.

EXERCISES

- Think about what you read and why you read it. Explain to your colleagues why reading is important.
- As part of your studies you may be required to do a literature review of your topic. Are you confident about how to do this? And about which resources you can find and where these are? If not, check with your supervisor and colleagues.
- Do a mini-literature review of three main topics in your research. Do one for the subject area, one for the methodology, and one to prepare you for explaining what your contribution is to the field.

PART III

How do I find out?

This part considers the practicalities of doing action research. It contains the following chapters.

The chapters contain practical advice and exercises for doing action research. They are meant as useful guides and ideas to get you started. At all times you are encouraged to develop your own ways of doing things.

At this point in your action enquiry you are asking, 'What can I do about the situation? How do I find out?' By asking these questions you signal your intent to learn how to take focused action and to use the learning to inform your practices.

Thinking about doing an action research project

This chapter is about planning for personal, social and organisational change and improvement. Seeing these processes also as processes of enquiry turns change into a form of research. The chapter considers what such planning processes involve. Undertaking this kind of forward thinking is essential to ensure you involve everyone in all aspects of the change, help them make the best use of their knowledge and talents, and do not waste time and other valuable resources.

Planned change processes usually involve different phases:

1. A review of the current situation to see what is working and what is not, and to be clear what this means in a particular context.
2. A consideration of what needs to be done practically to support people involved in change.
3. A consideration of any ethical issues involved.

The chapter is in three sections that address these issues:

1. What do review processes involve?
2. Feasibility planning
3. Ethical issues

The chapter also provides exercises to help you see what these ideas might mean in practice.

1. What do review processes involve?

Action research is itself a process that begins with a review phase, and the review and evaluation are built in systematically, as follows:

- We review our current practice,
- identify an aspect that we want to investigate,
- imagine a way forward,
- try it out, monitor what we do, and
- take stock of what happens.
- We modify what we are doing in light of what we have found, and continue working in this new way (or try another option if the new way is not appropriate),
- continue to monitor what we do,
- review and evaluate the modified action,
- test the validity of the claim(s) to knowledge, and
- develop new practices in light of the evaluation. (See also McNiff, 2016a.)

When thinking about personal and organisational change, therefore, the first step is to review current practices. Elliott (1991) calls this as a 'reconnaissance' phase where you take stock of the current situation to see what is going well and what is not. Because practice is always values-laden, this means first considering the values you or your organisation live by, and assessing whether and to what extent these are being lived in practice.

Thinking about personal and organisational values

Think first of your personal and organisational values. Values are those things that give our lives meaning: they become the guiding principles for action. If you believe in justice, you will act in a way that encourages justice.

Do this in three steps. Think about:

- your personal values;
- your organisational values;
- to what extent you are living these values in practice.

Step 1: Your personal values

Ask yourself, what values inspire my life? Why do I do this work? What makes life worthwhile? Remember that values are often deeply contested in many ways, including the following:

- You sometimes deny your own values: you say you believe in full participation yet find yourself excluding others.
- Different people hold different values even in groups with the same aims: some believe in free speech for all; others believe that only some should speak.
- Personal and bureaucratic values can differ: teachers and clinical nurses believe their work is directly with students and patients; bureaucrats believe they should deliver a product to customers.
- Ideological systems can differ: practitioners tend to work towards democratic education; corporations towards a market orientation.

Mary McCarthy, a participating teacher on the SBARP Project in Ireland, writes a reflective dialogue with her self:

Self: Why did you decide to continue with the action research programme this year?

Me: Because I was convinced of its relevance and importance for me in my professional development. It made me focus on my values and examine my classroom practice in light of those values.

Self: This all sounds a bit vague and pretentious. What 'values' did you discover you had?

Me: I learned that I wanted my classroom to be a happy, democratic place where the pupils and I would learn and discover together …I learned that I must listen more and talk less. I learned that a good rapport between the students and myself could not exist without mutual trust, understanding and respect. I hope that I always had those values but maybe they became cloudy over the years. (McCarthy, 1994: 38-9)

To check where you stand, try the following.

TASK

- Ask yourself 'What are my core values? What makes my work meaningful?' Write your answers in your learning journal.
- Think of an episode when you felt you really did live your values fully. Think of another episode when you did not.
- Write down three episodes today where you have lived your values.

Now think about your organisational values.

Step 2: Your organisational values

Ask the same kinds of questions as above, but now from a 'we' basis, because organisational values are (or should be) collective values. Ask yourselves:

- 'What are our organisational values? Are we clear that these inform our organisational goals? Are we achieving them?'
- 'If so, how do we show this? If not, what do we need to change?'

TASK

- Write down your organisational values and goals. Check that the goals match the values.
- Give some examples of how you feel you are achieving your goals.
- Write down how you could achieve your goals more effectively.

Step 3: To what extent are you living your values in practice?

Having established your personal and organisational values, consider to what extent you are living these in practice. Various strategies can help, including a SWOT analysis and asking critical questions.

Doing a SWOT analysis

SWOT stands for 'strengths, weaknesses, opportunities and threats', though you can change the terminology (for example, you may prefer 'limitations' to 'weaknesses'). Strategies like this can help you take stock of your current situation, as shown in Table 9.1.

Table 9.1   Example of an organisational SWOT analysis

Strengths	Opportunities
• What are our strengths? What are we doing well? • List some of the things you are doing well.	• What opportunities are there for improvement? What can we do about our limitations? • List some of the possible ways forward.
Weaknesses	**Threats**
• What are we not doing so well? What could we do better? • List some of the things you could do better.	• What might hamper us? What circumstances might prevent us developing new ways of working? • List some of the potential threats to the realisation of your values.

Asking critical questions

Asking critical questions such as the following can help:

- What am I/we doing well?
- What could I/we do better?
- What should I/we stop doing?
- What should I/we continue doing?
- What should I/we start doing?

TASK

Discuss these matters with colleagues, students and clients and get their feedback through using a range of data-gathering methods (see Chapter 13 for how to do this). This can help you record successful practices and any new actions you took to improve these, as shown in Table 9.2.

Table 9.2   Responses to a SWOT analysis

Question	Responses	Opportunities	Threats
What am I doing well?	I am good at counselling students.	Many students ask to see a pastoral tutor.	We have not sufficient staff to appoint pastoral tutors to all students.
What is the organisation doing well?	We have a strong collaborative culture.	Existing staff are committed to ongoing collaboration.	Any new appointees must agree to collaborative working, which may itself require some kind of staff professional education initiative.
What could I/we do better?	I could develop my listening skills.	I can access resources from the staff library about improving listening skills.	I may need some supervision of my own: can any existing staff member help me?
What could the organisation do better?	The organisation could provide supports for closer collaboration among staff and students/clients.	The organisation could provide a free beverages machine.	The organisation may not be willing to provide unlimited free beverages.
What should I stop doing?	I should stop missing appointments with students and for staff meetings because of work overload.	Many opportunities exist for meeting with all students.	Some students may wish to monopolise staff time.
What should the organisation stop doing?	The organisation needs to have a better policy on employees' workloads.	The organisation can develop a reputation for fair employment practices.	The organisation may come under pressure to provide more equitable conditions of employment.
What should I start doing?	I should implement a policy of specific times for meeting with students.	Greater opportunity to fit in more meetings with students: students know their appointment times and will be more likely to keep to planned schedules.	Some students may not respect timings, which means I need to be much firmer.
What should the organisation start doing?	The organisation should encourage a policy of timetabled and timed supervision sessions.	Greater opportunity for more students to access supervision.	The organisation may not be willing to implement this policy.

You may be surprised at what you find out by doing this kind of exercise, possibly something like the following:

- We are able to do our jobs well but do not have the time or resources to do them as well as we would like.
- We have good relationships in our organisation but could improve these through stronger collaborative working.
- We need to be much more imaginative about how to develop collaborative working practices.

These ideas can give rise to action research questions of the form 'How do I/we... ?', such as:

- How do we find time and resources to develop high-level practices?
- How do we, as the senior management team, support the development of strong collaborative working practices?
- How do we, as an organisation, develop imaginative strategies for involving students in organisational planning?

These kinds of investigative processes can help to ensure ongoing personal and organisational improvement.

> Writing in a South African context, Lesley Wood says:
>
> [I]n South Africa, few principals have been exposed to the kind of learning that would enable them to lead in a transformative way, since autocratic and hierarchical methods of assessment have until recently been the norm in most schools ... Values refer to the ideas we hold about what we believe to be good and right ... However, values remain abstract unless we make a conscious decision to live them out ... I argue that, if school leaders choose to base their practices on values that are aimed at making the world a better place for all, their behaviour and practice will become more virtuous. This ideal is not easy to achieve, unless there is commitment to continual critical self-reflection and the will to change. (Wood, 2013: 53, 56)

Let's now consider how feasible it is to support such ongoing change.

2. Feasibility planning

Consider the feasibility of doing an action research project in your setting. This involves thinking again about:

- possible opportunities and constraints;
- what resources you may need.

Possible opportunities and constraints

Think first about any possible pitfalls to watch out for. Thinking critically about a real-life situation can give rise to all sorts of questions, including the following.

Identifying a concern and research question

Ask yourself about whether you can realistically do anything about your identified concern, and whether you will you be allowed to. What might happen if you want to encourage greater staff participation in organisational decision making? This would involve evaluating whether good relationships exist. Be careful not to upset managers who may try to block your enquiry. You cannot change systems immediately though your enquiry represents a first step towards greater democracy.

> Three colleagues from UiT, the Arctic University in Tromsø, write about the marginalisation of practice-based research as the impetus for their action research. They say:
> 'We appreciate that, like thousands of others, we are caught in the living debates [about] the kind of knowledge that is legitimated as contributing to valid theory and the systems of power that enter into those debates. This gives us the reasons and further impetus to continue our research into how we can highlight the value of practical knowledge in health-care education and healthcare services as much as abstract propositional knowledge. We wish to foreground the need for practitioners' voices to be heard in public debates about what counts as high quality healthcare practices and how such quality should be judged.' (Norbye et al., 2013: 77)

Aim to keep the project small and manageable and focused on your own practice, and work with only a few colleagues. Remember that large organisational change begins with small personal change: your research contributes to wider understandings. All social change begins with small groups of people talking together.

Explaining why your chosen focus merits investigation

Why is this a concern? Is it realistic to think you can do something about it? Sometimes external constraints such as unnecessary bureaucracy will force you to spend time doing paperwork rather than with children or patients. Sometimes internal constraints will make you believe you cannot do anything, or you will lack confidence or companions who share the same commitments. Be realistic and practical, and challenge any lack of self-confidence that may be holding you back: remember, your words count; your organisational presence counts.

Is it possible to gather data on a systematic basis?

Will you be able to gather data on an ongoing basis and have enough time during the working day to do so? Will you have access to people who can help you and will they be willing to do so? Will you have organisational support? Will people believe that you are researching yourself rather than them? What will happen when key participants leave or withdraw from the research, or parents and managers refuse to sign permission slips and progress reports? Sometimes you will be required to stipulate what results you will achieve from your action research: what happens when the results do not materialise? How do you persuade others that learning can take time and it is often not possible to achieve identified outcomes?

Lise says:
'I was trying to keep my reflective journal on the Ward and was told by a manager, "If you have got time to write, go and do some work." This, I feel, indicates that certain institutional ways of recording information seem acceptable but others can be met with hostility and suspicion.'

Is it possible to do anything about a problematic situation?

Consider your options before deciding to take action. Do you need someone's approval, or have you to go through a permissions process? Will your university's ethics committee approve your research proposal? Will managers and fellow workers give you permission to gather data from your workplace setting or interview patients and parents?

Also consider whether you will have enough stamina, time and resources and the support of family and friends. What will you give up in order to find time for your research? Will you do the required module reading if it means missing the football match on Saturday?

In an interview, the director of a long-term action research project reflected on whether developing the project had been worthwhile, as follows:
'I was so excited by what we were doing and the positive feedback we were getting from the teachers. But then there was also the awful reality of persuading governors and trustees to see the benefit of what we were doing. It went from a wonderful level of excitement to the sheer slog and hard work of trying to convince those that had to be convinced – the trustees, the institutional directors who were looking for outcomes and were frustrated that we weren't immediately getting results as they saw it, the sheer slog of organising meetings and writing up the minutes, and trying to carry other projects at the same time – it wears you down. At times it felt lonely for me as programme director: at other times it was really very good and I am glad I had the experience.'

Will other people be available to help you in testing the validity of your knowledge claims?

How will you test the validity of your claim that you are influencing someone's learning? You can influence your own learning by questioning and changing your own assumptions and you can influence the learning of others you work with. Will your participants give you honest answers, or might they feel constrained by organisational rules? How will you gather data and generate authenticated evidence? What will this look like? Will you have access to a skilled supervisor and books and other resources to give you advice?

Showing that your conclusions are reasonably fair and accurate

Will you have access to external critical friends and validation groups who will consider whether you are conducting your research rigorously or forgetting important elements? Will they be willing to meet with you regularly? Will they have time? Will you? How will you deal with critique? Will you be prepared to rethink your position and challenge your own prejudices? How will you react when they show you that your findings are mistaken?

Will you be able to modify your concerns, ideas and practices in light of your evaluation?

Always be prepared to be open to what the data reveal. Sometimes the data will show us disconfirming data, things we would rather not see, which will mean changing practices. These are important data because they point to more appropriate directions for your research and how you can strengthen it.

These may seem like unnecessary questions but you do need to be aware of potential difficulties. However, keep your determination. Your new insights are essential to helping others learn. You will develop those insights by studying your practice and improving your capacity to learn.

Thinking about resources

Resources can be understood as time, equipment and people.

Time

Doing your project will take time. Some organisations encourage practitioners to do action research and make time for it within the working day, and some allocate research time. You will need time for reading and reflecting, attending meetings to negotiate access, gathering data, producing progress reports and writing the final report. Putting your project into your life means taking something out. What is negotiable with family, friends and colleagues? Remember, also, that it is possible to become obsessed with reading and thinking. Make sure you take time out for recreation and relaxation, and prioritise family and friends. Be prepared to dip into your private time and do not complain later.

Etain Gibson, who works at St Mary's University, Twickenham, speaks about supporting PGCE students who are studying English. She says:

'English is a subject with a high level of information, so I decided to try presenting the theory via an audio lecture prior to involving students in the practical sessions. I monitored what appeared to be effective and what not. Generally they found the lecture useful, but there were serious time constraints given the heavy workload in PGCE master's programmes. It was also important to keep in mind the quality of students' experience, so I had to adjust the pre-session theoretical tasks accordingly and also ensure these were relevant to students' different needs. Keeping all these factors in mind made the situation quite difficult to handle but everyone seemed to think it was worth the effort.'

Equipment and resources

Equipment means money, so check beforehand whether you can use your organisation's equipment or must buy it yourself. Can you use their stationery, camera, video equipment? Will the organisation supply a computer and an IT expert to help with graphics? What about photocopying and reprographics? Can you access online resources such as refereed research journals? Draw up a list of necessary equipment and resources and check availability.

You will also need your own library of key texts, depending on how thoroughly you want to develop your studies. Buy these yourself if necessary. If your organisation has a policy of supporting professional learning see if it is possible to develop a staff library, or develop one yourself if you are the budget holder, to include subscriptions to journals such as *Educational Action Research* and *Reflective Practice*.

People

Although the focus of your research is you as you investigate your individual 'I', you are never alone. You are always in company with others who are also studying their individual 'I's'.

People to involve are participants, critical friends and validators, supervisors and interested observers.

Participants: Remember that your research participants are not objects to be investigated; they are equals. Your research is about you studying you, not them, to see if you are influencing their learning and your own, so check how they respond to you as you interact with them. Ask 'What am I learning with and from you? What are you learning with and from me?' Your participants will mirror yourself back.

Nqabisa Gungisa, a teacher who achieved her master's degree as a member of the Khayelitsha group in South Africa (see the story about this group in Chapter 12), tells how she invited her students to give her critical feedback on some innovative pedagogical strategies she had developed. One of those strategies was to provide additional classes on Saturdays, where she even provided breakfast for the students. She writes:

'I asked my learner participants to write me anonymous letters, reflecting on the effectiveness of my innovations, including the Saturday tutorial classes, learners' class presentations, group discussions, investigative exercises and projects. I also asked them to comment on our working relationship and how they felt about my interest in their attendance and the completion of other work given to them by other teachers. From their feedback I can now claim that I have managed to foster a culture of self-discipline and encourage them to believe that they can liberate themselves from their previous self-perceptions as without worth. I can also claim that I have influenced them to develop a good sense of responsibility. Here are some of their responses to my questions, as recorded in my field notes:

- "First I thank you, teacher, for giving up your time. Coming to these classes has given me hope that if I can continue working like this I can pass my mathematics exam."
- "I would like to thank you for your time and also for offering us something to eat. Since I have been attending your classes I have learned a lot and now I am able to do my homework on my own, something that I never did before in my whole life."' (Gungisa, 2008: edited with permission)

Critical friends and validators: The aim of your research is to make a knowledge claim, specifically that you have learned how to improve some aspect of your practice. This claim must be justified to avoid it being seen as your opinion. If you say 'I have influenced the quality of relationships in my business', you will need to produce evidence to show that this really is the case. This public testing is especially important in action research where knowledge claims are grounded in subjective experience. Submit your data and findings to rigorous critique at all stages and ask critical friends to give you stringent feedback. Critical friends can include colleagues, parents, clients, students or anyone else who is going to give you a sympathetic but critical hearing. You may have one or several critical friends, depending on your needs and circumstances.

Validation groups: Aim to convene a validation group for the duration of your project. This group will number about 3–10 people, but see what is possible. Their job is to meet at key stages of your project, especially at the reporting stage, to listen to your knowledge claims and scrutinise your evidence. They should agree or not whether your claims and evidence are believable. Be prepared for people to raise questions about taken-for-granted aspects, which may mean re-thinking. Validation groups meet with you of their own free will, so never abuse their commitment. Thank them properly, and acknowledge them in your dissertation.

Supervisors: These can be your best friends and provide invaluable support. They are given limited time for supervision in their job allocation and most have too high a caseload. Listen to their advice and be courteous. They expect you to challenge but from an informed position. Most supervisors do more than their contractual obligations, so do not take advantage by expecting responses to emails during weekends or out-of-office hours, or for them to respond to umpteen drafts of assignments. And remember to say thank you.

Interested observers: These are people who are interested in your work but not directly involved, such as your manager or the parents of students who are your research participants. Treat them with consideration. Again, they do not have to give up their time and energy for your research, so thank them properly and let them know they are appreciated.

3. Thinking about ethical issues

Involving other people in research demands ethical awareness: this is not just a matter of courtesy but also a legal obligation. Involving children and vulnerable people requires special attention. Involving them in your research without prior permission or clearance is dangerous practice. Check whether your profession publishes ethical guidelines and study them. Also say in your report that you have done so and have adhered to the guidelines rigorously.

Ethical considerations involve three main aspects:

- Negotiating and securing access.
- Protecting your participants.
- Assuring good faith.

Negotiating and securing access

You must negotiate and get formal permission for your research, in writing, from your university ethics committee and from your organisation. You must also get permission from participants if you wish to involve them. Organise letters for all participants. Give a letter to those persons who have difficulties in reading and read it through with them. Seek and get permission from parents or legal caregivers to involve children or vulnerable people, as well as from the children or vulnerable persons themselves. Keep letters requesting and granting permission for reference. Place a copy of letters to participants as an appendix in your report, and have your original letters available if readers want to see them. You may decide in some cases on limited disclosure: check procedures with participants and your supervisor. This is not just about courtesy but also about avoiding potential litigation. An example of a letter requesting permission is shown in Figure 9.1. You can modify this for your own purposes.

Protecting your participants

Do not name or otherwise identify your participants, unless they wish to be identified. Many participants in action enquiries will wish to be named and have their contributions acknowledged. When participants do not wish to be identified, give them numbers or initials such as 'Participant 3' or 'Colleague J'. This is important when using video data, when people are easily identifiable. Difficulties can be avoided by being open about what you are doing, and seeking and obtaining permission beforehand. Also emphasise that you are researching your own practice and not theirs. Be careful about naming your location: check with your manager or principal. Often people will be delighted to be identified and have their contributions acknowledged. If so, go ahead and identify them, but ensure you have their written permission first. Promise your participants that you will protect their interests and maintain confidentiality for those who wish it. Never break this promise and remember that it could be expensive if you do. Also promise that participants may withdraw from the research at any time and if so that you will destroy all data about them.

Let your participants know you are to be trusted. Draw up and give an ethics statement to every person involved. Include a tear-off slip for their signature to show they have received it, and keep these carefully (see the example in Figure 9.2).

Assuring good faith

Always do what you say you are going to do: maintain good faith. Create a reputation for integrity and protect it. People are more willing to work with someone they trust.

Having observed all ethical aspects, you can now exercise your duty to yourself and go ahead and do your project. Ensure that you protect and exercise your own academic freedom, to speak from your perspective as a person claiming originality of mind and telling your truth with universal intent (Polanyi, 1958). Your work is important, and you have a responsibility to others to publish your findings so that they can learn with you and from you, with the intent that they should do the same for others.

Your institutional address

Date

Name of recipient

Address of recipient

Dear [Name]

I am hoping to undertake an action research study into how I can improve lines of communication in my department. I would be grateful if you would grant permission for my research to proceed.

Two copies of this letter are enclosed. Please sign and date both. Keep one copy for your files and return one copy to me.

With thanks.

Your Signature ....   Print Name ....   Date ....

✂--

I hereby give permission for [your name] to undertake her/his research in [name of organization].

Signed ....   Print Name ....   Date ....

Figure 9.1   A letter requesting permission to conduct research

To whom it may concern (or Dear colleague, or Dear [Name]),

I am undertaking an action enquiry into how I can improve lines of communication in the department, and am asking you to be a participant in the research.

I will give priority to your interests at all times. I promise the following:

Your identity will be protected at all times unless you give me specific permission to name you.

You are free at all times to withdraw from the research, whereupon I will destroy all data relating to you.

I will check with you all data relating to you before I make it public.

I will make a copy of my research report available to you prior to its publication.

Two copies of this statement are enclosed. Please sign and date both. Keep one for your files and return one copy to me.

Your Signature ....   Print Name ....   Date ....

✂--

I have received an ethics statement from [your name].

Signed ....   Print Name ....   Date ....

Figure 9.2   An ethics statement

Summary

This chapter has given advice about what to think about when planning to do an action research project, specifically what is involved in review processes and the feasibility planning of an action enquiry. It has considered what action planning involves, and set out the details about what you need to think about at each point. It has also engaged with what is involved in ethical issues and how to get clearance for your research.

The next chapter considers what is involved in action planning.

──────────────── **EXERCISES** ────────────────

- Are you clear about what you need to think about before doing your action research project? Have you thought about doing a SWOT analysis or a similar exercise? Write answers to the questions in Table 9.1 and compare your findings with your colleagues. Ask for their critical feedback.
- Be clear about whether your project is feasible. Look at the questions about feasibility planning. Have you the necessary resources and supports for your project? Check out all these things before starting.
- Are you clear about the need for respect for ethical issues? Will you get clearance to do your research project? Check with your supervisor, workplace manager and colleagues. Make sure all your participants are fully informed about what you are doing and why you are doing it. Are you clear yourself about what you hope to gain from doing your project?

Planning to do your action research

As an important first step to your research, draw up an action plan: action plans can have considerable benefits for managing processes of change. This chapter offers advice on how to do this. You can easily adapt the advice to many other areas of your work. Chapter 11 extends the ideas into carrying out your action plan and Chapter 12 into evaluating the quality of your resultant action and learning.

The chapter is in three sections:

1. What is action planning?
2. What does action planning involve?
3. Some words of caution about action plans available online

1. What is action planning?

Action planning is the term used for planning how to manage a systematic process of personal or organisational change. It is a process that allows you to do the following:

- Consider what you need to do in relation to identified needs.
- Plan and take an appropriate course of action.
- Provide for systematic monitoring and review with a view to modifying practices.

This means you can identify areas for improvement, imagine how to make the improvement possible, monitor the processes in action and assess the quality of outcomes. You can do this by asking critical questions such as:

- What is my/our concern?
- Why am I/are we concerned?

- What can I/we do about it? What will I/we do about it?
- How will I/we gather data and generate evidence to show progress?
- How will I/we ensure that any conclusions I/we come to about progress are reasonably fair and accurate?
- How will I/we modify practices in light of the evaluation?

Table 10.1 is an example that shows this process in action.

Table 10.1 Action plan for a project to encourage listening among primary school children

Question	Response
What is my/our concern?	I need to encourage my primary school children to listen to others more carefully.
Why am I/are we concerned?	Listening is important to show that children respect one another and that they engage with their own deep learning.
What can I/we do about it? What will I/we do about it?	I will try specific strategies to help the children see the importance of listening and its regular practice. These strategies will include focused discussion time during which I will offer verbal and non-verbal cues to reward attentive listening. I will identify three children who have been especially inattentive to others in the past, on the basis that they may provide strong case study data to show whether they develop good listening practices. This may also indicate that my pedagogical practices are moving in the right direction.
How will I/we gather data and generate evidence to show progress?	I will monitor children's progress through observation, audio and video recording, interviews with identified children and video. I will also monitor my own learning process through recording key actions and insights in my learning journal and through taped conversations with critical friends. I will analyse my data using specific categories of analysis and interpret the results in collaboration with others.
How will I/we ensure that any conclusions I/we come to about progress are reasonably fair and accurate?	I will invite two colleagues to act as external observers and critical friends; their task will be to observe me while I work with the children and record the processes involved. I will try to convene a staff seminar, which will double as a validation group meeting, during which I will present the results of my research and seek their critical feedback.
How will I/we modify practices in light of the evaluation?	The feedback, I hope, will contain comments about how I am encouraging specific children who have previously not listened attentively to do so now. I will think more about other strategies and their usefulness over the coming time.

2. What does action planning involve?

Action planning involves imagining ways in which you can address the needs and priorities identified earlier in your review phase (outlined in Chapter 9). In relation to those needs and priorities, check that you are clear about which steps are most relevant to action planning processes, as set out in Table 10.2. Also take care that you do not see the idea of 'taking action' simply as about doing activities (as in Table 10.2) but also recognise that this includes reflecting on the planned activities (as in Table 10.3): reflection on the reasons and purposes of taking action transforms the initiative from everyday action into research.

Table 10.2   Steps in action planning and their relevance to action planning processes

Action step	Relevance to action planning processes
Clarify aims.	You identify what you hope to do.
Explain rationale and purposes.	You explain why you wish to do it and what you hope to achieve.
Identify objectives and targets.	You identify aspects of what you hope to achieve.
Plan for activities and milestones.	You plan for what you hope to achieve at key points.
Consider resources.	You consider what you may need to help you succeed in the project.
Draw up timelines.	You draw up timelines for what you will do and when.
Articulate criteria.	You articulate those elements you expect to appear when you do certain things.
Articulate standards of judgement.	You anticipate what will happen to show whether the criteria have been realised.
Explain procedures for monitoring practices, data gathering, analysis and interpretation.	You explain how you will keep track of what you and others are doing and how you will analyse and make sense of your data.
Begin formal evaluation.	You begin the process of judging the quality of what you have done.
Imagine modification of actions.	You imagine how you might change your actions and thinking in light of your evaluation: this leads to ...
Identify future priorities and action plans.	You identify what needs to be done next and how it will be done. And the cycle continues ...

These kinds of steps are found in most everyday action plans. A problematic is that they emphasise the action (what to do, how to do it), and do not sufficiently emphasise the research (why do it and what is learned from the doing). It is important therefore to ensure that action steps are understood also as research steps, as shown in Table 10.3.

Table 10.3   Integrating action and research steps

Action steps with an action focus only	Action steps with a research focus also
Clarify aims.	What is the concern?
Explain rationale and purposes.	Why is it a concern? Reasons and purposes for the research?
Identify objectives and targets.	What do we want to achieve in the short, medium and longer term?
Plan for activities and milestones.	What can I/we do about it? What specific targets should we identify for different stages of the project?
Consider resources.	What and whom do we need to support us?
Draw up timelines.	When will we aim to carry out our actions? How do we organise our time?

(Continued)

Table 10.3   (Continued)

Action steps with an action focus only	Action steps with a research focus also
Articulate criteria.	What do we expect to happen? What are our minimum (and maximum) expectations? What values do we wish to realise in practice?
Articulate standards of judgement.	How will we check that our actions are having the desired effect? How will we judge these effects?
Explain procedures for monitoring practices, data gathering, analysis and interpretation.	How will we monitor and document our practices? What kind of data do we need? How will we gather these? How will we analyse and interpret these?
Begin formal evaluation.	How do we check that we are having the desired effect?
Imagine modification of actions.	Have our actions revealed new areas for examination? Have new questions emerged through the process?
Identify future priorities and action plans.	What have we learned? What is the significance of our learning? What do we need to do now?

Seeing action plans as research plans, too, ensures that you adopt a mindset where action generates learning and learning in turn generates new actions. This is the nature of action research.

TASK

Work through this plan with a colleague and draw up your own action plan relevant to your situation.

The worksheet in Table 10.4 may help you to complete this task. Work with a colleague to complete it in relation to your own situation.

Practical issues

Make sure you are clear about the implications in each of these action research steps, as set out in Tables 10.1–10.4. Each action step is shown also as an action research question. These steps are expanded here to help you think about some of the issues.

Step 1: Clarify aims

Action research question: What is the concern? What do I wish to investigate?

Be clear about what you are hoping to do in this project. Is it:

- to improve practices such as developing new ways of working?
- to improve learning such as inviting all participants to maintain a learning log?
- to evaluate where you or the organisation are and where you hope to go next?
- other outcomes?

Table 10.4   Worksheet: Framework for framing and doing your action research

Issue/question	Your response
What really matters to me? What do I care passionately about? What kind of difference do I want to make in the world?	
What are my values and why do I hold them?	
What am I interested in investigating?	
Why do I wish to investigate it?	
What data can I gather to show the situation as it is, and the reasons for my concerns?	
What can I do about it? What are my options?	
What will I do about it?	
What kind of evidence will I produce to show the situation as it unfolds?	
How do I ensure that any conclusions I come to are reasonably fair and accurate? How do I test the validity of my provisional claims to knowledge?	
How do I anticipate modifying my ideas and practices in light of my evaluation?	

Clarifying aims also helps you to clarify why you are doing this project. Is it:

- for personal improvement and career prospects?
- for organisational self-evaluation?
- to support colleagues' professional education?
- other outcomes?

Write down your aims for the project and how these might be related to others' or the organisation's aims. As always, keep everything small, focused, manageable and realistic. Identify only a few aims, and check that you know why these are important and whether they are achievable. In action research the aim always involves improving learning as well as improving action. Examples of aims are:

- I am aiming to improve my time management.
- We need to improve collaborative working.

These aims give rise to research questions:

Research aim	Research question
• I am aiming to improve my time management.	• How do I improve my time management?
• We need to develop collaborative working strategies.	• How do we develop collaborative working strategies?

It is important to focus on learning as much as on action, especially if the aims are not realised, as often happens. The learning itself is an outcome that can be brought to other situations and contexts.

Step 2: Explain rationale and purposes

Action research question: Why is it a concern? What are the reasons and purposes for the research?

Be clear about why the project is necessary, otherwise it will be a waste of time. This means identifying reasons and purposes for doing the project. This gives rise to the following:

Research aim	Reasons for the research project	Purposes of the research project
I am aiming to improve my time management.	My timekeeping is rather poor: I seem never to get to meetings on time, which is giving me a bad name.	I need to improve my timekeeping in order to get to meetings on time and be seen to be on top of my work.
We need to develop collaborative working strategies.	We are working as separate entities in our organisation, so people don't know what others are doing. This is leading to frustration and low morale.	We need to improve our capacity for information sharing and systematising work practices.

Now link these points with a value: values become the guiding principles for living and taking action.

Research aim	Reasons for the research project	Purposes of the research project	Value as the basis for planning to take action
I am aiming to improve my time management.	My timekeeping is rather poor: I seem never to get to meetings on time, which is giving me a bad name.	I need to improve my timekeeping in order to get to meetings on time and appear on top of my work.	High standards in professional conduct: this value is being jeopardised.

Research aim	Reasons for the research project	Purposes of the research project	Value as the basis for planning to take action
We need to develop collaborative working strategies.	We are working as separate entities in our organisation, so people don't know what others are doing. This is leading to frustration and low morale.	We need to improve our capacity for information sharing and systematising work practices.	Collective work, responsible action: these are not being realised in practice.

Step 3: Identify objectives and targets

Action research question: What do we need to know and be able to do in order to achieve our aims?

Objectives are the more specific aspects of your aims and refer to what you need to know and be able to do in order to achieve your aims. They are often written in the language of capacity building ('will be able to …' or 'will understand …') in terms of knowledge, skills and understanding. They also identify targets to be achieved that will show these aspects in action. In relation to the examples used above, objectives look like this.

Aim	Objective	Knowledge	Skills	Understanding
Improve timekeeping practices.	Develop good timekeeping practices.	Will demonstrate knowledge of how to maintain good timekeeping.	Can articulate why good timekeeping is important.	Understands the need for good timekeeping.
Develop collaborative ways of working.	Develop collaborative working strategies.	Will know how to relate to others.	Will be able to relate to others, e.g. through initiating conversation.	Will understand the need to relate to others and be able to explain this.

Step 4: Plan for activities and milestones

Action research question: What do we hope to achieve at key points? How will we achieve these?

Articulate the activities that will help you realise your objectives in practice. Remember that you cannot achieve everything overnight, so organise your project in terms of what you can realistically achieve in smaller chunks of time: perhaps think in terms of the short, medium and longer term. Articulate these as specific targets and possible outcomes, which may take the form of incremental steps as follows:

Short term

Targets	Activities	Anticipated outcomes
Improve timekeeping this week.	Get to all meetings on time this week.	Good timekeeping for the week.
Create environment for conversations this week.	Get two groups of people to talk together.	Sharing of working practices by the two groups.

Medium term

Targets	Activities	Anticipated outcomes
Improve timekeeping for this month.	Get to all meetings on time this month.	Good timekeeping for the month.
Offer incentives for collaborative working.	Talk with managers about installing a free beverages machine in a social space.	Free beverages machine installed in a social space.

Long term

Targets	Activities	Anticipated outcomes
Good timekeeping practices firmly established.	Punctual attendance at all meetings.	Senior managers notice new professional attitudes and mention promotion opportunities.
Alert other departments about access to free beverages in a designated social space.	Talk with colleagues over a coffee about how to develop inter-departmental working practices in designated social space.	New inter-departmental working practices initiated and planned for development.

These are idealised stories but they are achievable. However, be aware that things may not go according to plan. If things fall apart, as they sometimes do, be patient, use your imagination, and talk with others about how to get back on track, or whether to change track altogether.

Step 5: Consider resources

Action research question: What do we need to support us?

Resources refer to what you need to support the implementation of your plans. Draw up a list of resources required. Think in terms of 'Wh–?' questions as practical heuristics, and about availability. Be realistic because costs may be involved.

Aim	Who needs it?	What do I/ we need?	When do I/ we need it?	Where do I/we need it?	Which do I/we need?	Availability? High-low probability
Achieve good timekeeping.	Me.	I need a system of alerts: An alarm clock? Mobile phone?	Immediately.	Close at hand: possibly phone?	Best available.	High.
Develop collaborative working.	Our organisation.	We need a good coordinator.	As soon as possible.	Ready availability.	Person with experience and understanding.	Medium depending on whether recruited from current personnel or brought in.

Step 6: Draw up timelines

Action research question: When do we aim to carry out our actions? How do we organise our time?

Good action plans always have a timeline built in to ensure, as far as possible, the achievement of aims according to identified times and the successful outcome of the project. Because you are doing a project in a limited time, work out an action plan in terms of when actions will be completed. Spend time planning activities before doing them, and think about possible pitfalls and alternatives.

Aim to draw up a timeline for your project as in the example below, or better still, devise your own. Doing this will itself take time, so factor this into the overall action plan.

Example 1

Aim of project: developing collaborative ways of working

Time	Action	Time allowed
Week 1 (insert dates)	Meet with planning group to discuss project and its feasibility. Decide on action frameworks – aims, rationale, objectives, targets. Decide on practicalities: time, people, resources. Appoint roles and responsibilities in planning group. Decide how to draw up the action plan. Person appointed to collate feedback and draw up draft plan.	Two weeks for consultation and drafting action plan. Negotiate date of next meeting.

(Continued)

(Continued)

Time	Action	Time allowed
Week 3 (insert dates)	Meeting of planning group to consider draft action plan. Discuss feasibility. Negotiate time for reflection. If appropriate begin to allocate roles and responsibilities for implementing the action plan. Next target: produce overview of personnel, roles and responsibilities.	Two weeks reflection and consultation. Draft recommendations for roles and responsibilities. Negotiate date of next meeting.
Week 5	Planning group to outline implementation of project. Planned implementation June–September.	To be negotiated.

Aim to draw up action plans wherever appropriate for successful completion of your project. A good action plan will keep you on task and focused. You will be able to check off jobs once they are done.

Step 7: Articulate criteria

Action research question: What do we expect to happen? What are our minimum (and maximum) expectations?

The idea of a criterion (plural 'criteria') is part of discourses to do with assessment of quality: a criterion is something you expect to be present or appear. You expect a hotel to be clean, warm and comfortable: cleanliness, warmth and comfort become criteria; you buy a coat in terms of its cost, fit and colour, so cost, fit and colour become the criteria for selecting that coat. Criteria are usually set in advance: they are things you expect or require. A criterion for passing a driving test is that you stop at red lights. A criterion for producing an action research assignment is that you show scholarly engagement. In action planning a criterion becomes a marker by which you can assess whether or not objectives have been achieved: these act as signs to show us whether something is working.

When drawing up your action plans you nominate specific criteria that denote success, hence they are sometimes called 'success criteria'.

Example

Criterion	Am I/are we achieving the criterion?
Punctuality	Am I more punctual? Yes. I get to all meetings on time.
Collaborative working	Are we encouraging collaborative working? Yes. We talk about how we can improve our working practices over a coffee from the new beverages machine.

Step 8: Articulate standards of judgement

The idea of standards of judgement is also part of discourses in assessing quality (be aware that the idea of standards is used variously in the literatures). A criterion is something you set in advance and you expect to see realised, whereas a standard tells you whether the thing is being realised. If warmth is a criterion for choosing a hotel, a standard is whether or not a particular hotel is warm. You say, 'I expect the hotel to be warm' (you state a criterion) and you ask, 'Is the hotel warm?' (a standard). Standards can also indicate degrees of quality, so if you have to choose between hotels you ask, 'How warm? How clean?', and you choose depending on the degree to which a hotel comes up to your own standards.

In terms of your action plan, you would indicate the extent to which aims and objectives had been met and how well they had been met. For example:

Criterion	Standard
Punctuality	Did my punctuality improve? How often was I punctual? On a regular basis? Sometimes? Always?
Collaborative working	Are we working collaboratively? To what extent? Can we quantify this? Can we show differences in qualitative matters? Can we produce quantitative and qualitative data to show the differences?

Step 9: Monitoring, data gathering, data analysis and interpretation

Action research question: How will we monitor and document the actions? What kind of data do we need? How will we gather these? How will we analyse them? How will we interpret them?

These matters are dealt with in detail in Chapter 13.

Step 10: Evaluation

Action research question: How do we check that we are having the desired effect?

These matters are dealt with in detail in Chapter 12.

Step 11: Proposed modification of actions, which leads to future action plan

Action research question: Have our actions revealed new areas for examination? Have new questions emerged through the process?

These matters are dealt with in Chapters 12 and 18.

Step 12: Identifying future priorities and action plans

Action research question: What have we learned? What is the significance of our learning? What do we need to do now?

These matters are dealt with in detail in Chapters 19 and 20.

The next section gives some words of caution about action plans available online.

3. Some words of caution about action plans available online

If you go online and key in 'action plans example', or words to this effect, you will bring up dozens of action plans, including templates of various kinds and advice on how to fill them in. Many are published by universities as part of their courses and can be most helpful: for example, from the University of Kent (www.kent.ac.uk/careers/sk/skillsactionplanning.htm) and the University of Leeds (https://library.leeds.ac.uk/downloads/file/311/example_smart_skills_action_plan).

However, do be aware of what you are looking at. The templates for most online action plans focus entirely on actions leading to behavioural outcomes. They tend to take the form:

Action step	Time	Material/ resources	Person responsible

Or:

Aim	Objective	Target	Target date	Progress

These action plans emphasise the need for intentional targeted actions (doing things): most do not mention research (understanding how and why to do things). Most also tend to assume that actions will take a sequential, one-dimensional direction in order to arrive at a given outcome. This view actually denies the nature of action research as a process of enquiry: while a process of enquiry does need to be conducted in a systematic, coherent way, it is neither one-directional nor does it anticipate or focus on behavioural outcomes. It focuses on learning, which inspires new actions, which then inform future actions.

Also, many published action plans (in books and on the Internet) use the acronym 'SMART', first outlined in the 1980s' literatures of management and employer–employee relationships, and often credited to different people including Peter Drucker. The letters are also given different meanings in the literatures, but all generally mean the following: 'Specific', 'Measurable', 'Achievable', 'Realistic' (or 'Relevant'), 'Time related' (or 'Trackable'). These are instrumental criteria that are to do with assessing the achievement of actions: they do not aim to assess quality in research or learning. For this, different criteria and standards are required. These are generally of a form that aims to show how values transform into criteria and standards of judgement. If you believe in participation and democracy you should look in your data archive for those episodes of practice that show the practices of participation and democracy, that is, the realisation of values.

Sadly this view of focusing on the achievement of behavioural outcomes is becoming dominant in universities so those forms of action research that have been co-opted by universities also tend to focus on behavioural outcomes. Questions I have been asked by participants on courses include:

Question	My response
How many cycles must I do for my project to be seen as good quality action research?	There are no fixed rules about this, but if you are doing a course it is wise to complete at least one cycle, so that your reader can see how you address methodological issues. Some institutions require you to complete two cycles, but institutions have different requirements. Check with your supervisor and do what is necessary to get the degree.
Does the question always need to communicate that there is a problem?	No, not always. You can conduct an enquiry as an evaluation where you check what is happening and evaluate it.
What happens if my question changes during the enquiry?	That's fine. Most people find that their questions change during, and probably through the process. New learning emerges. It is important to document your learning in your learning journal and explain in your dissertation how and why this happened and how this may have changed the focus of the enquiry.
We are doing a group project. Is this allowed?	Yes, and there should be more of them, because a main feature of action research is that it is collaborative. However, take care when it comes to making knowledge claims. You can speak in terms of 'we' if you, as a group, genuinely came to new collective interpretations and understandings, but stay with 'I' if you are referring to your personal learning.
Do I need to ask other people to identify a research issue and a question for me?	No, you can do this yourself. Look at what is on your desk, and identify one burning issue that you need to do something about: this could be a distressed child or patient, or the need to manage your time better. Make sure you can do something about it; that it is important to do it; and you must do it. Keep it small, manageable and focused. It is a waste of time trying to influence the overall organisational structure; choose something where you can have an influence. This is itself will contribute to changing the organisational culture.
My institution is funding my research and they have asked me to identify specific outcomes. What do I do if those outcomes don't materialise?	This is a feature of some institutionalised forms of action research, where action research is seen as a kind of traditionalist 'input-output' process. Try to explain to funders that you cannot predict outcomes with certainty though you will certainly try to influence practices in this direction. Emphasise instead that a more valuable 'outcome' is improved individual and organisational learning.
How do I handle it when things go wrong?	They often do; the best plans fall apart. Keep a record of how you handled things and use this as data when you write up your dissertation.

Anticipating that it is possible to identify specific outcomes of a process of enquiry assumes that there is a 'gold standard' by which all accounts may be assessed. It also assumes that you will know what you should know before you know it. These are false premises and have serious implications if you see action research as a process of enquiry, not as a procedure to be implemented: but you do need to show that you are achieving designated university-approved criteria in order to get your degree, and these often take the form of identified outcomes.

I also have to say that, when people write to me about their institutional studies, my standard response is to say, 'I cannot get involved in your institutional enquiry: that would be unprofessional and unethical. Consult your supervisor: this is what they are there for.' It is essential to maintain ethical conduct; this, for me, becomes a major value-as-standard that all professionals should adopt.

The next chapter deals with how to implement action plans from an action research perspective.

Summary

This chapter has looked at what is involved in action planning, and given practical guidance about how to draw up action plans. Spending time on planning can contribute to the long-term success of your project. Some cautionary words have also been offered about 'ready-made' action plans to be found online, and about some idiosyncratic views of what doing action research involves. You will need to inform yourself and come to your own decisions about what to think and what to do.

The next chapter looks at the practicalities of carrying out your action plans.

———————————————————— **EXERCISES** ————————————————————

- Are you clear about what action planning involves? Check with your colleagues about their perceptions.
- Write out responses to each of the action steps identified in the chapter.
- Draw up an action plan for your own project, specifying a timeline and all the practical elements of doing your project, as outlined here.

Carrying out your action plans

Now you are ready to begin doing your research project so here are some ideas about how you can carry out your action plans. This chapter sets out the different questions to ask and offers ideas about each one. This shows your research as a whole: doing so includes stating clearly what you wish to do and achieve, your reasons and purposes for doing it, and how you will evaluate whether you have achieved your aims. It also means being reasonably clear about how you will achieve your purposes.

The chapter examines each step in an action enquiry, identifies the job to be done, and suggests tasks for doing it. It is organised in terms of the questions you ask, as follows:

1. What is my/our concern?
2. Why am I/are we concerned?
3. What kinds of data will I/we gather to show why I/we am/are concerned?
4. What can I/we do about it?
5. What will I/we do about it?
6. What kind of data will I/we gather to show the situation as it is and as it develops?
7. How will I/we analyse and interpret the data? How do I/we generate evidence from the data?
8. How will I/we test the validity of my/our knowledge claim(s)?
9. How will I/we ensure that any conclusions I/we come to are reasonably fair and accurate?
10. How will I/we modify my/our concerns, ideas and practices in light of my/our evaluations?

1. What is my/our concern?

Job to be done: identify what the research issue is; identify a research question

Go back to the issue you identified in your action plan, or identify another issue that has arisen in the meantime. Make sure it is an issue you can do something about. You cannot change the organisational system you work in or the policy around, say, the inclusion of patients in hospital decision-making practices. However, you can change your current practice and you can include patients, with appropriate permissions, in your enquiry.

At this point identify what you wish to research, keeping your issue small, focused and manageable. In the following exercise, take the examples of (1) finding ways to manage your time more successfully, (2) improving the quality of your educational leadership, and (3) encouraging good staff relationships.

Turn your research issue into a research question, beginning with 'How do I/we … ?'

Research issue	Research question
Improving my time management	How do I improve my time management?
Improving the quality of my educational leadership	How do I improve the quality of my educational leadership?
Encouraging good staff relationships	How do we encourage good staff relationships?

Your claim to knowledge is directly linked with your research issue and your research question. You ask at the beginning of your research, 'How do I manage my time better?' and you claim at the end, 'I have learned how to manage my time better'. Your data and evidence show the processes involved in moving from your question at the beginning to your claim at the end.

Remember that your research issue, and its question, may change over time. This happens frequently in action research given that it is a developmental process where nothing stands still. Your question, 'How do I improve my time management?', may have developed from 'How do I find time to do my research?', and may now develop even further and become the start of new action enquiries. These are generative transformational processes where one question transforms into another, more complex question.

TASK

Write down your research issue and turn it into a research question.

---

2. Why am I/are we concerned?

Job to be done: explain your reasons for doing your research

Say why this is an issue for you. The beginning of an action enquiry for many people is that they are not living their values in their practices as fully as they would like. If this idea sounds right for you, link your research question with a value. Here are the same examples as before, now articulating the values that inform the question.

Research issue	Research question	Underpinning value
I need to manage my time more effectively.	How do I manage my time more effectively?	Integrity: demonstrating responsible practice; responsibility towards self and others.
I need to improve the quality of my educational leadership.	How do I improve the quality of my educational leadership?	Responsibility in organisational wellbeing.
We need to encourage better staff relationships.	How do we encourage better staff relationships?	Good staff relationships are core to organisational wellbeing and success.

Linking your research issues and questions with their underpinning values can give you the rationale and explanatory framework for your project; you explain your reasons and purposes – why you need to manage your time more effectively, why you need to encourage better staff relationships and what you hope to achieve through doing so. You write these reasons and purposes into your dissertation. Here are some more examples:

Research issue	Research question	Value	Anticipated knowledge claim
Improving the quality of my relationships with my colleagues.	How do I improve the quality of my relationships with colleagues?	Relationship and empathy: community; recognising the other.	I have improved the quality of my relationships with my colleagues for better working practices.
Encouraging students' interest in history.	How do I encourage students' interest in history?	Importance of understanding the basis of current situations: need to create a better society.	I have encouraged my students' interest in history for the creation of a more sustainable world.
We need to create a resources centre that will benefit our community.	How do we create a resources centre that will benefit our community?	Need for knowledge; learning; access to information; sustainability of community.	We have created a resource centre that is benefiting our community.

Remember that while all practices are informed by values, not all actions are practices. Smiling or tripping over are actions but not practices. A practice is purposeful, values-laden and socially oriented. Your task is to show how your practice is more than simply action, it is praxis: it is considered, committed and morally oriented. Keeping this in mind will also help you justify your work by explaining how it is informed by the values of compassion and dialogue.

The case studies in this chapter come from teachers in Qatar. A team of five professionals, including me, was hired by a UK-based organisation to develop a government-sponsored professional education project in Qatar from 2009–2010. (We published the case studies of some of the teachers in *Action Research for Teachers in Qatar* [McNiff, 2010]: this can also be freely downloaded from www.jeanmcniff.com/qatar.asp.) Each of the teachers shows the process of their action research. Specific examples are given below.

3. What kinds of data will I gather to show why I am concerned?

Job to be done: Systematically gather a range of data from different sources

Aim to gather data throughout your project and at all stages with an eye to the issue you are investigating and its underpinning value. Watch out for key pieces that may get turned into evidence. The differences between data and evidence are explained fully in Chapters 14 and 15. Briefly, 'data' refers to all the information you gather about an issue, while 'evidence' refers to those special pieces of data that show the issue in action and how criteria relating to the issue may be achieved. Evidence is therefore embedded in artefacts such as books, emails, memos, transcripts, computer files, videos, pictures, text messages and social media. Keep a lookout for those pieces of data that show what you are looking for: if you were looking for the exercise of kindness and other values you could look for their realisation in specific pieces of data. For example:

Value	Data source showing the realisation of the value
Kindness	• Shown in a text message from a friend saying she is experiencing kindness from her colleagues following an illness. • Evident in the minutes of a staff meeting where colleagues offer to help one another.
Good relationships	• Evident in the transcript of a conversation between two colleagues saying how much they enjoyed working together. • Evident in an email from a manager to all staff sending New Year good wishes.
Justice	• Evident in field notes from your conversation with a colleague where they say they have negotiated a good pension plan. • Evident in a memo from a colleague thanking you for speaking up on their behalf during a recent workplace bullying episode.

Also remember the differences between 'thin' data and 'thick' data, as explained in Geertz (1973). Producing a photo of colleagues laughing together and claiming this showed good relationships is thin data: it would not stand alone as evidence because it could be open to misinterpretation; colleagues could have been laughing for several reasons. The photograph would need to be backed up by at least one other piece of data, and preferably more – perhaps a text message or an email saying what a good time they had (see 'triangulation' on page 189). These multiple data sources would produce thick data, which are what you are looking for.

TASK

Write down some ideas about where you would look for data to show the following in action:

- Examples of the values that inspire your life and work.
- Your research issue and research question.
- The reasons for your concern/for undertaking your research.

Check ideas about the relevance of your data with critical friends, and keep records of conversations using audio or videotape recording, which can also stand as evidence in your dissertation. Note especially whether you question your own assumptions about your interpretations of the data. For example, in your enquiry about improving the quality of relationships in your organisation, you may receive a text or email from a colleague explaining that caring relationships are not prioritised. An entry from your personal log might note that you need to take action to develop better relationships. Aim to gather data that represent the social situation and show your response to the situation. Your aim is to show how you are improving your understanding as the basis of action focusing on improvement.

In her account 'From skills to knowledge in basic mathematics', Anbarah Al-Abdallah explains why she wished to help her underachieving fourth grade students (9-10 years old) in mathematics develop learning strategies for high levels of attainment. She writes:

> I began to research ways to help the children develop computation skills, beginning with simple addition. My research question became, 'How do I help low achievers to improve their performance in addition?'

She gathered extensive data to show the situation as it was using the following techniques:

- Diagnostic test scores.
- Pretest and post-test scores.
- Students' work.
- Student interviews.
- Participation checklist.
- Reflective journal.
- Attendance sheet.
- Photographs.

She outlines how she analysed the data, and ends her account by commenting on her own professional learning from doing her action research, as follows:

> I have changed my perceptions of students: I thought they were helpless, but I now see them as impressive learners. I appreciate the need to move beyond skills and behaviours and focus on enabling students to develop understanding and knowledge.

4. What can I do about it?

Job to be done: outline how you might take action

Now is a good time to consult with others who may or may not be involved in your research about possible future action. Getting their reactions helps you check out your perceptions and possible prejudices. Are the difficult relationships real or do you perceive these as such because you are feeling under pressure? Getting others' opinions on possible courses of action can help avoid inappropriate action. Here are some examples of how this can be done.

What do I need to find out?	Whom do I consult?
I need to find ways of making staff meetings more democratic.	I consult all staff at a staff meeting; I request ideas for possible strategies.
We need to ensure that all children understand the importance of good handwriting.	I consult a small group of experienced staff: I ask them to act as an advisory task force on encouraging good handwriting.
I need to develop my communication skills.	I consult a trusted colleague who can act as professional coach.

Making a decision to act takes thoughtfulness and a consideration of all options. For example:

Research issue	What can I/we do?
My colleague has written me a letter saying she is experiencing a lack of understanding from others following her extended leave of absence. This denies my values of care and compassion. What can I do?	I can: • explain her situation to management and encourage their understanding. • encourage her to approach peers and senior colleagues and explain her position. • tell her to buck up. • encourage peers to be more understanding.
Some parents wish to get more involved in their children's education in our day centre. We are always aiming for greater participation so need to create more opportunities. What can we do?	We can: • partner parents with staff to help monitor their children throughout the morning. • enlist the help of parents in acting as playground monitors. • invite parents to attend staff meetings.

TASK

Think of a situation where you must take action and have a number of options. Write out the situation and list your options. Consult with others about which one to adopt and why.

5. What will I do about it?

Job to be done: outline your options for action and potential benefits and hazards; and try one out.

Having considered your options, try one out. Choose one option only and follow it through. If it seems to be working, continue. If not, try something else. Do not get discouraged if things do not go according to plan, or if you make mistakes. Mistakes can be valuable sources of learning. Changing options, however, can be uncomfortable. It is usually easier to stay as we are, but if the way we are is not right, we have to do something about it. No one else will: it is our responsibility. Using the examples above, you could write:

Chosen option	Follow-up plan
I will encourage peers to be more understanding.	I will speak with individuals and small groups, suggesting how they can be more supportive of our colleague. I will arrange for someone to sit with her during coffee breaks.
We will invite parents to attend staff meetings.	We will explain to parents the way that staff meetings are usually conducted. We will ask them how they would like to contribute and how we can ensure that their voices are heard.

Suleiman Al-Fugara writes about 'Developing Inclusion in Schools: How do I integrate students with additional educational support needs into mainstream schooling?' He outlines some of the actions he takes to ensure that students with additional educational support needs are fully integrated into the life of the school:

'I ensure that students with additional educational support needs are properly accommodated within classes. I sit with them, note their strengths and limitations, and teach integrated classes. Colleagues and I have developed a special strategy. We already award certificates to students who reach high levels of achievement, and we now award the same certificate to students with additional educational support needs who make any significant progress. We give certificates to parents who work closely with the school, and arrange for students to present the certificate to their fathers at a whole-school ceremony. Sometimes, however, bearing in mind MacBeath's (2006) cautions that integration can be stressful, we arrange for children with additional educational support needs to have their own space: for example, we arrange separate examinations areas, with teachers' support, to ensure they receive appropriate encouragement.'

Keep careful records, both of action and of learning. For example, you could write in one column of your reflective journal 'What did I do?', and in a second column 'What did I learn?', as in Table 11.1. Leave a space after entries, or a blank third column so that you can later respond to the question 'What is the significance of my action and my learning?'

TASK

Identify an option for action and explain your choice to others.

Table 11.1 Table to show process of reflection on action

What did I do?	What did I learn?	What is the significance of my learning?
I encouraged peers to be more understanding.	I should also have focused on encouraging the victim. I could have spent more time with her myself.	Externally imposed solutions do not often work. Personally developed solutions tend to lead to more sustainable outcomes.
We invited parents to attend staff meetings.	We should also have prepared staff for working with parents.	Throwing people together is seldom effective. More effective is careful preparation for people to make their own decisions.

6. What kind of data will I gather to show the situation as it is and as it develops?

Job to be done: describe how you gathered data and explain why you chose specific data-gathering methods

Aim to gather data: you can do this at any time, on an opportunistic basis as when you record field notes, or as formal data-gathering episodes at scheduled intervals, the frequency of which you decide. For a three-week project you may need to gather data every two or three days; for a three-month project, every week would probably do. Make sure all data are relevant to your research question. When asking, 'How do I encourage participation?' aim to gather data to show aspects of participation (or possible non-participation).

Remember that you are not trying to impose change in the sense of directly 'impacting' on someone. Change can work like this, when one person gets someone else to do something, or does something to them such as cut their hair. You are aiming for sustainable change, rooted in the values of relationship and negotiated forms of living. Sustainable change happens when people decide for themselves what is best for them and in relation to their wider social circumstances.

Perhaps think not about change but about exercising influence (as outlined in Chapter 6). Do you do this? Do you keep in mind that people think for themselves, that they decide whether to be influenced or not? Many people are told that they cannot think for themselves and must think in a certain way, and they come to believe this. Do you want people to internalise what you think or to think for themselves? How do you find ways of freeing your own thinking in order to help others to think for themselves?

Maintain careful records of your social action and your learning. You can use the same data-gathering methods throughout your project or many. Be imaginative. Do not instantly opt for a questionnaire. Think creatively: choose interviewing, artwork or video conferencing. Keep ethical considerations in mind and get permission from participants to use their words or work as data. Ask them to sign and date their work, and then sign and date this yourself. This is an important form of authentication.

Sort your data regularly and consolidate them at intervals. Remember that you are showing processes of development where people, including yourself, come to do things differently. Show how these processes unfold and also show their potential influences in others' speech and actions. Comment explicitly on these processes in your dissertation. Also analyse and interpret your data in terms of agreed categories to produce evidence to support your knowledge claims. Chapters 14 and 15 give detailed information on generating evidence from data; the next section also explains this briefly.

TASK

Write down where to find evidence of your influence in (1) your learning, (2) your actions, (3) other people's learning, (4) other people's actions. Your sources may be the same or different from your earlier rounds of data gathering.

How do you judge the effects of the exercise of your influence and whether you are achieving your research goals? Write down the value that inspired your work and say whether you are living towards it, at least in some instances. Where could you find instances of this?

---

7. How will I test the validity of my provisional knowledge claim(s)?

Job to be done: Explain how you tested the validity of your provisional knowledge claims and the importance of doing so

How do you make judgements about the quality of your influence and whether you are achieving what you hoped to achieve? Write down the original value that inspired your work and say whether you feel you are living towards it, at least in some instances.

Here are two examples:

Example 1

Data that show values	What kind of evidence might I find?	Value under consideration
A participant's research diary	Diary entry where she thanks you for your support while settling in at work	Support: Need to support newcomers
Transcript of a tape-recorded conversation with a student about whether she is making progress	Extract where the student says you have helped her become more confident	Self-confidence: Importance of helping people develop confidence in themselves
Video of self-assertion workshop you have presented	Clip of a shy person standing up for herself in a problematic conversation with others	Self-assertiveness: Need for people to value and speak for themselves

(Continued)

(Continued)

Example 2

My value	Where do I look for data?
Fairness and high academic standards	As a student I would look in my marked assignments to see the realisation of my supervisor's values of fairness and high academic standards: I would look for data showing my supervisor's insistence on accurate grammar and punctuation and justified critique.
Freedom	I would look for data to show that my supervisor encouraged me to think for myself.
Academic freedom	I anticipate that my supervisor will challenge statements that appear only as opinion.

Remember that the focus of your enquiry is you. You are monitoring your actions and learning, as you try to influence further learning in relation with other people. You are not at this point evaluating other people's practices. You are evaluating your practice to see whether or not you feel justified in claiming that you are achieving your own high standards.

Here are some examples of possible claims to knowledge and the standards used to make judgements about those claims.

My claim	Value as criterion	My standards of judgement	Evidence: what will the data show?
I have encouraged good working relationships in my organisation through insisting on professional courtesy.	Professional courtesy	My data archive contains instances of people's testimonies that they have learned from me the importance of professional courtesy.	I will find text messages and emails from colleagues saying that they have learned from me the importance of professional courtesy.
I have influenced the quality of communication in our school.	Good communication; relationship; empathy	My data archive will contain instances to show people communicating well and pleasantly.	I can produce instances of practice, including emails and text messages, to show that colleagues are communicating well and pleasantly. My values of relationship and empathy are being realised as standards of judgement.
I have encouraged occupational therapy students to make thoughtful professional decisions.	Capacity to make thoughtful professional decisions	My data archive will contain instances to show occupational therapy students acting with discernment in making professional decisions.	Professional portfolios and assignments show the exercise of original thinking and critical judgement. My value of professional decision making and discernment is being realised in practice.

TASK

Look through your data archive for those pieces of data that show how you are addressing your values.

Hayder Yahya Al Shorman asks, 'How do I help my students in Grade 12 Advanced Chemistry to improve their academic standards?' He implements an extensive staff development plan and concludes his account by reporting on his own learning. He writes:
   'I have learned the following:

- Teachers need to be prepared to change their practices to improve educational processes.
- As a professional I need to evaluate my practice continually.
- Accepting the need for self-improvement is key.
- Collaborative working is essential for improving teaching and learning.'

His recommendations are:

- 'All teachers should be prepared to improve their practices, and be open to processes of change.
- Action research puts teachers at the centre of their professional learning, and in control of their professional lives; teachers need to accept the challenge of taking responsibility for their practices.
- Action research can have significant influence for systemic improvement when factored into the lives of teachers through the provision of additional time and opportunity.'

8. How will I ensure that any conclusions I come to are reasonably fair and accurate?

Job to be done: demonstrate the authenticity of your research and the potential quality and significance of your knowledge claims

Throughout your project, aim to test the validity of your knowledge claims against the critical feedback of others, to show that those claims are, as far as possible, unprejudiced, authentic and not simply a matter of opinion or wishful thinking. Do this as an ongoing process: regularly check your ideas and findings against the critical feedback of critical friends, participants, supervisors and other interested persons, and at formal meetings such as a validation group (see Chapter 16). You hope your listeners will agree that your research demonstrates methodological rigour, ethical practice and a sense of social hope, and that you have presented your thesis with due regard for clear expression and academic conventions. They may comment on the quality of your methodology, your observation of good ethical practice, the authenticity of your data, processes of generating valid evidence in relation to articulated standards of judgement, and the entire conduct of the research. This process of public critique is essential to all forms of research, and vital in action research where claims to knowledge are rooted in subjective experience. Be prepared for disconfirming feedback that tells you what you do not want to know, for example, that things are not going as you think: it can help as a valuable steer to your project and prevent you from making unjustified claims. Decide for yourself whether to act on the advice of critical colleagues, otherwise be prepared to defend your decisions and future actions. To ensure that a validation group will see what you wish them to see, write down your provisional knowledge claim and where your validation group can find appropriate evidence in your text, as follows.

My anticipated claim	What I hope my validation group will see
I will claim that I have improved the smooth running of my organisation.	I hope they will see evidence of the smooth running of my organisation in my records and strategic action plan. I hope they will see an improvement in productivity and income this year.
I will claim that I have encouraged students to be more responsive in class.	I hope they will see videos of my students taking part in lessons and taking a proactive peer teaching role.
I will claim that I have improved the quality of my academic leadership.	I hope they will see increasing numbers of faculty enrolling for academic study. I hope they will see a stronger publications output.

TASK

Write down your provisional claim and what kind of evidence your critical friends and validation groups will see to help them make judgements about what you have done and its potentials for achieving your purposes.

---

9. How will I modify my concerns, ideas and practices in light of my evaluations?

Job to be done: Set out how you perceive the potential of your research for influencing new, more socially and democratically oriented personal and social practices

What do you anticipate you will do differently in light of what you have learned through doing the research? Make some educated guesses. Also remember that it takes courage and commitment to let go of old ways and head for the future. The fact that you are prepared to critique your own practices indicates your determination to keep raising critical questions in order to challenge prejudice and defend those people less fortunate than yourself: these are your guiding principles for action.

If you feel your new way of working is reasonably satisfactory, you will probably continue working like this for as long as it remains satisfactory. This may not be for long, however, because people change all the time and their circumstances change with them. A core feature of action research is to see how one research question can transform into another, and how one issue can act as the grounds for new issues. Nothing is ever static. We are constantly changing ourselves and our contexts. For example:

Example 1

Research question: How do I manage my timekeeping?

Engaging with this question can give rise to new questions such as:

- How do I protect research time?
- How do I negotiate with others about my work schedule?
- How do I manage the process of writing reports?

Example 2

Research question: How do I encourage young children to become active learners?

Engaging with this question can give rise to new questions such as:

- How do I encourage self-confidence among young children?
- How do I manage relationships in my class?
- How do I enlist the help of parents during classwork?

This kind of transformation can help you organise your ideas and practices as ongoing cycles of action and reflection. Focusing on one issue can lead to new learning. This learning can feed back into action, and the action can act as the grounds for new learning. It is an ongoing spiral of spirals that helps us to realise our potentials for unlimited new ideas and boundless forms of new practices. We create our futures as we live our presents.

This returns us to the idea of why we should demonstrate publicly how we hold ourselves accountable for what we do. By using our research projects to evaluate our work, we show how we are ensuring that today is the best we can be and do, and this gives us hope that tomorrow will be even better.

Summary

This chapter has taken you through an action research process, step by step, with ideas and examples of how you can do this for yourself. You are encouraged to adapt the suggested questions into questions about your own circumstances, and to use your imagination about how to do your action research.

The next chapter considers how the quality of your practices and research may be evaluated.

EXERCISES

- If you are planning to do a project, write out responses in the future tense to each of the questions in the chapter. If you have completed your project, write out responses in the past tense to describe what you have done at each point in your project. Get your colleagues' opinions about whether you have done this clearly and coherently. Can you trace the golden thread through your plan?
- Use these writings as the basis for your assignments and dissertation.

Evaluating the quality of your plans, practices and research

Evaluation is about establishing the value or quality of something. In any organisational setting it can apply to a range of areas, including the quality of provision, of leadership or of a curriculum. In this book the focus is on evaluating the quality of your own research-informed practices. Three issues therefore arise. You need to demonstrate:

- the quality of your plans (what you intend to do), the quality of your practices and research (what you have done), and the quality of your knowledge (what you have learned through the practice and research);
- the validity of your claim that this is what you have done and learned;
- how this is communicated through your explication of how you have come to know it.

This chapter focuses on the first point; the second, which is about assessing the validity of knowledge claims, is dealt with in Chapter 16; and the third, which is about communication, in Chapter 18. Questions now arise, which this chapter addresses, as follows.

1. What does evaluation involve?
2. How is it evaluated? Evaluating your own work
3. Examples of personal and organisational self-evaluation practices

1. What does evaluation involve?

Doing evaluation is never a neutral process. While evaluation is generally understood as establishing the value of something, different people prioritise different values, and therefore hold different views about what counts as 'good'. Consequently, evaluation processes are always politically constituted and involve the exercise of power, mainly about who is entitled to say what and who counts as 'right'. This has implications for you because action research is in itself a form of self-evaluation where you ask, 'How do I evaluate what I am doing? How do I improve it as necessary?' This immediately raises questions about who is qualified to say what counts as good and how practices are judged in relation to what is decided. Many questions arise, three of which suffice at this point:

- Who evaluates?
- What is evaluated?
- How is it evaluated?

Who evaluates?

Two primary perspectives are evident in current evaluation policies and practices: in the first perspective, 'value', and therefore evaluation, is understood in terms of a pre-defined, fixed set of properties or rules to be applied; in the second, where value and evaluation are seen as open transformational practices, rules are negotiated by the parties involved. The first perspective may be seen in dominant contemporary approaches to evaluation, a primary example of which came to prominence in the early twentieth century, when Frederick Taylor (1911) introduced the long-lasting (and for some) sinister idea of scientific management. The idea was that people's work could be judged by a manager carrying a stopwatch: a worker would achieve so many units of work in so much time. People were seen as automata whose output could be judged in terms of designated targets. The influence of this idea is evident today around the world and in multiple fields: whereas in Taylor's day the main field was industry, today it is everywhere, including across the professions. People's capacities and learning are judged in terms of how many targets they achieve in a given time. Implications of this approach include the standardisation of practices and people; de-skilling, demoralisation and de-professionalisation; and the controlled centralisation of thought. When this view enters evaluation, it establishes the idea that an external evaluator makes judgements about other people's practices. The stopwatch is accompanied by a checklist, and becomes an instrument for measuring the achievement of behavioural targets and pre-specified outcomes. Callahan's (1962) *Education and the Cult of Efficiency* is as real today as it ever was.

This model of evaluation-as-inspection permeates most, if not all professional contexts where practitioners are inspected by authorised 'experts'. Those 'experts' hold 'expert knowledge' which, according to the dominant orthodoxy, may be applied to others' practices. On this view, evaluation comes to take the form of inspection, conducted by those official experts. This approach can be terrifying for those whose practices are being evaluated. Drawing on the work of Foucault and others, Ball (2003) speaks of 'the terrors of performativity', the expectation that practitioners have to abide by stringent frameworks that dictate how they should act. This control by terror is part of a wider strategy which aims to control the public mind, often perpetrated through the media. In academic contexts it is done primarily through the scholarly and policy literatures where dominant stories maintain that only a particular kind of knowledge and theory is accepted as high status knowledge, implying that only a particular kind of knower is acceptable as a high status person. All are required to buy into the system, willingly or under duress. Chomsky (1991) speaks about this as the process of manufacturing consent: if people do not consent willingly their thinking must be manipulated in a certain way so that they do consent. For those who espouse this view, says Easterly (2013), the imposition of a theory of evaluation is more important than the spontaneous theories practitioners produce of their own development.

The above refers to the idea of a constrained vision, as outlined in the Introduction. An unconstrained vision, on the other hand, which is the nature of action research, works from a different perspective. Because of its underpinning values of justice and democracy, practition-ers are able to exercise their own voices about who should evaluate, and on whose terms this should be done. This is the view promoted in this book. However, in order to justify this stand and merit popular confidence that their own theories should be taken seriously, practitioners must themselves show that they are competent to judge their own work, test its validity, and produce publicly warranted evidence to show that their findings are credible and trustworthy. This means making their explanatory and evaluation processes rigorous and robust, and produc-ing strong evidence to show that as practitioner–researchers they are capable and competent to self-evaluate. From this perspective, practitioners become their own experts. According to Russell, 'The most important characteristic for a school [or any organisation] to develop ... is the capacity to improve from within. Self knowledge is needed; the power of any external interven-tion is limited, and should be focused on generating a school's [or organisation's] capacity for sustainable self-renewal' (Russell, 1996: 70).

What is evaluated?

Evaluation therefore includes not only demonstrating the validity of the researcher's claims about the work but also the validity of their claims to be capable of doing the job. While shifts in evaluation practices have happened in recent years, as shown for example in the schools' self-evaluation movement (MacBeath, 2006), the debates continue, with massive repercussions for real-life practices. This amounts to a struggle between whose views should be seen as the 'right' way forward: whether organisations should continue to implement official policies, which still err towards a conservative constrained vision, or to accept and support the development of more open exploratory forms of practitioners' initiatives to evaluate their own practices. The dominant orthodoxy is that the focus of evaluation should be on outcomes rather than on the develop-ment and support of learning processes, or on how those learning processes may themselves be developed and supported. In a recent (2016) UK White Paper on 'Excellence Everywhere' (see www.gov.uk/government/uploads/system/uploads/attachment_data/file/508447/Educational_ Excellence_Everywhere.pdf), most of the text focuses on structural and organisational issues, with statements of the kind 'We will establish more privately owned schools; we will provide highly skilled leaders'. Little is said about learning other than that greater emphasis will be given to subject knowledge; little is said about improving the quality of learning of teachers or students, or how they can be supported to improve this themselves.

2. How is it evaluated? Evaluating your own work

This focus on an outcomes-based model of evaluation assumes that the achievement of articu-lated goals may be evidenced through technical exercises such as randomised controlled trials.

A main criterion frequently used to judge practices, generally but especially in higher education contexts, is whether the work can be demonstrated as having 'impact'. The quality of research is judged in terms of whether it may be generalised to like practices and replicated in similar circumstances. These practices are reflections of Bernstein's (2000) views about how knowledge is pedagogised (that is, formed as specific pedagogic structures that often work as symbolic forms for the control of knowledge and identity). Technicist approaches view curriculum as an accumulation of information, and practices as the accumulation of skills. The task of the professional educator is to get this information across to trainees, frequently using didactic and delivery-oriented methods. The demands are to achieve targets, cover the syllabus, finish the textbook, and deliver the curriculum. It becomes a case of getting a functional job of work done, and delivering a product, rather than about working with people with real lives. Evaluation becomes a practice of experts, done to trainees. This denies the obvious (though frequently officially denied) fact that local people know what is right for them and can work out their own solutions to local problems. It also denies the emancipatory principles of a commitment to communicative action (Habermas, 1987) where all may participate in deciding how they should live together and how social practices may be judged.

The struggle is high profile today, given that established evaluation practices ally themselves with corporate power, also communicating messages that 'everyday' practitioners should accept the situation. Yet this view can be changed. It would be naïve to think that the current global shift towards technicisation will budge overnight, but this does mean that those who resist need to be all the better informed about how to take focused, longer-term action in order to achieve legitimation, including through being awarded a degree. This has implications for you as a practitioner, because it means that, if you wish to be seen as capable of evaluating your own practices, you must show that you can do so effectively. And given that, as someone studying on a course, you are now also in the context of higher education (itself now a member of the corporate community, with its own rules in the form of established academic criteria), you need to show that you can achieve those, too.

This book argues that practitioners should judge their own practices and willingly hold their evaluations up to public scrutiny, including by the community of scholars, and demand that they should be listened to. Like Senge (1990: 4) they believe that 'The organizations that will truly excel in the future will be the organizations that discover how to tap people's commitment and capacity to learn at *all* levels in an organization' (1990: emphasis in the original). All should be prepared to evaluate their own personal and social practices and test their findings against the critical scrutiny of knowledgeable others. This, of course, challenges the authority of those who like to be positioned as experts and managers, although it can be wonderfully liberating for practitioners who wish to position themselves as persons doing a worthwhile job of work in company with others who are doing the same. But making this shift requires considerable courage and energy; nor is help available from even the more progressive literatures on organisational self-evaluation, that again produce the theory of how this may be accomplished without offering systematic advice or support for how it can be done. While they may write about self-evaluation in scholarly texts, few authors are able or prepared to show that they do it themselves. This all means that practitioners need actively to engage by undertaking self-evaluation practices, demonstrating how self-evaluation may be achieved and producing validated evidence to show that their efforts may be justified in terms of encouraging the emancipatory and collaborative practices of those whose thinking they wish to influence. These efforts are essential if the realisation of the infinite potentials of human capabilities for self-determination are to shift out of the rhetoric and become reality.

So what does it mean to evaluate your own work? Here are some ideas.

3. Examples of personal and organisational self-evaluation practices

A colleague, whose doctoral studies I was supporting at the time, once said to me 'You write about action research but you don't actually do it'. I hope, in this book and elsewhere, to have roundly refuted this perception. For me, action research is not only about doing projects, it is more about living a life of enquiry and making your learning from those enquiries public. However, I have done formal projects, a lot of them, and continue to do so. These projects have been both small and large scale, and have usually involved helping other people to self-evaluate their own practices and improve them as appropriate. My help takes the form of the provision of intellectual and practical resources, as well as negotiating politically constituted situations so that they can achieve their certificates and degrees; this last has involved engaging mainly with the politics of higher education contexts where the aim usually is to keep so-called 'practitioners' in their place. My hope always is to bring the university to those who position themselves as 'everyday' people and those people to the university. And I fulfil my research obligation of 'making public' by writing papers and books like this one, to show the research base of the learning that emanates from the experience.

Here are three examples of projects conducted by people I am associated with, focusing here on self-evaluation strategies and stages in projects. The first and third are taken from Ireland; the second from South Africa.

Project 1: National Centre for Guidance in Education (NCGE): (Ireland)

The NCGE is an agency of the Department of Education and Skills, with responsibility to support and develop guidance practice in all areas of education and to inform the policy of the Department in the field of guidance (see www.ncge.ie). Based on my work in Ireland with the SBARP and other projects, and in Northern Ireland, I was invited to join them in a consultancy role, as a member of a team of supporters, from the mid-2000s until 2013; today I remain associated with them and supportive of their work. Throughout our time together we supported thousands of guidance counsellors in Ireland to explore their practices and develop focused strategies for improving it as appropriate. We adopted throughout an action research approach that enabled guidance counsellors, individually and in groups, to interrogate the assumptions that underpinned what they were doing and develop new practices based on their findings. The work had widespread influence in schools and colleges and continues today. It has influenced other national initiatives in Ireland, such that self-evaluation is now part of everyday school life. An irony is that, because action research itself has been packaged by higher education and government institutions, many professional education initiatives have also been packaged: on one agency website, for example, the focus has shifted from the investigation and evaluation of practices to the preparation and delivery of subject-oriented self-help resources.

However, a beautiful example of what can happen when practitioners decide to evaluate their practices is in the form of the NCGE's *Evidence Based Handbook: Guidance Case Studies* (Darbey et al., 2013: available online at www.ncge.ie/uploads/Evidence_based_handbook-final.pdf). In this four guidance counsellors tell about their learning how to do action research for self-evaluation and how their ideas influenced whole-school development initiatives, both in the area of guidance and in subject areas. Achieving this level of influence was far from easy and involved negotiating personal, collegial and institutional challenges, yet they were quietly yet significantly successful.

As a team, we supporters provided workshops, with appropriate materials such as the ones in Chapters 9, 10 and 11 in this book, where guidance counsellors learned how to evaluate their own practices and produce public accounts that showed how they held themselves accountable for their own practices. Linda Darbey, coordinator of the project in the Dublin office, arranged for support in the form of email feedback to participants on assignments, team planning and review sessions, and assessment panels. The entire initiative was grounded in the premise that:

> School guidance planning is very much an exercise in self-evaluation which specifically focuses on areas in need of improvement. At its core is a strong value of examining one's practice on an ongoing basis, leading to a guidance practitioner becoming a critical and reflective member of a guidance service support system which contributes greatly to a positive school climate of student learning. (Darbey et al., 2013: 2)

In the NCGE *Handbook*:

- Gearóidin Brady writes about how her school's work in County Donegal is part of the 'Delivering Equality of Opportunity in Schools' scheme. She says: 'It is important that children living in areas of social disadvantage are given every opportunity to succeed in school, contributing to breaking the cycle of disadvantage' (p. 3). She and her colleagues undertook their individual and collaborative enquiries into how they could achieve this aim.
- The focus of Niamh Dwyer and colleagues was a review of the pastoral care system for first-year students. Niamh summarises her learning from the project as: 'In conclusion, I can say that in implementing this action plan I did influence the situation of 1st year students, their parents and teachers in terms of raising their awareness about the different types of learners and the different methods of learning for those learners' (p. 21).
- Dymphna Foody and colleagues looked at the entire range of guidance provision in their school. Dymphna offers a list of recommendations for Guidance Counsellors beginning a planning process, including 'Begin: don't see this as taking on extra work, but as getting real and relevant support to do what needs to be done in your school'; 'Believe in what you are doing'; 'Persevere: things will not always go according to plan. Learn to recognise and accept the minor victories'; and 'Evaluate honestly: if something is not working don't be afraid to scrap it and return to the drawing board' (p. 37).
- Peter Hyde writes about the need not to feel threatened by change but to engage with it as a process of self-empowerment. He also comments on the wider organisationally beneficial effects of studying one's own practices: 'Although action research may commence with an individual wanting to improve the quality of his or her practice it can lead to, and contribute to, other practitioners wanting to improve theirs. This does not always happen ... but when it does happen I have experienced it to have brought about meaningful improvements both in my practice and that of others in the school' (p. 53).

The entire philosophy of action research for whole school evaluation may be summarised as follows: 'The evaluation process is a school self evaluation exercise and is not dependent on an external voice' (Darbey et al., 2013: 2).

Project 2: Khayelitsha, South Africa

In 2003 I visited South Africa to deliver a workshop on action research. After the workshop, a colleague invited me to observe some of the consultancy work he was doing in Khayelitsha, a large township near Cape Town, containing perhaps half a million disenfranchised people, many living in squalid conditions. I have written about this experience elsewhere, but the most important elements are that, from talking with some of the teachers there, I negotiated with St Mary's University College (now St Mary's University, Twickenham), where I had an institutional position, to teach a master's programme. This was the same programme I was already teaching at the university, through which eight senior lecturers gained their master's degrees, all with distinction. The programme in Khayelitsha initially attracted over 50 teachers, but in the event only 10 stayed the course and gained their master's degrees. During that time, all the teachers kept reflective diaries of their learning as part of their assignments, and I did the same. So a large data archive of collaborative self-reviews exists, especially as self-evaluation was built into the course and self-evaluation accounts appear throughout the assignments (see www.jean mcniff.com/khayelitsha). I also arranged for two members of the group to travel and co-present at the American Educational Research Association's annual meeting (see www.jeanmcniff.com/ items.asp?id=81 and www.jeanmcniff.com/items.asp?id=5). Their papers were well received and they gained individually from the experience.

As part of the evaluation process participants presented their work to peers in the group: these presentations were recorded, so that the videos could be brought back to the accrediting institution for assessors there also to comment on the quality of the work. Colleagues from higher education settings in South Africa also visited our weekend workshops whenever possible, listened to participants' presentations and offered critical comments: this provided powerful external evaluation to counterbalance and offer objective comment on the authenticity of participants' own self-evaluations. One of those visitors was Professor Lesley Wood, now at North-West University, who wrote the following after her observation of our work:

Practice: Students demonstrated a good understanding of their practices and definitely have grown in terms of their self-perceptions as agents of change. They are more pro-active and self-directed then before. They do understand the need to be self-critical and demonstrate evidence of this. Many gave examples of how they have influenced learners in the wider school environment.

Research: Although all students appeared to understand the process of action research and its theoretical foundations during oral conversations, few were able to demonstrate this in their presentation. Only one or two students referred to theory to explain their interventions

(Continued)

(Continued)

and values. Many failed to present a clear evidence base. There was also little explanation of their values as standards of judgement, and, although they mentioned critical friends, they did not really show how they tested the validity of their claims. This may be covered in the assignments but it was not clear from the presentations.

Presentation: The students are to be commended on their presentations, as most were clear and well communicated. Students were confident and were both supportive yet critical of each other's work.

This kind of critical external commentary can do much to help practitioners strengthen the quality of their work and produce the kind of reports that examiners are looking for.

Project 3: Early Learning Initiative, Dublin

The third example returns us to Ireland, and the work of Josephine Bleach, Director of the Early Learning Initiative in Dublin, who was introduced in Chapter 1. Her account appears in a Special Issue of the *Educational Action Research Journal*. She speaks about the importance of evaluating large projects using a range of evaluation methods.

Josephine writes:

'As a local project, we had to produce robust evidence that we were implementing a programme and achieving our outcomes to the NEYAI (National Early Years Access Initiative) funders. This required us to have explicit criteria against which the authenticity of our data and evidence could be checked within the broader exercise of testing the validity of our claims (McNiff, 2010) ... Gathered systematically, over several action research cycles, these data were used to provide indicative evidence of effectiveness and causality. This also enabled us to be confident that we were engaging in virtuous practice; that is [from an Aristotelian perspective], doing the right things with the right people for the right end and in the right way ...

'Multiple methods were used to create evaluation data on the programme. This allowed for triangulation, which created confidence in the accuracy of the findings. Quantitative and qualitative data were collected through evaluation forms following each training session and numeracy week. This was supplemented by qualitative data collected during on-site visits and the quantitative data from the child assessments. Three different forms of assessments were used to measure children's numeracy outcomes ... Baseline and follow-up assessments were completed on a group of children aged three to four years. The results were compared with children of the same age taking part in other NEYAI projects along with a more socio-economically advantaged sample.' (Bleach, 2013: 27–8)

These examples show that, if you wish to be seen as sufficiently capable and competent, both as a practitioner and as a researcher, to evaluate your own work (which you are), you have to fulfil certain conditions and develop strategies for achieving those conditions.

The main conditions include the following:

- Demonstrating scholarly and practical expertise: you need to show that you are:
  o contributing to knowledge of the field;
  o demonstrating critical engagement;
  o demonstrating methodological rigour in research;
  o demonstrating capacity in writing and communication

Procedures for achieving these are outlined throughout this book.

- Developing strategies for self-evaluation, including the strategies outlined especially in Chapters 10–12.
- Learn to notice: Mason (2002) and Berger (2007) speak about the need to be aware of our surroundings and our responses to them, actively to pay attention, to notice.
- Learn to reconsider and reframe (Schön and Rein, 1994): do this through listening to others' feedback and paying attention to critique.
- Be prepared to interrogate your own assumptions critically: use your reflective journal, using exercises such as the one on page 172 of this book.
- Reflect on your reflection: learn not to take your first reaction, and to wait for the second to arrive, as it usually does.
- Convene groups of critical friends: learning evolves through companionship.
- Leave your thoughts for a few days: when you go back you may find that new insights have developed.
- Learn through writing, as outlined in Chapters 18 and 19.
- Give your work to others to read: develop a reading group and actively look for critical feedback on your ideas and writing.
- Keep your courage strong: this can be difficult, especially when you know that your thinking and circumstances are going to change, and will continue to do so.

Above all, perhaps, it means having the courage to swim against the current (Berlin, 1997), in spite of the strength of it. But there is also exhilaration in the idea that you are in the good company of millions of other practitioners who share your desire for educational change yet do not have the intellectual or practical resources to support them, as you do, or actually know how to do it. You do, and it is your responsibility and privilege to develop the tradition of self-evaluation, support others, and proceed with energy for its dissemination.

Summary

This chapter is about evaluating the quality of your practices and research. It explains that different models of evaluation exist: action research is a process of personal and organisational self-evaluation, which is different from established models of outsider evaluation. Self-evaluation requires honesty and self-critique. Examples are given to show these ideas in practice.

The next chapter considers how to monitor practices in order to gather data.

---------------------------------- **EXERCISES** ----------------------------------

- Are you clear about the differences between an external and an internal approach to evaluation? Are these always separate or can they – and should they – be integrated within the same enquiry? Explain your views to a colleague.
- When is an external approach appropriate to whole-organisational evaluation? When is a self-evaluation approach more appropriate? Why?
- Write out how you evaluate your own practices and how you would like them to be judged by others. In what way can you justify your claim that your practices are good quality?

PART IV

How do I generate evidence to test the validity of my knowledge claim?

All research, including action research, aims to make knowledge claims. In action research the aim is to say that you now know more than you did before, and explain how you came to know it. This is often about how you have learned about your practice by studying it: you are able to describe and explain what you are doing, and also explain the importance of doing so.

Claims to knowledge need to be tested for authenticity, so that the claim does not appear as personal opinion or supposition. Evidence must be generated from data, and this must have been rigorously tested by competent researchers. This means gathering quality data from which you will select pieces to stand as evidence.

This part contains the following chapters.

Chapter 13   Monitoring practices and gathering data

Chapter 14   Working with data: analysing, authenticating and interpreting

Chapter 15   Generating evidence from the data and making knowledge claims: summary chapter

Each chapter offers practical advice about what to do in order to generate strong evidence.

Monitoring practices and gathering data

When evaluating practices, it is not enough just to talk about what you have done: you also have to show what you have done, describe the processes involved and explain why you chose those processes. This capacity for meta-analysis contributes to showing that you are a competent researcher as well as a competent practitioner.

This chapter is about what you need to do and think about in order to gather useful data, and not waste time gathering irrelevant data that you may well discard later. You therefore need to decide what you are looking for and where and how you might find it. This will involve decisions about how to monitor what you are doing in order to track developments over time, and which data-gathering methods to use.

The chapter is organised to respond to these three questions:

1. How do you monitor practices?
2. How do you gather data?
3. How do you organise, store and manage data?

1. How do you monitor practices?

In your action research you are looking for specific episodes of practice that show:

- how you are influencing your learning;
- how your learning influences new actions;
- how your actions influence other people's learning;
- how their learning influences their actions (refer back to Figure 6.1).

This may be seen as an integrated, self-organising system of reciprocal action and learning that works at multiple levels. Your task is to be clear about the interrelated nature of the system and explain how one aspect influences the others, and how this can give rise to new cycles of action and reflection.

Episodes of practice that show how you are influencing your learning

First, consider what you are looking for and where you might find it.

What are you looking for?

Influencing your own learning means looking for times when you exercised critical engagement about what you were thinking or reading. You began to interrogate what was being said and done to see whether it was believable. Critical thinking is a core responsibility of being a researcher. Whenever you read or hear a news item, think 'Whose voice am I hearing? Whose words? What are they telling me? Why should I believe them? What are their credentials?' We are bombarded with information from all directions: the media, social networks, literatures, everyday discourses. Check before you believe what you hear: people can be skilled in manipulating words and communicating false messages. Learn to watch out for false words and use your own thinking to block them.

Also watch out for times when you block your own thinking, perhaps by taking a particular stand or being uncritical. You may react automatically to certain groups of people simply because you live in a particular culture or because you have seen a film representing them (often incorrectly). This is often the basis for all kinds of tribalism, from adopting a stance towards people with different ethnicities to cheering for a particular football club.

Demonstrating critical thinking is vital in research, because you must justify everything you say and how you do this. To re-emphasise, there is no moral code that tells you which moral code to live by, unless you are committed to a specific moral code set out, say, in a holy book: we all have to think for ourselves. It is also vital to adopt an enquiring stance towards your research, and not use it to reinforce your prejudices or show that your opinion is right. The best dissertations show how the author developed their own thinking, as well as developed their actions appropriate to their changing context.

As a member of a team of 16 early years lecturers with backgrounds in teaching, health, social work and law, Carla Solvason, senior lecturer at the Centre for Early Childhood at the University of Worcester, developed a professional education project for student teachers involving innovative staff pedagogies. The project appeared encouraging, with increased engagement from students. Aware also of the need for ethical research, Carla began to think about what ethical practices actually involves. She writes:

[I began] to reflect on the form of language we use with students concerning matters of ethics. We frequently use the terms 'ethical' and 'sensitive' ... but I wonder whether

> we should be broadening the range of our ethics-related terminology and embedding it more specifically within our teaching ... perhaps we should be aiming to explore this thorny concept far more thoroughly and to develop a more public discourse of ethicality within our teaching. Possibly we need to explore with the students what, exactly, it means to be 'mindful', or to be 'self-aware,' or how to recognise 'human dignity' when they consider their reflections on practice. (Solvason, 2016: 41-2)

Be aware also of the propensity to jump to conclusions. Kahneman (2011: 6–7) explains how we often make unwarranted assumptions, which then inform our judgements and consolidate into biases. He provides the following example:

> As you consider the next question, please assume that Steve was selected at random from a representative sample:
>
> An individual has been described by a neighbour as follows: 'Steve is very shy and withdrawn, invariably helpful but with little interest in people or in the world of reality. A meek and tidy soul, he has a need for order and structure, and a passion for detail.' Is Steve more likely to be a librarian or a farmer?
>
> The resemblance of Steve's personality to that of a stereotypical librarian strikes everyone immediately, but equally relevant statistical considerations are almost always ignored. Did it occur to you that there are more than 20 male farmers for each male librarian in the United States? Because there are so many farmers, it is almost certain that more 'meek and tidy' souls will be found on tractors than at library information desks. However, we found that participants in our experiments ignored the relevant statistical facts and relied exclusively on resemblance. We proposed that they used resemblance as a simplifying heuristic (roughly, a rule of thumb) to make a difficult judgment. The reliance on the heuristic caused predictable biases (systematic errors) in their predictions. (Kahneman, 2011: 6-7)

Kahneman proposes two systems of thinking for making judgements: what he calls 'System 1', which is based on intuition and recall from past experiences and involves 'fast thinking', and System 2, which is a more deliberative process of analytical 'slow thinking'. He suggests that many of us tend to work with the fast System 1 practice of jumping to conclusions based on our immediate recognition of past experiences: test this yourself by listening to a party political broadcast and consider how your thinking is being subtly manipulated towards a particular version of reality.

Where do you look for it?

Look in those places where you showed critical thinking. This could be your reflective journal, where you record both what you did and what you thought of what you did. Do an exercise such as in Table 13.1.

We all do silly things and make mistakes. There is no shame in accepting responsibility for past actions: the harm is in not acknowledging them or the fact that we are capable of doing them, and then to continue doing them.

Table 13.1   Data to show differences in 'then' and 'now' thinking

Record of my thoughts in my reflective journal, 3 March 2016	Record of my thoughts in my reflective journal, 10 August 2016
I am finally getting to grips with understanding the difficulties that foreign nationals experience when learning English.	Having travelled to Japan during the summer to brush up on my Japanese I recognise how mistaken my earlier understandings were. I simply did not appreciate the cultural complexities involved.
My students appear to be learning much better now that we are using paired work.	This week a group of children told me they were bored with paired work and could we please do something different.

Look at videos of yourself in conversation with others and reflect on your actions. Ask yourself 'What was I thinking at the time? Why did I say that?' This means being aware also of the context; we say and do things according to what seems right at the time and in response to what is going on.

You can draw on many other sources to show yourself exercising critical thinking: emails and social media: websites; responses to others; notes to self; diary entries.

To develop your capacity for critical thinking, read books on critical literacy such as Brookfield (1987), Lankshear and Knobel (2011) or Gee (2005). Those authors, like Kahneman, show the dangers of taking words at face value without stopping to consider what the words mean in real-life contexts.

Episodes of practice that show how your learning influences new actions

Be clear about what you are looking for and think about where you will find it.

What are you looking for?

Look also for those data that show you taking action based on your thinking. Do you always act on what you hear in a political broadcast? Politicians are known to tell lies deliberately: so are friends and spouses. If you are a teacher or person with position power others will tend to believe you. Do you exercise that power with discernment?

Many authors speak about the need to think before acting, including Arendt (1958), Schön (1983) and Kahneman (2011, as above). Yet while it is vital to think first about what you do, it is also vital to do it. You can reflect for ever and get paralysed through the process. You have to accept responsibility for your own stand. Stand up for what you believe in but try not to hurt anyone else in the process.

Where will you find it?

As above, look in places where you have recorded what you did on the basis of what you were thinking. You can also look for those episodes recorded by other people who record how you acted.

Anabarah Al-Abdallah, introduced in Chapter 12, explains how she involved other people to record progress. She says:

'Engaging in their learning through using the [program] Touch Math seemed to have enabled my students to raise achievement and improve their confidence. To test the validity of my conclusions I asked the school coordinator whether she agreed, and how we as a maths department could use the program for other grades. I also presented my research to sixteen peers on the professional education course we were attending. All agreed that I was justified in making my claims.' (See www.jeanmcniff.com/qatar.asp)

Episodes of practice that show how your actions influence other people's learning

Think about how you will gather data that show other people reacting to you.

What are you looking for?

Look for data that show how your actions influence other people's learning. When you help someone learn how to do something you influence their actions. The aim of professionals and the basis of good pedagogical practices is to help others learn how to help themselves. The word 'teaching' covers any situation where others learn from and with you, whether this is in a formal classroom or down a coalmine. People learn from and with you and use their learning actively to improve the quality of their own and others' lives.

Where do you look for it?

Look for data that show you helping others to learn and do things for themselves: find an email from a student saying they have got their degree because of your help; a thank-you card from a parent saying you helped their daughter learn to walk again; a Facebook message saying how much your kindness is valued. These data attest to how you have acted in other people's interests so they can now think and act for themselves.

Julie Pearson, a senior lecturer from St Mary's University, Twickenham, tells how she learns to support students in Primary Physical Education. She says:

'My core values of inclusion, freedom and care influence my practice that is about developing processes of learning rather than arriving at an end product. I extend the original description of assessment as "to sit beside" (Stefanakis, 2002) to counteract the traditional assumption of teaching and learning where students "download" and reproduce teachers' skills and knowledge. I include the voices of those I teach to reflect the value of co-creating knowledge within a practice.' (Pearson, 2016)

Episodes of practice that show how other people's learning influences your actions

Here are some ideas about what to look for and where to look for it.

What do you look for?

Look for those data that show you learning from what other people do, which they in turn have learned from you. This is a mutually reciprocal process and key to social evolution. We learn from and with one another and then pass that learning on to others. It is a non-stop process of the cyclical interactions of learning and acting.

Where do you look for it?

Aim to exercise professional integrity by acknowledging how other people's learning has helped you develop your own actions and learning. In everyday living you acknowledge others' influence through improving your practices; in academic studies you acknowledge the influence of other people's ideas for your studies and writing. You can find such instances in the acknowledgements page of a dissertation, in accurate referencing of other people's ideas, or in a letter to a newspaper where people thank you for your charity work.

> Susanne Winther is a nurse and PhD student at Aalborg University Hospital, Denmark. She tells how colleagues and she developed an action research project involving staff from an intensive care unit and staff from eight general wards as co-researchers. She writes:
> 'The aim was to develop safer and more professionally conducted patient transitions and handovers, and to generate knowledge and encourage insights among the staff about the processes involved.'
> She and co-researchers ran three workshops to discuss how handovers could be managed more successfully. Among other things, they invited former patients and relatives with the aim of learning from their experiences and contributions. She writes: 'It was evident that the workshops had a decisive influence on the co-researchers' engagement, particularly the workshop with the patients. Staff often referred to the patients' stories and were keen to collaborate across the practice communities to find new ways to reduce and resolve the problems that patients and relatives experience. They produced suggestions and action plans that they are now testing out.' (Winther, 2016)

Thinking about these processes of mutually reciprocal action emphasises the pluralistic nature of living: we are always in the company of others; we live in complex webs of time–space interrelationships where what one person does inevitably influences others. This is the nature of being human. It is reason for celebration and also to think before we act; we never know whose lives we will touch so our only course of action is to act well and with thought for the other.

2. How do you gather data?

Gathering data involves: knowing where and when to look for data; observing what is going on; recording, storing and sorting the data; and knowing how to retrieve the data. Many of these processes overlap, so take the following advice as a guide.

This section deals with the following points:

- Gathering data.
- Organising, storing and managing data.

Gathering data

At this point you are observing what is going on and finding ways to record it. Remember that you are not simply looking at action, but trying to show and record how learning enters into action.

Techniques to observe and record the action

Many techniques are available for monitoring actions and showing how and what kind of learning is going on. Here are some of the most common. Following Creswell (2007: 130) they are organised as:

- observations;
- interviews;
- documents;
- audiovisual and multimedia presentations and performances.

(You can also find many examples of gathering and analysing data from the reports of teachers involved in the Qatar project, at www.jeanmcniff.com/qatar.asp)

Observations: field notes

You make notes on the move as you observe actions or listen to interactions. You can write them into a special notebook, or on the back of your hand and write them up later. Experiment with mind maps, spider diagrams and pictures. Use your smartphone to make notes on the move and use the record function to give you hands-free access; use this as an ongoing record of thoughts and actions. Use driving time to think and keep audio notes. Watch out for opportunities and record events immediately as field notes. If you leave an idea without recording it you may forget it.

Kat Hobbs is a room manager in a nursery in a children's centre in London. She writes:

During the last year of my degree at Pen Green Research Base I wrote my dissertation about my action research; this included my reflections on my own practice whilst trying to understand how to improve an area in my setting. I have a huge passion for outdoor play and was interested in researching what children thought about the outdoor environment and playing there.

'At the time my setting was making changes to the outdoor area and therefore it was important that the main users of this space had their say. This was not an approach that had been used within my setting before which made me more determined to try it out. I also wanted to reflect upon the way I listened to children. I chose qualitative methods of data collection such as interviews and focus groups, and these provided me with extremely rich data. I also asked the children to photograph and draw elements of the outdoors they liked and disliked, wanted to keep or change. I made it clear from the start of my research that the children were researchers alongside me; it was vitally important that they wanted to be a part of the group and enjoyed their time researching with me.

'A colleague and I took a group of four children to another nursery's garden which, unlike ours, was filled with nature and wildlife. I observed them in both outdoor spaces, filmed their play and made written notes. On analysing the data I found that several themes emerged, so I turned to different sources and literatures to help further understand. When engaging in any form of action research I believe it is important to choose something you are passionate about as this will help develop knowledge and understanding. It also came as something of a surprise to me how totally consuming but rewarding this can be. This form of research is extremely worthwhile as the data produced can be very rich and can benefit practice immensely.'

Doodles and drawings

Try recording your observations in pictorial form, especially to show the quality of interactions. Draw stick figures; use the drawing app on your smartphone or iPad. Also use concept maps and spider diagrams that also show processes of tracking and linking ideas. Write up these notes as soon as possible after the event so you don't forget them.

Record sheets and observation schedules

These are the sheets you produce to gather data and maintain records, including observation schedules, analyses of actions and pictorial representations of action. The best are the ones you devise yourself, but Table 13.2 and Figure 13.1 show some ideas. Note that the tally marks refer to the number of interactions. Also note the use of the 'five-bar gate' to count in multiples of five.

Visual charting

Figure 13.1 shows an analysis in graphic form of the interactions among people at a meeting. Note how many times each person talks and who they talk with.

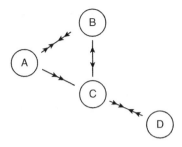

Figure 13.1   An example of interaction charting

Table 13.2   Examples of record sheets

Record sheet to show number of interactions between nurse and patient

Minutes	1	2	3	4
Interactions between nurse and patient	ЖЖ ЖЖ II	III	ЖЖ ЖЖ II	ЖЖ ЖЖ I

Record sheet to record number of times participants speak at a business meeting

Participant	Number of contributions
Mr Green	ЖЖ ЖЖ II
Ms Black	II
Mrs White	ЖЖ ЖЖ ЖЖ II
Mr Grey	ЖЖ II
Ms Pink	ЖЖ ЖЖ ЖЖ ЖЖ I

Interviews and surveys

Interviews are used extensively in action research to gain information from participants about their opinions and experiences. They are similar to live surveys and can take different forms including:

- Structured interviews: you ask closed or open-ended questions to solicit a specific response. You take notes or record the interview. Use a questionnaire rather than interview to ask closed questions or to get a 'yes–no' answer.
- Semi-structured interviews: you ask specific questions but invite the participant to give more extensive answers and record or keep notes.
- Focus group interviews: you record or ask an observer to keep notes.
- Electronic interviews: you use computers or other devices for text messages or emails. These can be audio or visual, telephone and online using web links, interactive messaging and face-to-face interactions.

In all interviews remember that you or someone else can keep notes and write these up afterwards. Also remember that transcribing can take ages. Be careful about ethical issues when interviewing, especially if you intend to make the data public. Remember the following:

- Pilot the interview before doing it live. Practise your interviewing skills with a colleague and get their feedback on your performance.
- Negotiate to record the interview. Never record without asking permission.
- Tell your interviewee what the interview is about and check if they agree. Tell them if you cannot tell them what it is about. Give them whatever information they need to make them feel comfortable.
- Aim to listen more than you speak. Learn to accept silences. Demonstrate empathy and be patient.
- Don't mislead or deceive people into giving you information.
- Give your transcripts back to your participants for them to check and edit, and negotiate the final document with them so that they are comfortable with what has been said.
- Never use transcript data without permission. This will lose participants' trust: once gone, it is gone forever.
- Maintain good faith at all times.

Documentary data

Documents take a range of forms including:

- logs, diaries and journals;
- letters and correspondence;
- public records and documents;
- questionnaires and surveys;
- audiovisual and multimedia materials and performance.

Logs, diaries and journals

These are the records you keep of personal action, reflection on the action and the learning arising from it. It does not matter whether you call them logs, diaries or journals, whether you keep a research diary and a reflective diary or use the same journal for both purposes. It can be helpful to differentiate episodes of action from episodes of learning, for example, by using different fonts or colours, as in Table 13.3.

Table 13.3 Learning generated through reflection on the action

What happened	What I learned
The parents' meeting was a success this evening. Perhaps the welcome cup of tea made a difference to the atmosphere.	We should pay greater attention to extending hospitality to parents and other guests.
K. came to the rehabilitation unit today. He is making good progress and has gained a lot of strength in his leg.	We learned that K. responds well to encouragement. He has made good progress since we decided on a policy of affirmation.

Text messages and emails

Social networking can be a rich source of data. Keep a record of a particular thread of an e-seminar or different contributions on social networking sites. These kinds of data can be difficult to track, so aim to keep on top of things and store them in easily accessible ways.

Public documents and records

Public documents and records record current and past practices, and include institutional archives, agendas and minutes of meetings and policy statements. They can provide valuable contextual information for your studies. Look for information in professional journals about current and past developments in the field. Use these records for establishing what is or was going on in the situation you are investigating and any social or political forces that helped or hindered your enquiry. Accessing and working with records is often called 'desk research' or 'archive/library research'.

Questionnaires and surveys

Do not rush into questionnaires. They may seem an easy way to collect data and many texts are available explaining how to construct them. If you do use them, do so to get a sense of trends and directions. Also pilot them many times to make sure they are providing the kind of information you need to move your enquiry forward. This advice also applies to surveys.

You can conduct closed, semi-structured and open surveys and interviews. Closed questions that look for 'yes–no' answers are easier to analyse, but do not give much information. More open questions that allow personal responses can be more difficult to analyse but provide rich information and insights.

Artworks

Encourage participants to produce their original visual representations as artworks and ask them to give their own interpretations of how their artworks represented their experience and learning. Keep records of these interpretations. Maria James (2013) asked students to find a publicly available artwork on the Internet, or to create an original piece of artwork, to record their emotions before a learning episode and another after the episode to show their changed perceptions both of self as learner and of the learning situation.

Audiovisual and multimedia materials and performance

These are used increasingly in formal action research accounts, usually as video and multimedia recordings. They show the living realities of interactions, including the responses of others to what is said and done, so they often capture live meanings more effectively than written texts. Many programs are available to record Internet-based meetings with recording functions for later viewing and analysis. Many organisations use Virtual Learning Environments (VLEs) to enable participants to interact and share ideas, with few maintenance cost implications.

Ingrid Bruynse is a teacher educator; she uses print and audiovisual media and training to address educational needs in South African public schools, where the two-language policy in schools has raised serious problems about the quality of learning and teaching in early grade education. The two languages used in South African schools are English, home language to a small minority, and Afrikaans, which has a complex position and history in South Africa: neither language is an African language. None of the local African languages are spoken as languages of learning and teaching for secondary schooling.

A new policy encouraging a third African language in schooling was introduced in 2015. To combat further confusion, Ingrid has been working with the National Department of Education to develop a teacher development programme to provide teachers with materials and methods for teaching African languages in their classrooms and for developing pedagogies for working with other languages.

Her company, Bright Media, is working with a focus group of teachers, using open content from a number of partners like the British Council, the South African Institute for Distance Education, the South African Broadcasting Corporation and the higher education providers to provide a collection of language resources and teaching methods and processes that can be selected by each of the nine provinces appropriate for their language and schooling needs and to support the policy implementation.

Performance

Most higher education institutions now accept performance as an integral part of professional education programmes; these include dance and music performances and photovoice presentations. They also accept multimedia recordings as part of evidence though explanations for these usually need to be produced as a regular written text, as part, say, of a professional portfolio or dissertation. Butler-Kisber identifies different forms of performance: poetic enquiry, photographic enquiry and performative enquiry. For her:

> Performative inquiry offers an important lens for thinking about inquiry that is embodied, relational, participatory, and geared towards action and social change. Promise lies in the continued exploration of this form of inquiry. (Butler-Kisber, 2010: 146)

3. How do you organise, store and manage data?

Whether you are working with physical data such as paper diaries or photographs or electronic media, aim to keep all the data well organised: early organisation pays off. First organise the data, whether physical or computer-based, into categories such as conversations, interviews, permissions, participants, blogs, spreadsheets, and other forms, and then organise these as files.

This would give you collections of data under their designated headings for ease of retrieval. Give each file a name, which should be short and easily remembered. It should communicate basic information about the data including:

- what the event is about;
- when it happened;
- where it happened;
- who was involved;
- anything else you consider important.

Always date your files, using a consistent format: 3 December 2016 or 3.12.16. This also applies when producing draft texts when analysing your data or producing a report. It is easy to confuse different versions of texts, so create a system that suits you and stick with it. Changing systems mid-stream can be confusing and may lead to errors. Try using colour coding: on my computer I mark the most recent version in red, the one before in mauve, and so on. This means sorting your work and keeping it updated: do this systematically and don't skip it. You can also use numbers and dates to keep yourself on track, as can combining your coding systems. Also maintain headers and footers on printed pages and update these regularly. Identifying data can save you hours of time and frustration so do this as a regular housekeeping job. This is especially important if you are doing collaborative work, when different people need to identify who has done what.

Now sort your files into folders. Give each folder a name, short and snappy as above, and put folders into folders. Do this hierarchically: have a generic folder into which you place folders containing files with specific content. On my computer I have a generic folder labelled 'Conferences': this contains all the information about the conferences I attend. Into this generic file I put a folder for each conference, and in each folder I put other folders containing letters about the conference, texts of presentation, information about the venue, and so on. It is up to you how you organise your material, but do organise it to keep yourself on top of things.

Backing up and protecting your material

- Always back up your files. Take care of your data and don't lose them. Make paper or electronic copies of really important data and keep these separate from your main data archive.
- Keep your data archive active. Visit regularly and maintain your systems on a regular basis. Move files around as the data gathering develops and becomes more complex.
- Keep confidential material in password-protected files. Say you have done this in your report; your reader will see that you took ethical matters seriously.
- Include appendices as end pages or a disc containing your data with your printed and bound text. Tell your reader where to find the disc. Also tell the reader why the data are important, why they should look at these and how to interpret them.

This last point brings us to Chapter 14, which is about analysing, interpreting and making sense of the data in order to generate evidence.

Summary

This chapter has discussed matters regarding monitoring practices and gathering data. The point was made that you should be clear about what kind of data you are looking for and where to look for them. The main things to look for are data that show how you are influencing learning; how your learning influences new actions; how those actions influence other people's learning; and how their learning influences their actions. These processes are reciprocal. The chapter also gave advice on organising, storing and managing the data.

The next chapter considers how to work with the data in terms of analysing, authenticating and interpreting them.

────────────────────── EXERCISES ──────────────────────

Think about what kind of data you will look for and where you will look for them in relation to the following questions:

- What data will show how I am influencing my own learning? Where will I look for these?
- What data will show how my learning is influencing my new actions? Where will I look for these?
- What data will show how my actions are influencing other people's learning? Where will I look for these?
- What data will show how other people's learning is influencing their actions? Where will I look for these?
- Will you look for data alone, or involve other people? How will you check that they are comfortable with what you are doing?
- Also think about how you will gather the data and how you will store them. Make sure to include these aspects in your methodology chapter and throughout your dissertation.

Working with data: analysing, authenticating and interpreting

You will now have substantial amounts of data, which you will need to turn into evidence to support your knowledge claims as part of the process of testing and establishing their validity or truthfulness. For example, if you say 'This way of working is better than previous ways', you will need to support that claim with evidence, otherwise what you say could be construed simply as your opinion. You will also need to show and explain the processes involved.

Selecting data to act as evidence involves three main processes: (1) analyse the data, (2) authenticate these, and then (3) interpret and make sense of them. You also need to explain the processes involved.

The chapter is organised to deal with these points:

1. Analysing data
2. Authenticating data
3. Making sense of the data

It also makes the point that working with and analysing data may be conducted from both a surface-level factual perspective and also a deep-level meaning-making perspective.

It should also be noted that, although these processes are presented here separately for purposes of analysis, they are not discrete processes: they act more as a continuum, where each element transforms into and merges with another. It should always be possible to relate one element to another and see how one is evident in the whole and how the whole informs each of its parts. Doing research is an integrated holistic process that enables a researcher to give meaning to their life.

1. Analysing data

Remember that evidence is not the same as data. 'Data' (notes gathered in the field) refers to those pieces of information about what you and others are doing and learning. These data are in your data archive. Your task is to select some of these pieces and explain how they count as evidence. These will be those special pieces of data that can be identified as specifically in relation to your research issue and your claim to knowledge. The pieces of data do not change their form, but they do change their status. A comment remains a comment and a picture a picture, but it now comes out of the larger body of data to stand as evidence. It is much the same as when you drag and drop a document on your computer or move a document from one folder to another. You drag the item out of the data archive and drop it into your evidence archive. The piece of data no longer officially keeps company with other data; it now keeps company with a knowledge claim, as shown in Figure 14.1, and thereby transforms into evidence.

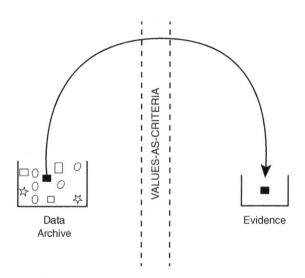

Figure 14.1 Drag and drop: transforming data into evidence

Remember also that evidence is more than illustration. Illustration is used when you select a piece of data (a datum) to show a point in action: you say 'We organised a meeting – for example ...', and you produce the minutes and transcript of what was said at a meeting. Or you produce documentation around a new work schedule or a video recording to show you mentoring a colleague. These are illustrations: they show practices in action but do not offer reasons or explanations for the practices. They do not help you to offer a value judgement about whether they show improvement in a practice; nor do they help you analyse the processes involved to explain why they should be seen as improvement.

Evidence is generated first through analysing the data. At a simplistic, technical level, analysing data may be seen as comprising two interrelated processes: content analysis and coding. Here is how these terms may be understood. First consider the idea of content.

Content

Content may be understood as what is presented to a reader; it is what you read. Almost everything you encounter in the world is content: a book, a picture or film, or an experience. Further, authors such as Derrida (1997) and Barthes (1970) speak of anything you encounter as a text to be read. Perhaps the idea of written texts is the most obvious kind, but a text can refer also to what you see and experience. The content of a book is what you read; the content of a film is what you see; the content of an experience is what you experience. You read these in different ways that involve different levels of consciousness and different forms of knowledge and capacities. Reading a printed text involves knowledge of language and the ability to decipher letters and words; reading a visual text involves knowledge of how things interact and the ability to appreciate what is involved in visual experience; reading a social situation involves experiential knowledge and the ability to understand the different personal, social, historical, political and economic forces acting on people that lead them to do certain things (this emphasises the importance of not jumping to conclusions and recognising that things may not be as you think they are, as in Kahneman, 2011). These matters are developed further in Section 3, on interpreting the data. They also have significant implications for writing, as discussed in Chapters 18 and 19. Also remember that each individual's reading of a social situation may well be different because of this.

When data are understood as field texts they show instances of what happens when people ask questions such as 'what, where, when, which, who, how, why is this happening?' These questions act as heuristics ('rules of thumb'). Data help us make sense of the narratives we produce as we speak about our experiences.

Data analysis therefore refers to analysing the content of any piece of text, when 'text' is understood as marks on a surface, such as writing or pictures (moving and still) or social interaction and performance. The aim is to interact with and make sense of what you read. This involves remaining aware of what you are looking for in your data: for you this is the demonstration of your criteria, which, in your view, may be seen in terms of your values. So say you are analysing a text to see whether it contains instances of the demonstration of values-as-criteria: if 'participation' is the value-as-criterion, you would for look for instances of participation. Similarly you could look at videos which show the live action of participation, or at records of social interaction as recorded, say, in your journal or as communicated to others through social media. Most forms of social media contain written, visual and interactive texts that require different forms of analysis.

Coding

You sort your content into categories and give the categories names so they can be readily identified. Take the example that you have too many clothes: some don't fit any more or are out of fashion, so you need to dispose of them in order to make room for new clothes. You first need to take stock of what you already have and what condition they are in. You therefore sort out shirts, trousers and jumpers and put them into their different categories. You put shirts in one pile, trousers in another and jumpers in another: this gives you three categories. Now give each category a letter: shirts (S), trousers (T) and jumpers (J). Sort them again to see how many blue, white and cream shirts you have, and do the same for the other garments. This will give you three sub-categories for shirts. Give each one of those a letter, which gives you six categories: S.1, S.2 and S.3. Do the same for trousers so that you have T.1, T.2 and T.3 (see Figure 14.2).

```
S = Shirts
S.1 = Shirts, blue
S.2 = Shirts, pink
S.3 = Shirts, white

T = Trousers
T.1 = Trousers, grey
T.2 = Trousers, black
T.3 = Trousers, brown
```

Figure 14.2   Coding strategies

This process is called coding (it can also be called 'thematic analysis', because 'codes' can also mean 'themes': see Alex Sinclair's letter below). Librarians do it with books; shops do it when ordering stock. The reason for coding things is to provide a shorthand system to ensure that you get the right product for the context. You can use different coding systems: colour coding or graphic coding (really whatever symbols you choose).

Do this with your data and remember that you are looking for certain things: here we stay with the example of participation. Look at a piece of data (a text) such as the transcript of a conversation and do a coding exercise. Go through the transcript and look for instances of participation; participation becomes a category. Give each instance a code: in this case, say you use underlining. This would give you the following:

Person A: We enjoyed our meeting today. Everyone took part.

Person B: Yes, it was a good experience. Even those who had been silent before spoke, some for the first time.

Your job as a researcher is both to analyse your data like this and also show the processes involved, so that your reader can see that you appreciate the need for the analysis of data as a way of demonstrating methodological rigour. It is really important to spell out to a reader why you have done this because data can be interpreted in different ways by different people so there is a need for this transparency. You can identify different items for coding purposes: these can be themes, ideas, concepts, keywords and, in the case of action research, values. Values come to act as your codes, so look for values-as-criteria when you search your data.

Below is an example of how you would do this kind of coding as part of your data analysis. Note the use of numbers for lines, which is also a common device in textual analysis; the use of underlining as a coding device is continued.

Example of textual analysis

1   A: How was your meeting today?

2   B: Great. A great improvement on yesterday.

3   A: Oh, why was that?

4   B: Because <u>more people took part than before.</u> We used a pairing exercise. <u>Even some of the quiet ones spoke up.</u>

6   A: That's great. Is this what you wanted to happen?

7   B: Yes, <u>I wanted to encourage participation and it looks as if it has worked.</u>

Here, is some correspondence with Alex Sinclair, at St Mary's University, Twickenham, about his understandings of coding, and how he uses it in his work as a science lecturer for students studying for a BA (when I am producing a text I tend to send work in draft to colleagues to get their critical responses). Also note the important point Alex makes about practitioners choosing their categories rather than lecturers or official researchers.

Jean to Alex

Hello again, Alex,

Am I right in thinking that analysing data is like organising a wardrobe into different categories/kinds of clothes – shirts, trousers, socks – and a number or other code is assigned to that category: this could be a colour code? You then do a content analysis of the items in that category, i.e. how many white shirts, blue shirts.

Ironically I know how to do it but it's the first time I am writing about it and explaining how it is done. There is a big difference between doing it and explaining how to do it.

Alex to Jean

Hi Jean,

Yes, this is my understanding of it.

With our third years we talk about analysing their data using themes (which are the same as codes) that have arisen from their literature review. This could obviously be themes of their own choosing, such as values, etc.

I don't know if it is worth mentioning but coming from my objective science background the idea that these codes/themes were chosen by the researcher and therefore were subjective/flexible was something that took me quite a while to get my head around. I remember one lightbulb moment coming away from a workshop on data analysis thinking that as long as you justify the reason for choosing your codes/themes then pretty much anything goes. This was quite a big turning point for me, not only in terms of data analysis but about the whole research process in general.

So in this respect the wardrobe could be coded into colours first and then coded again into types of clothes.

I know the grounded theorists are particularly keen on their coding and have specific names for the different layers – see Birks and Mills (2015) and Charmaz (2014) on Grounded Theory.

Three processes are involved here: first the production of data; second, the communication of key pieces of the data that may stand as evidence; third, a critical commentary on why the data should stand as evidence. These aspects are developed in Chapter 15.

Here is an example of a critical commentary.

Alex, who is also studying for his PhD, writes:

'The aim of my studies has always been to develop a curriculum for ecoliteracy (Orr, 1992): by this I mean encouraging others to see the need to develop practices aimed at protecting and safeguarding the wellbeing of the planet and its inhabitants. I am deeply concerned for planetary wellbeing; it is evident that the problems of ecological disequilibrium (Guattari, 2008) are being caused by anthropogenic pollution, natural resource depletion and the gross inequality between the world's richest and poorest. I could see that these problems stemmed from a divisive form of thinking that reinforced a perception of people as separate from one another and as separate from their planet. My own understanding of the relationship between the planet and its inhabitants (Abram, 2010 and Lovelock, 2006) is that we are in interde-pendent, symbiotic relationships. Nurturing these relationships therefore requires a mutually respectful attitude, what Lovelock (2006: xv) refers to as "a lasting relationship of mutual benefit". I believed that this idea could also be used in an educational context.

'The need to engage with this issue informed my studies for both my master's and PhD degrees, but itself required me to undertake a critical appraisal of the values and form of think-ing that underpinned my teaching. Because of this focus on mutual respect among people and between people and their planet, I have always aimed to develop mutually respectful and trust-ing relationships with those I taught and worked with. The idea of mutual respect has therefore become the main criterion for judging the quality of my teaching. Now, nearing the completion of my doctoral studies, I believe that, like Glenn (2006), "I am developing a theory of practice that locates the possibility of learning in the relationships that are created between people". So, as well as monitoring and analysing developments in my students' ecoliteracy I have also monitored and analysed whether the manner in which I encouraged this development is com-mensurate with my value of mutual respect.'

Now think about what authenticating data involves. At a minimum it involves:

- authenticating data, which also involves the authorisation of the authentication;
- triangulation.

2. Authenticating data

Authenticating data is vital because data can show both what you hope to see and also what you would prefer not to see. Those data that provide unwelcome representations are called 'disconfirming data'. They can be dealt with in different ways: you can

- pretend they don't exist, which amounts to dishonesty in reporting and an abdication of researcher responsibility;

- rejig them by producing additional bits of data that challenge the first set of data (equally dishonest);
- take them seriously.

You are recommended always to take them seriously because they can show that you are on the wrong track and need to rethink and act in a different way. It also adds to the methodological rigour/transparency you are hoping to demonstrate. Especially you need to examine the assumptions that led you to think that these were useful data that could possibly stand as evidence, and question why you thought as you did at the time. Disconfirming data help us to examine the potential clash between what Argyris and Schön (1978) call 'espoused theories' and 'theories-in-use'. 'Espoused theories' are what actors claim they base their thinking and actions on; 'theories-in-use' are the actual theories they use to guide their actions. There can often be a conflict between the two as when, for example, you say you encourage participation but then show in practice that you don't.

You now need to explain how your data may be seen as authentic and actually show what you wish them to show. Here are some of the procedures for clarifying that you are acting responsibly and producing data that have been authenticated at source, and whose authenticity has been endorsed by others.

Authenticating data

Aim to show the authenticity of the data by ensuring that it has some kind of authorisation from the data source. You can do this using a range of techniques. You could demonstrate the internal authenticity of a piece of data by, for example, ensuring that there is a signature on a photograph, a time and date on a video or a mark of confirmation of ownership from the producers of a film. The manufacturer's logo on products aims to show the authenticity of the product.

Authorising the authenticity of the data

The authenticity of the data then needs to be approved and agreed by the community, including your community of research peers in multiple contexts: this amounts to a co-authorisation process. This would take the form of, perhaps, an additional signature on a photo from a disinterested participant, or a similar endorsement of a video. The minutes of meetings are generally sent out to all participants at the meeting who are then at liberty to approve them or not: this is an example of external authorisation. A core strategy for avoiding any challenges to such authorisation is to avoid its happening in the first place: a main strategy for this is triangulation.

Triangulation

One of the most common devices for demonstrating and establishing authenticity is to use triangulation at all stages of your research, especially in data gathering, analysis and interpretation.

The idea of triangulation came originally from map-making, where mappers could identify the location of a place by taking bearings from known objects, using the concept of triangles. They imagined how intersecting lines on a landscape could be coordinated to show the place they wanted to be. To do this you would identify a line from, say, a tree to your right and a hill to your left, and draw imaginary lines between the hill, the tree and you: where the lines intersect would give you the place you wanted to be.

The same principle may be used in data analysis. It means that:

- data about the same event should be gathered from multiple sources: to show participation in action you could produce data in the form of videos, diary entries and observers' comments;
- authentication of the data would be obtained from different sources. Different observers agree that the data are thick data rather than thin data (see page 146): that it shows meaningful actions rather than trivial ones;
- authentication is authorised by different sources: different observers agree that the data show what they say they show.

This idea coincides with that of Yin (2009), who cites Patton (2002) as identifying four kinds of triangulation:

1. Of data sources (data triangulation).
2. Among different evaluators (investigator triangulation).
3. Of perspectives (theory triangulation).
4. Of methods (methodological triangulation). (Yin, 2009: 116)

For your project you are concerned only with items 1 and 2. You do need to ensure that you produce multiple forms of data, identify multiple data sources and get multiple opinions from different people. By explaining in your text how you have carried out these authenticating/ authorisation processes you can be reasonably confident that readers will take you more seriously than if you were to produce just one form of data or identify only one data source. This is another way of demonstrating methodological rigour, which is a main requirement in producing evidence.

3. Interpreting and making sense of the data

Go back to the idea of content as a text, and the idea that data are part of a text through which you read the world and make meaning of your place in it and contribute to it.

Action research is about trying to make sense of things, to understand. We do this to find ways to contribute toward re-creating the world in relation to events and circumstances that are themselves always shifting: we make the world according to our understanding of it. We tell stories about this process as our research (what we are doing and how we are learning to understand better) and these stories are complemented by other people's as they do the same. Nixon et al. (2016) say that recording our stories takes the form of a palimpsest, a parchment that is written on over and over again.

Interpretation can happen at multiple levels and from multiple perspectives: here are two of them, a surface-level factual perspective and a deep-level analytical perspective.

A surface-level factual perspective

Interpreting data from a surface-level factual perspective can take the form of responding to the questions: who, what, where, when, which, how, why? You can ask these questions in relation to any and all forms of data, as follows:

Who?	What?	Where?	When?	Which?	How?	Why?
Who did it?	What did they do?	Where did they do it?	When did they do it?	Which aspect did they do?	How did they do it?	Why did they do it?

Using the example of participation, this generates the following (there would, of course, be many other possible questions):

Who participated?	What did they do when they participated?	Where did they participate?	When did they participate?	Which contribution did they make?	How did they participate?	Why did they participate?

When interpreting data the first five questions give you information about the content: the questions 'how?' and 'why?' give you the reasons and purposes for any actions undertaken. This is what you are looking for: not simply information but also insights that will help you understand your place in the event and the quality of your influence in the other's understanding. You need this kind of contextualising information to help you make judgements about the quality of what you are doing.

Further, remember that all interpretations are situated: you are a person in a particular space and time, so your interpretations/understandings are influenced by that specific space–time. It is the same for others: they also are located in their individual and collective space–times, so their interpretations/understandings are products of their contexts. To try to impose your contextualised understanding on their contextualised understandings is asking for trouble: it will lead to an amazing broth of misunderstandings. Also there is no Big Book of Understandings that will help you grasp other people's understandings: you have to test your understanding against what you consider is a wider good in relation to your own values. Whether other people share your values or you theirs is a matter of negotiation, of dialogue where you each try to see the other's point of view.

Jonathan Vincent at York St John University, who is studying for his PhD, writes:

'[Our Stratus Writing Project is] a participatory action research project working with university students on the autistic spectrum. Our project used autoethnographic

(Continued)

(Continued)

> narratives as a means of identifying [participants'] unique insider knowledge about autism and experiences of higher education. Our research process aimed to be fully participatory, where data were collected, analysed and disseminated by the students themselves. [The Project] asserted that the autistic students themselves are authoritative and carry revealing wisdom about their own lives ... The analysis ... represented an opportunity to construct new and valid meanings in a humanizing way. Megan, one of the participants, summed it up in her evaluation when she said, "The greatest success from my point of view was having a voice. We weren't treated like research subjects but research partners in the process ... right from the beginning through to presenting at conferences."' (Nixon et al., 2016: 117-18)

This is one of the major difficulties in interpreting research data. Many researchers fall into the simplistic trap of thinking that data may be interpreted in terms of their own understanding, without acknowledging that those interpretations should be seen as provisional and open to challenge; they must always be held lightly. According to Kahneman (2011), 'fast, on-your-feet' thinking where you tend to jump to conclusions raises questions about the quality of judgements (you will say the first thing that comes into your head based on prior experience), whereas 'slow', reflective thinking encourages you to step back and consider alternative interpretations. You show this process of slow thinking when you show your report to participants and invite them to have access to your interpretation of the data. This adds time to the research project, but demonstrates good research practices in that you show how you are observing ethical practices through inviting their critical responses. And remember to explain what you are doing to your reader, too, so that they can see that you are not just acting but that you are also aware of what you are doing and can offer explanations for it.

A deep-level analytical perspective

This kind of reflective action can also help you explain how you are interpreting data from a deep-level analytical perspective. This means engaging in multiple levels of reflection and analysis, re-reflection and further interpretation based on the reflection (something like the multiple storeys in a high-rise building, as follows).

Imagine a multi-storey secret intelligence headquarters, MI52 (probably by the River Thames). On the roof are antennae and satellite dishes which receive incoming information; this information arrives in many forms, including bursts of sound or visual images:

- On the top floor, Floor 5, the information collected on the roof is transcribed by decoders into written words, sound recordings and pictures so that it can be fully understood by anyone. They pass this information on to ...
- ... Floor 4 below, where intelligence operatives cross-check the authenticity of each piece of information against other sources: this is known as triangulation. They communicate their authorisation of the authenticity of the data and pass it on to ...

- ... the next floor down, Floor 3, where the information, which now takes the form of pictures or speech or written words, is sorted by analysts into information categories such as political, military or economic, according to where it is intended for use. They pass it on to ...
- ... Floor 2 below, where experts in these areas analyse each piece of information to see how they can interpret it and best make sense of it. They pass it on to ...
- ... the next floor down, Floor 1, where specialists receive the information and decide how it may inform policy and future action. They pass the information on to ...
- ... the ground floor, where action is planned and orders given by people with names such as M. They then send those orders down to the basement, and ...
- ... from the basement garage, James Bond drives away in his Aston Martin to carry out orders and take action. Pow!

And all the time, the people on every floor are working in relation to other people: they discuss and decide how to code, decode, analyse and interpret information while simultaneously trying to make sense of what they are doing in the process. They all have different interpretations of what they are doing in the process of analysing and interpreting. Further, the building that houses MI52 is part of a wider complex of buildings in a city within in a country within a world of multiple voices, each speaking from within a particular historical, social, political, economic and so on context. We live in a world of unstable, un-grounded meanings, where the only grounding is the one we decide for ourselves and negotiate with those whose different social and values commitments we share most closely. Meanings constantly shift their shapes; we are always in a particular moment that is singular in time and space and will change its shape in relation with the circumstances of the next moment.

Yet, as stated throughout, you have to take a stand at some point and go with a particular interpretation, especially when you decide to take action in the world. However, when it is a case of writing a dissertation, you need to show that you respected the shifting patterns you were part of and held your conclusions lightly, always recognising the dilemmas of context and personal bias. This, for me, is a core difference between writing a story and writing a narrative (an idea explored in McNiff, 2017): you can write a story from a particular standpoint; you can use your authorial voice and tell a particular story from your point of view, but you write a narrative from a situated voice; you can use your researcher voice where you acknowledge the constantly shifting scenarios that make any ultimate choice problematic; this is part of a researcher's responsibility.

And in writing this I am automatically taking a stand. It is stories all the way down: you can never get away from them. Which is in itself a story ...

We now move to the next step, which is to investigate what 'evidence' means and looks like, and this provides the focus for Chapter 15.

Summary

This chapter has offered advice about analysing, authenticating and storing the data. It has talked about different techniques for analysis and interpretation. The point is made consistently that data analysis and interpretation always need to be seen as part of the wider aspect of doing research, and specifically with a view to generating evidence.

The next chapter moves into matters of generating evidence from the data, and provides an overview of the steps required to do so.

—————————————————————— **EXERCISES** ——————————————

- Think about the different ways in which you can analyse and make sense of the data. Think especially about which themes you will draw out of your research and what kinds of code you may allocate to them. Write out how you intend to do this, and produce examples of how you have done this in your project.
- Check that you understand how to interpret the data. What kinds of questions may help you? Discuss these issues with colleagues and get their critical feedback.
- Are you clear about what triangulation involves and why it is important? Remember to explain these matters to the reader in your dissertation.

Generating evidence from the data and making knowledge claims: summary chapter

You have analysed and begun to interpret your data: the task now is to turn the data into evidence to ground and test the validity of your knowledge claim(s). Producing evidence is part of the process of establishing the validity, or truthfulness/believability, of a claim. If you say 'This way of working is better than previous ways', you will need to support that claim with evidence, otherwise what you have said could be construed as your opinion.

This chapter takes the form of a summary that pulls together all the action steps and procedures involved in generating evidence from the data and making knowledge claims, outlined throughout and especially in Chapters 13 and 14; revisit these and look at the examples given. These processes can appear complex but they are vital, because together they (1) show the process of your enquiry from start to finish and also (2) constitute demonstration of the concept of methodological rigour: this is a core criterion by which the quality of your dissertation is judged. The chapter also offers further ideas about key issues.

It is written from the perspective that you now need to look ahead and think actively about writing your dissertation, so key points are highlighted for special attention. It is important to let the reader know that you know these things. In the same way as school students need to explain the processes that led them to certain conclusions, so too do you need to explain to your reader that you know the importance both of demonstrating certain aspects of doing research and saying that you know why it is important to know these and articulating this clearly.

A key point is not to confuse data and evidence: when you write your dissertation, let the examiner see that you know the differences and that you know the importance of knowing the differences. As a reminder, 'data' refers to the pieces of information you gather about what you and others are doing and learning. All these data are in your data archive. Your task is to turn some of these pieces of data into evidence. Evidence refers to those special pieces of data that you identify specifically in relation to your research issue and your knowledge claim and that you have negotiated with others to show their part in your research. In terms of your action research, you have also produced data to show your learning, how your learning has influenced your actions, how your actions have influenced others people's learning, and how they have used their learning to influence their new actions. These are mutually reciprocal processes that may be analysed technically, as in earlier chapters, but when put together, will form a coherent story. Remember also to say that you have checked with participants that you are representing them appropriately. You are also holding your own story up to public scrutiny.

Generating evidence is a rigorous process that involves the following broad steps:

1. Stating what the knowledge claim is.
2. Identifying criteria and standards of judgement.
3. Selecting data, and analysing, interpreting and authenticating these.
4. Generating evidence.
5. Explaining how the evidence may be used to test the validity of knowledge claims (this is also the focus of Chapters 16 and 17).

The chapter is organised as five sections that address these issues in a summarised form.

1. Stating what the knowledge claim is

Remember that the aim of any research is to make a knowledge claim; this claim is that you are making a contribution to knowledge of your field; doing your study has enabled you to develop knowledge of your field. When you write your report, you state what your claim is. You say, 'I [claim to] have contributed to knowledge of my field of nursing/rural development/heating engineering'. Making a claim to knowledge means that you are saying that you know something now that was not known before. This knowledge is being put into the public domain for the first time and is adding to the public body of knowledge. The knowledge may be about a substantive issue, such as a new clinical nursing practice, or it may be about the process of creating new ideas and explanations. If it is about substantive issues, the knowledge is usually about practice. If it is about making sense of things, it is usually about theory. Knowledge generated through action research is about both practice and theory. You offer descriptions of what you did (your practices) and explanations for why you did it (your theories). Your descriptions and explanations together become your personal theory of an aspect of your practice, such as leadership or teaching.

Your claim to know in relation to practice would be something of the kind:

- I have developed a more manageable work schedule than my previous one.
- I have improved my mentoring practices.
- We have developed better communications in our office.

Your claim to know in relation to theory would be something of the kind:

- I have developed my understanding of the need for a good work schedule.
- I have created my theory of mentoring practice.
- We know how and why to communicate better in our office.

Both kinds of claims are related. One cannot stand without the other. Your theory of practice (explanation for practice) has been created from within the practice. You can describe and explain your improved mentoring practice because you have studied your mentoring practice and worked systematically to improve it. You know what you have done and how and why you have done it.

The need to show how you are contributing to theory as well as practice is important in all action research, and especially in any texts submitted for accreditation. The criteria for accreditation usually state that a candidate must show that they are making a claim to knowledge of their field. If the report shows that the candidate is making a contribution only to practice and not to knowledge, the report could well be rejected.

2. Identifying criteria and standards of judgement

As noted in Chapter 14, making a judgement about something involves identifying criteria and standards of judgement: these are different though intimately related. Tell your reader that you know the difference: the criteria tell you in advance what is expected in a thing or action; the standards of judgement tell you whether or to what extent a criterion is being achieved. The criteria for safe driving, for example, would involve observing traffic flows and driving within speed limits. A driving instructor would probably bring a checklist of criteria to a driving test; these would take the form of 'can do' skills and knowledge. The instructor would tick the items off when the learner driver did these things. Whether or not the driver passed the test, however, would depend on whether and how well the instructor judged the driver to have done them. Did the driver negotiate the traffic flows? How well did they negotiate them: did they drive responsibly within designated speed limits? The instructor uses these values of safe and responsible driving as their standards of judgement. When you make judgements about your practice it is not enough simply to work to criteria in the form of achieving targets, such as 'I took the patient's temperature' or 'I completed my work on time', although these are initial elements. You also have to explain the nature of what you did and why you believe it should be perceived as good quality.

Consider the following examples.

Context	Criterion	Standard of judgement
My name is Elke. I am a community nurse. Part of my job is wound care in the community.	The dressing is changed aseptically and with minimal distress to the patient.	The old dressing was removed effectively, the wound was cleaned and the new dressing applied gently.

Context	Criteria	Standards of judgement
My name is Seamus. I am involved in a well-digging project in Sub-Sarahan rural development projects where local people have to walk miles to get water.	I judge the quality of my practice in the following terms: cleanliness of the water; convenience for all villagers; democratic access to water.	• The water is clear and bacteria-free. • The well is centrally situated for all villagers. • No one person controls access.

(Continued)

(Continued)

Context	Criteria	Standards of judgement
My name is Abdullah. I am a heating engineer who services domestic boilers.	I judge the quality of my practice in the following terms: • Safety of the boiler. • Effectiveness of the service. • Cleanliness in doing the job.	• There are no leaks in the system. • I leave the boiler in good working order. • I ensure that I leave no mess in my working area.

When we make a judgement about something, we do so in relation to specific standards. Having standards is important to ensure that our work is good quality. However, you need to explain why questions need to be asked about which standards are appropriate, who sets the standards, and who says who should make decisions about these things.

Which standards? Whose standards?

Many debates about quality argue that practices should be judged in terms of practitioners' performance, in relation to specific skills and competencies; these often appear as targets. In many market-driven societies, ambulance drivers and fire crews have to reach their destination in a specific amount of time, and hospitals must achieve a designated turnaround of patients. The emphasis on quantity can, however, jeopardise quality. Stories are told of patients not receiving quality care because doctors have to achieve their quotas of patient appointments. This approach to target setting and performance is part of the current managerialist and consumerist culture that prioritises profitable performance over people.

Explain to your reader that professionals use different kinds of standards to judge the quality of their work, related to the values that inspire the work, and in relation to any professional values and standards agreed by your community of practice. A business manager may judge the quality of their leadership by how well they encourage motivation and purpose among employees. A teacher may judge their success by whether and how well they enable young people to learn. Professional values are to do with care and respect for enabling the other to think and act for themselves and with a responsible regard for other people. Most action researchers will try to find ways of living these values. So a manager judges their work in relation to employees' increasing motivation and purpose, and a teacher judges the quality of their work in relation to students' capacity to develop independence of mind and capacity in decision making.

As a practitioner–researcher, your job is to set your own standards of practice and judgement, and show how you are fulfilling them; you will also need to show how you are working in relation to policy recommendations. In terms of your practice, do you show how you live out your values of compassion and social purpose? In relation to exercising judgement, do you use these values as your standards? Furthermore, do you articulate these standards and communicate them to others, so that others can see how you judge your practice and negotiate your judgement with you? If you are submitting your work for higher degree accreditation, the validating institution will have its own criteria and standards of judgement. You will have to show how you fulfilled these, as well as any that you set yourself.

3. Selecting, analysing and interpreting data

Having established your criteria and standards of judgement, you now need to search your data archive and find instances of values in action. A business manager may show the quality of their leadership by selecting instances from the minutes of a meeting in which they urged people to have faith in themselves, promising that they would support them. They also select an email sent to them by a colleague to say that they are organising a staff get-together as a direct consequence of their support of inter-departmental collaboration. The teacher may produce a thank-you card from a former student, now a solicitor, expressing their thanks to the teacher for helping them get through a difficult learning episode. These physical artefacts may be seen as containing participants' testimonies to practitioners' capacity to live their values in practice.

Demonstrating the authenticity of the data

In Chapter 14 we looked at triangulation as an important means of observing procedures for establishing the authenticity of specific data to indicate that certain things have happened. To develop the theme, and now in relation to strengthening the quality of your dissertation, you will need to show that you are aware of the need for the following points and have done them. These are:

- demonstrating the authenticity of the data;
- negotiating the authenticity of the data;
- negotiating the validity of the evidence.

A frequent error that practitioners make when writing their reports is to say they have done something without producing the evidence that they have done it. They tell but they do not show. Your job as a practitioner-researcher is to do both: you need to tell your reader what you have done and then show that and how you have done it (that is, produce evidence to back up claims).

In relation to showing your reader the authenticity of your data and that you have not fabricated these, show how you have taken steps to authenticate them and explain to your reader why you are showing them. You can do the following:

- Print the time and date on a photograph, email or text message.
- Ask the sender to sign and date a written note.
- State the time and date at the beginning of an audio recording.
- Keep systematic records of meetings, conversations or virtual learning experiences.

Also add a commentary whenever you produce any piece of data in your report. Explain to your reader why it is important to produce the data and how the data can now stand as evidence. How you do this is up to you, but aim to keep your data under control and explain to your reader how you have done this. It is of course possible to fudge the data, but this happens in all kinds of research and is part of wider debates about the ethical responsibilities of researchers and ensuring quality in research.

Negotiating the authenticity of the data

Explain how you showed your data to your critical friends and reviewers and invited them to agree with you (or not) that your data were authentic. They would look for the signs that show authentication (signatures, times and dates, and so on). Also explain to your reader what you have done and why you have done it. Explain why you have used triangulation and its usefulness as a strategy for generating evidence from data. The more sources you can show, and the more explanations there are for doing so, the greater the robustness of the evidence and your claim.

Negotiating interpretations of your data

Explain to the reader how you have negotiated the interpretations of your data with participants, and with critical friends and external readers. You have taken care to show the increasingly sophisticated nature of interpretation: from straightforward reflection to re-reflection and re-framing. You are reasonably confident that you are reporting agreed interpretations accurately but you still hold open the options of possible error. Emphasise that you appreciated how interpretations are always influenced by those of participants, and your own circumstances and by wider influences. It is important to emphasise that what you are reporting are provisional conclusions, not definitive ones, as these may be open to further interpretation, including the interpretations of your reader.

Negotiating the validity of the evidence

The next section contains explanations about how to generate evidence from the data. Again you will explain how this has to be negotiated, and now the discourse will change: you will no longer speak about testing and demonstrating authenticity but validity. You will move from the technicalities of authentication to the moralities of claiming and demonstrating that you are telling the truth.

4. Generating evidence

To recap on the process of generating evidence to test the validity of and to support knowledge claims, an initial step is to search your data archive and find artefacts that contain data, such as audio-recorded comments, pictures, field notes, email exchanges and minutes of meetings. You take out of these data those specific instances that you feel show your values in action, such as a special comment, a picture or an email. You use those data in your dissertation, but now you need to explain how they represent both your capacity to realise your values in practice and your capacity to articulate and communicate your specific standards of judgement.

Further, to raise the standard of demonstrating methodological rigour and ethical judgement even further, you also explain the need to triangulate your evidence and how you have done so. This involves getting interpretations of data from different sources and showing what those interpretations say. Your sources would include those participants whose testimonies you are using, as well as comments from critical friends. This process can be most rewarding when others agree with your interpretations: similarly it can prove bothersome when they disagree because you will then have to go back and start again. Explaining to an examiner that you have done this will impress them greatly so if it turns out that you have to start again, take a deep breath and do so.

You also test the validity of your interpretations against theories in the literature, to show how you are agreeing with them, developing them or challenging them. Also, your explanations to the reader of what you are doing will act as a consistent running commentary in your dissertation that offers an ongoing evaluation of the quality of your practices and theorising.

5. Explaining how the evidence may be used to test the validity of knowledge claims

Take care both to show the process in action and to explain it to your reader. In your dissertation you will specifically articulate the fact that you are producing evidence in relation to your articulated standards of judgement: this explains why you have selected those data and not others. You will explain that you know what you are doing and why you are doing it. You will also explain that the values and principles which underpin your work (your ontological commitments) have now emerged as dynamic standards of practice, and you are articulating and communicating these to others as the standards by which you have judged the validity of your claim (your epistemological standards of judgement) and the validity of your contribution to new knowledge. You will also need to ensure that any evidence you select can be shown as authentic or genuine. A text message would carry the date and time of sending; a letter or photograph would carry the signature of the sender. This is part of demonstrating your methodological rigour.

Elke says:

'I can produce evidence to show the validity of my claim that I have developed an effective wound-dressing technique in the following ways:

- I can produce my written clinical records of the progress of the wound.
- I can ask the patient to give me a score out of 10 for levels of comfort while I was changing the dressing.
- I can produce photographs to show the healing of the wound without any signs of introduced infection.'

Seamus says:

'I can produce evidence to show the validity of my claim that my well-digging is effective in the following ways:

- I can show a video of a local official carrying out tests on the water.

(Continued)

(Continued)

- I can show a video of myself and a group of villagers toasting each other with a glass of water.
- I can ask the villagers if they would do a recorded conversation outlining the situation before and after we dug the well.'

Abdullah says:

'I can produce evidence to show the validity of my claim that I service domestic boilers effectively in the following ways:

- I can show my records of system pressure before and after my work.
- I can produce the form signed by the customer to say that the boiler is working effectively.
- The form also contains the customer's comments on their satisfaction with the cleanliness of my work.'

The strategies outlined in the last three chapters have shown the importance of producing authenticated data and turning them into evidence. These are carefully disciplined processes whose implementation needs to be shown in reality and not just spoken about. The whole point of evidence is that it is about producing physical artefacts and explaining the processes involved in their production.

However, the process of testing the validity of knowledge claims is not yet over: you now have to test the validity of your provisional understandings against the judgement of informed others. This means going public, putting your knowledge claims and findings into the public domain and inviting public critique about their quality. In the case of getting a degree, it means writing a dissertation, where the 'others' will be your examiners. You will need to convince them that you are telling them the truth about what you have done and why you have done it. The next part of the book deals with these matters.

Summary

This has been a summary chapter, revisiting ideas about the different techniques involved in analysing and interpreting data in order to produce authenticated evidence, and how that evidence can contribute to the task of producing verifiable and justifiable knowledge claims.

——————————————— EXERCISES ———————————————

- Check that you are confident about all the matters outlined in this chapter. Ask your supervisor or colleagues about any aspects that are not absolutely clear.
- Write a summary paragraph for each section in relation to your own research.

PART V

How do I test and critique my knowledge?

This part deals with testing the validity of your knowledge claim and establishing its legitimacy in the public domain. Validity is about establishing the believability or trustworthiness of a claim, which is largely a methodological procedure. Legitimacy is about getting the claim accepted by the wider public, including by the scholarly community. This then becomes largely a matter of power and politics, because people have different opinions and tell different stories about which kind of knowledge is valuable and who should be accepted as a knower.

The part contains these chapters.

Chapter 16   Testing the validity of your knowledge claim

Chapter 17   Establishing the legitimacy of your knowledge claim

In terms of your own action enquiry into the nature and uses of action research, you are now at the stage of evaluating the quality of your understandings and practices: you are asking 'How do I test the validity of my knowledge claim? How do I show that any conclusions I come to are reasonably fair and accurate?' You do this while anticipating that you will be producing a dissertation shortly, where you will need to show your reader that you have actively engaged with these questions in the interests of demonstrating methodological rigour and ethical responsibility.

16

Testing the validity of your knowledge claim

Having generated your evidence and established its authenticity, you now have to seek validity for your knowledge claim and the legitimacy of the account. Authenticity, validity and legitimacy are different things. Authenticity refers to the genuineness of something, such as a piece of evidence, as outlined in Chapter 14. Validity refers to testing and establishing the truth-value or trustworthiness of a claim as outlined in Chapter 15: this is a matter of observing appropriate procedures for demonstrating methodological and ethical rigour and negotiating interpretations and representations. Legitimacy refers to getting the account accepted in the public domain. You do this by getting people to listen to you and take your work seriously, in the hope that they may be open to learning from it or trying out something similar for themselves. Establishing legitimacy is a matter of power and politics, because people may or may not want to listen to your views, in spite of your having demonstrated the validity of your work.

While Chapters 14 and 15 dealt with establishing authenticity and genuineness, which are elements in the process of testing the validity of knowledge claims, this chapter deals with actual procedures for testing that validity. The next chapter deals with procedures for establishing legitimacy. Also remember that, as always, although these matters are set out here as separate for purposes of analysis, they are actually intertwined and inseparable in the real-life contexts of getting people to see the importance of your research and work.

The chapter is organised as two sections:

1. Procedures for testing the validity of knowledge claims
2. Examples of validation procedures

1. Procedures for testing the validity of knowledge claims

This section deals with procedures for testing the validity of knowledge claims and contains the following:

- Different approaches to testing validity
- Arranging for critique
- The responsibilities of critical friends
- The responsibilities of validation groups

By showing and explaining that you have triangulated your evidence and tested its validity, you have satisfactorily demonstrated to yourself the internal validity of your claim to knowledge. You now need to get other people to agree that your claim to validity is credible: you need to establish its external validity. The business of going public is key: if you wish to have the usefulness of your work acknowledged you have to talk with other people and get them to engage. This means that when you write your dissertation or otherwise put your claim into the public domain, you have to offer an explicit articulation of the procedures used to demonstrate its methodological rigour, including observation of ethical considerations. Doing this provides other people's critical assessments against which the validity of your claim can be tested. Once other people agree with you, you can begin to regard your claim as valid (but see next paragraph) and proceed with greater confidence. However, it may turn out that in the process of public testing others may not agree with you, which means you may have to go back and think again. When this happens (as it often does), many people react negatively: they tend to see critique as critique of themselves and not of their ideas. Critique is, however, essential for ensuring high quality scholarship, so actively look for this and welcome it. In my own case, as demonstrated in Chapter 4, whenever I produce a text I send it to as many colleagues as possible, asking for their critical responses, and I act on their feedback. I also ensure that I acknowledge their help as fully as possible: they are important allies in the business of putting ideas into the public domain. Critical responses can be invaluable for pointing out slippages in an argument or inconsistencies in procedures. Seeking out critique is essential if you wish to present a coherent argument and demonstrate attention to detail, and a major responsibility for all researchers.

Remember also that there is a big difference between validity and legitimacy: validity means showing the truthfulness of a knowledge claim; legitimacy means having the claim accepted. Validity is to do with producing evidence and demonstrating rigour; legitimacy is to do with power and control. I have already cited the example of Galileo who produced strong evidence to show that the earth went round the sun: he could demonstrate the validity of his findings. However, this went against the orthodoxies of the regime then currently in power (the Church) and he was threatened with torture, so he withdrew his claims. Or the infamous 'hand of God' goal in the 1986 World Cup: invalid but legitimised. This can also be the case in institution-based research, when researchers do things their own way and reach conclusions agreed by the establishment, yet are denied legitimacy. Michael Polanyi, a Nobel prize-winning scientist, explains how he came to conclusions without going through formal procedures, which was not permitted in traditional university life:

> The Professor of mathematical physics, to whom my paper was assigned (to verify the mathematics), had never heard of my subject matter. He studied my work bit by bit and then asked me to explain a curious point: my result seemed correct, but its derivation faulty. Admitting my mistake I said that surely one first draws one's conclusions and then puts their derivations right. The professor just stared at me. (cited in Mitchell, 2006: 5)

Similarly, the tutors of John Nash, Nobel Prize laureate in mathematics, said he was unteachable because he could not explain the procedures whereby he reached accurate conclusions (Naser, 1998).

However, it has to be acknowledged that in some cases your findings may be mistaken and your claim open to challenge. In this case, accept your error graciously and go back and do it again.

'My name is Velda McPhee and I am a health visitor in Mpumalanga, South Africa. I counsel local people on sexual health in the wider effort to stop the spread of HIV and AIDS. I believe I am making progress in some places, in that a lot of village women now practise safe sex, and insist that their husbands and partners do so as well, but this can be difficult in the face of strong traditions. These include the idea that women should not avoid contraception but agree to the practice of producing babies. They also include the idea that it is 'manly' for a husband or partner to have many relationships outside marriage; and women – even educated women – go along with these traditions and so sustain them.'

(All names in the story are pseudonyms although the story is based on real people.)

Different approaches to testing validity

Testing and demonstrating the validity of knowledge claims remains an important topic in the literatures. It is especially important for action research because in many cases the quality of action research is still judged in terms of traditional social science criteria, including objectivity (when the research is assumed to be value-free and conducted from an externalist perspective), replicability (when findings may be replicated in similar circumstances) and generalisability (when findings may be generalised for use by different groups in different contexts). It is becoming an even more serious issue now that universities are taking a metrics approach to demonstrating quality in teaching and research. Sadly, because action research is now embedded within university programmes, it, too, is vulnerable to such challenges.

Strategies in the literatures

In recent times, many researchers have offered their own perspectives on how to demonstrate validity in social science research and in action research. Some of the most common forms found in social science research are listed below, together with examples of what you could write to show the enactment of the criteria. Look first at Table 16.1.

Table 16.1   Forms of validity, meanings and examples in action

Form of validity	What it means	How you could show it
Catalytic validity	This term, coined by Patti Lather in 1991, expresses the idea that the experience of a study would enable people to move to new, more productive positions.	Having established collaborative working practices in the school as part of my research it was rewarding to see how other staff began to follow suit. I could claim catalytic validity for my research.
Construct validity	This refers to the idea that what a researcher says they are doing really can be shown to be the case – 'it does what it says on the tin'. It is therefore important to use multiple ways of establishing that their conclusions are believable, and not just them imposing their existing constructs on the reality they are observing.	My research showed that parents could make a valuable contribution to their children's education; my data from interviews with parents, teachers and children confirmed this to be the case. I could claim construct validity for my research.
Face validity	An issue appears as basic common sense; you recognise its truthfulness at face value.	Playing hockey can be dangerous: the number of hockey accidents reported in the research showed this assumption to have face validity.
Ironic validity	The researcher does not take things simply at face value but interrogates underlying assumptions.	I sought to establish the ironic validity of my knowledge claim by testing my assumptions about the high incidence of hockey accidents against statistical evidence and from soliciting the critical feedback of others.
Rhizomatic validity	Another term coined by Lather that refers to the interconnected nature of human enquiry and the power of a study to have influence in multiple directions.	Our collaborative research shows that other people's thinking has been influenced and they are adopting our recommendations. We believe we can claim rhizomatic validity for our research and claims to have influenced their thinking.

Additionally, prominent researchers such as Bullough and Pinnegar (2004) and Feldman (2003) have focused on demonstrating quality in self-study action research. They agree with the assumptions expressed in this book that establishing quality and demonstrating validity are grounded in a researcher's ontological values; Feldman also argues that validity has to be linked with one's moral purposes in the world.

Other contributions specifically in relation to action research include the following.

Richard Winter (1989)

The work of Richard Winter (1989) is widely respected and sets important precedents for the action research community. He says that action research accounts should demonstrate the six principles of action research (see Table 16.2, similar to Table 16.1, to show how the criteria may be communicated in action terms).

Table 16.2   Winter's (1989) criteria in action

Criterion	Communicating the criterion in action terms
Offer a reflective critique in which the author shows that they have reflected on their work and generated new questions.	Our research with young offenders led us to reconsider the reasons for their initial offending.
Offer a dialectical critique which subjects all 'given' phenomena to critique, recognising their inherent tendency to change.	Government policy on environmental education needs to take account of wider issues of climate change and international efforts to combat its development.
Be a collaborative resource in which people act and learn as participants.	Through our collaborative research we were able to show that we developed a new approach to a literacy curriculum.
Accept risk as an inevitable aspect of creative practice.	We had not catered on finding that students did not wish to attend additional Saturday classes.
Demonstrate a plural structure which accommodates a multiplicity of viewpoints.	We agreed on the new buildings plan, bearing in mind that we had to cater for the needs of wheelchair participants.
Show the transformation and harmonious relationship between theory and practice.	Having finally learned how to make pancakes and reflected on the processes involved, I have changed my mind about being a chef and decided to become a biscuit maker.

Heikkinen et al. (2012)

Drawing on the work of Winter (1989, 2002) and others in the action research literatures, Heikkinen et al. (2012: 8) identify five validity criteria:

- *The principle of historical continuity.* Inspired by work from Yrjö Engeström (1987) and Kemmis et al. (2011), this principle requires evidence to show how the action has evolved historically: 'The development of action does not begin in a vacuum, and action never ends' (2012: 8).
- *The principle of reflexivity.* Inspired by Winter's (2002) work, this principle shows the relationship of the researcher with the object of their enquiry.
- *The principle of dialectics.* Also inspired by Winter's (1989) work, this principle shows how the researcher's insights develop in dialogue with others.
- *The principle of workability and ethics.* Inspired by the work of Davydd Greenwood and Morten Levin (2007), this principle asks how well the research succeeds in creating workable practices.
- *The principle of evocativeness.* Inspired by the work of Michael Quinn Patton (2002), this principle asks how well the research narrative evokes mental images, memories or emotions related to the theme.

Herr and Anderson (2005)

Herr and Anderson link validity criteria with the goals of action research. They identify the following forms of validity:

- *Dialogic and process validity*: the research demonstrates the generation of new knowledge.
- *Outcome validity*: the research demonstrates the achievement of action-oriented outcomes.
- *Catalytic validity*: the research influences the education of both researcher and participants.
- *Democratic validity*: the research produces results that are relevant to the local setting.
- *Process validity*: the research contains a sound and appropriate research methodology (2005: 55).

These are all useful ideas for helping you appreciate the need to establish the validity of your research and knowledge claims. You also should aim to set your own criteria for judging the quality of your action research. Do this drawing on your values and see how they come to act as your criteria and standards of judgement. Aim also to show their dynamic nature as they weave through your entire research project. Also remember the need to be open to critique and to seek it actively in testing the validity of your knowledge claims. Here are some ideas about how you can do this.

Arranging for critique

If you are on a professional development or award-bearing programme, you will probably be assigned a supervisor to offer you guidance and critique. Their main job is to guide you and invite you to question your own assumptions: this is a strong form of offering critique so do not get anxious when they ask problematising questions about your work. Their job is to encourage you to extend your thinking. Do not expect them to tell you that your work is good unless it is good.

Also seek out critique from groups of critical friends. The kind of constructive, unsentimental feedback you are looking for will probably come from people who are sympathetic to what you are doing but are also aware of the need to challenge your thinking, especially in relation to your own assumptions and established ways of thinking. These people will probably be drawn from your circle of colleagues, peers, students, parents, friends or interested observers. There are no rules about who to invite.

Having identified your participants, invite them to act as critical friends and companions. Explain carefully in advance what this will involve. They will need to meet with you throughout your research, listen to you explain what the research is about, look at your data, and consider contextual aspects and the internal coherence of the research. Above all they should be prepared to offer critical feedback so that you can see things you may have missed or misinterpreted, or to find new directions. It is their job to help you to see whether you are extending your thinking and developing new insights, or whether you are finding ways to justify and continue your existing assumptions.

'I regularly invite women from the villages to work with me in establishing the validity of my findings, and my thinking, about how best to proceed. Sometimes they agree that we are making progress through the counselling and workshops that I provide. Sometimes they feel that we could do more by working together more coherently. They offer advice about what seems to be working and what could be better.'

Critical friends

Ideally your critical friends will agree to stay with you for the life of your research, but this is often not possible. Some may drop out, others in. You will need one or two people who are prepared to stay the course, to give you feedback about how original issues have developed, especially in terms of your own learning. While ideal, this may also not always be possible. It also emphasises the idea of getting baseline data at the beginning of your research project in the form of, say, a critical conversation with a colleague to say why you are doing the research and what you hope to achieve. This can act as your guiding star to keep you on track throughout your project. It is also useful to write out your own mission statement at the beginning and check back regularly to see if you are still on track to fulfilling it, or whether your thinking has changed sufficiently that you need to go back and reassess your mission statement.

You may meet with your critical friends singly or in groups, depending on your needs and their availability. Treat them carefully. They are valuable people, essential to your research, and you need to maintain their goodwill. Write to them about meetings and give them plenty of advance notice. Send a thank you note after your meetings. Never abuse their kindness. They are giving their time and energy for free and this needs to be acknowledged.

After each meeting with a critical friend, write a brief record of the event and sign and date it. Give two copies to your friend and ask them to countersign and date these. One copy is for their files and one for you. This copy can stand as a powerful piece of evidence when you come to show the integrity of the procedural aspects of your research.

'A core group of five women and I have built close working relationships. I have given them extra training in prevention measures, so they can take over my work when I am away visiting other villages. I have also given them books and other resources to develop their subject knowledge. They maintain records of our meetings together, so that they can learn from our developing insights together. They in turn act as critical friends to one another. When I return, we hold validation groups together, so we can all evaluate our individual and collective work and improve it where necessary. Therefore, as well as acting as critical friends to me and one another, the group of women have formed themselves into a task group whose job is to clear their village of disease.'

Validation groups

Your validation group will consist of up to about 10 people, depending on the size of your project; in some cases it can be larger (see below) but enough to get some kind of personalised contact. You may invite any or all of your critical friends to join this group, and you can also recruit new people. Again, they may be drawn from your professional circle, but now you should aim to include people who are not directly involved in your research or associated with you, such as the head of another department or someone from the business community. As before, they should be competent to offer you educated feedback, not be unnecessarily picky, but be seen as capable of offering an informed and reasonably unbiased opinion. An observation about my own practice: wherever possible I arrange for students to present their research to a group of peers or faculty who have already been briefed to respond in a supportive but critical manner. I also use my public presentations as a form of validation exercise to test out my own emerging ideas, and invite email correspondence from participants about the ideas being explored. This strategy really does work.

The job of your validation group is different from that of your critical friends. They should aim to meet with you at regular intervals to listen to your research account. Accept that not all members of the group may be available on all occasions, but try to ensure continuity. Their job is to read your account so far, listen to you, scrutinise your data and evidence, consider your emergent claims to knowledge and offer critical feedback. Validation meetings are seldom cosy or comfortable experiences for researchers, because the aim is to raise questions and critique, and not to approve anything without solid evidence that shows its internal validity. This means that when you present you have to articulate the standards of judgement used and show awareness of the problematics of generating evidence. Your validation group would expect you to articulate the potential significance of your work and indicate some of its possible implications.

Validation groups can convene to consider work in progress and also final drafts prior to submission. Meetings to consider work in progress act as formative evaluation meetings: those that consider final drafts act more as summative evaluation meetings. For formative evaluation meetings, prepare and provide a progress report that outlines the research design, work done so far, any preliminary findings, provisional conclusions on those findings and comments on how satisfactorily the research is proceeding or suggestions for possible new directions. For summative, final evaluation reports, set out your main findings and claim to knowledge (you may make several claims), and why you feel justified in making that claim. This involves an explication of methodological issues, such as research design and processes, and how evidence has been generated from the data to support the claim. It will also contain epistemological issues of why you feel justified in claiming to have developed your own theory of some aspect of your practice. This means that you can describe what you did and how you did it, and also explain why you did it and what you believe you have achieved in terms of your educational and social goals. You are able to articulate the standards of judgement used in making your knowledge claim, and explain their part in developing your theory of practice. Showing how your work can constitute a theory of practice is essential if you wish it to be seen as a potential contribution to educational theory.

As with critical friends, do not take your validation group for granted. Tell them their help is appreciated. Give advance notice of proposed meetings and enquire about their availability. Try to negotiate travel expenses for them, but say if this is not possible and thank them for their effort and commitment.

'I believe that the work the women and I are doing is having an influence on the health practices of the women in the village, and a drop in the incidence of HIV and AIDS. A key feature of its success is the involvement of the five local women. They have been able to work with their neighbours and develop the kinds of intimate relationships that I cannot. I would like to write up and disseminate the work, emphasising the centrality of collaborative working in any community effort. So I have secured the encouragement and enthusiasm of our district health visitor as well as from the regional university to help me establish the credibility of the work. They have agreed to visit with me twice a year, to listen to our research, scrutinise our evidence, and offer advice about how the work may be developed further and how it may be written up and disseminated in the wider public domain.'

In advance of the meeting, send a briefing sheet to each member of the group (see the example below). After each meeting, write up a record of what was said, sign and date it, and send two copies to each member of the group. Ask them to countersign and date these, keep one copy for their files and return one to you. Keep this safely. Produce it in your final report as evidence both of what was said in response to your claim to knowledge and also of the care you paid to all aspects of your research. Place these papers in your appendices (keep all identities anonymous unless people wish to be named, and provide written statements from them that this is their wish), or place them in your evidence archive and refer to them at an appropriate place in your dissertation.

Try to enlist one of the group as a minuting secretary. Detailed minutes are unnecessary but you will need a reasonably accurate record of points made and actions recommended. If no one volunteers, keep the minutes yourself, though this can be difficult given that you will be focusing on responding to questions. If someone does volunteer, give them an exemplar sheet like the one below to help them.

Remember that in validation meetings you will have little control over what happens and what people will think and say. This is why careful preparation is important. You must prepare a case for establishing the validity of your work, your credibility as a researcher, and the legitimacy of your knowledge.

2. Examples of validation procedures

Here are some ideas about how to draw up a briefing sheet for a validation meeting and how a validation meeting might be conducted.

VALIDATION MEETING BRIEFING SHEET

If you are presenting your work, please check:

1. Have you said at the beginning what you are claiming to have achieved through the research?
2. Have you made clear:

   - your research question?
   - your reasons for doing the research?
   - the conceptual frameworks you have used?
   - your research aims and intentions?
   - your research design?
   - an awareness of ethical considerations?
   - the methodology you chose and why?
   - how you monitored practice?
   - how you gathered data, interpreted the data and generated evidence?
   - the criteria and standards of judgement you used?
   - how you came to some provisional conclusions?

3. Are you explaining that you are now testing your claims to knowledge? Are you inviting critical evaluation of the claims?

(Continued)

(Continued)

4. Do you show how doing the research has led you to develop new forms of practice and new learning?
5. Do you show the significance of your work in terms of your possible contributions to new practices and new theory?

If you are listening to a presentation of research, please check:

1. Does the researcher make a contribution to knowledge? In what way? If this is a presentation by a doctoral candidate is the contribution original? In what way?
2. Does the researcher demonstrate critical engagement throughout? In what way?
3. Does the researcher demonstrate an awareness of ethical considerations?
4. Does the researcher make clear the standards of judgement used to test claims?
5. Does the research contribute to new educational practices and new educational thinking? In what way?
6. Does the researcher present the work in a way that clarifies its significance and future potentials?
7. Does the researcher show critical engagement with the ideas of others?

Minutes of a peer validation group meeting, 20 November 2015, Carnegie Bridge, Mpumalanga

Present

Velda McPhee (presenting)

Margaret M. (town resident, deputy health counsellor)

Maria G. (town resident, deputy health counsellor)

Alice M. (town resident, deputy health counsellor)

Fia X. (town resident, deputy health counsellor)

Carrie M. (town resident, deputy health counsellor)

Jean-Philipe Latour (hospital representative)

Tamana Makole (university representative)

Robert Maidment (publisher)

Velda McPhee presented her research account to the validation group covering all aspects of the briefing sheet supplied. She was closely questioned about the validity of her claim to knowledge and critical issues were raised about:

-   The justification of her standards of judgement – some members of the group requested further evidence to be supplied at the next meeting in relation to Velda's claim that she was encouraging the growth of new knowledge and new health practices through the involvement of a women's group in the village.
-   Her claim to be developing a new approach to dealing with HIV and AIDS – further evidence was requested.

Recommendations of the validation group

Velda should continue her work and her research in its present form, but attend to the issues raised by the validation group. Further evidence to be supplied at the next validation group meeting on 9 March 2016.

Velda should work closely with Robert Maidment (publisher) on preparing her work for further dissemination.

She should also work closely with Tamana Makole in preparing to give a series of talks to health workers at the regional teaching university.

Summary

This chapter has considered matters of testing the validity of knowledge claims. These included arranging for critique, which highlights the responsibilities of different contributors in the research, including critical friends and validation groups. Examples of and advice about validation procedures were given.

EXERCISES

- Are you clear about the need for testing the validity of provisional knowledge claims and how to do it?
- Check that you appreciate what different forms of validity you can claim for your research.
- Make sure you have involved critical friends and validation groups throughout the process of doing your research, and describe such meetings in your dissertation. Also say how you have periodically conducted validation meetings and invited critical feedback on your findings. Also say how you may have changed your thinking and actions in light of the critical feedback.

Establishing the legitimacy of your knowledge claim

Chapter 16 was about testing and demonstrating the validity of knowledge claims. This chapter is about getting your work, including your claims, publicly accepted, thereby securing their legitimacy. This can be tricky because, while you have some control over validation processes by showing that you have met research and institutional criteria, you have less control over legitimation processes, because you are in an established institutional system with its own accrediting processes and epistemological traditions. Therefore, to be successful you need to be confident about the nature of your contribution and how to work with and within institutional systems.

A great strength for you is that you are both a practitioner and a researcher; this means that your research can contribute to advancing knowledge of the field of practice and of theory. You should therefore be confident about the potential significance of your work for different people, and be able to make a case for its acceptance. It is where your philosophical and political commitments come together: your commitment to demonstrating the usefulness of your research for human wellbeing and connectedness merges with your political commitments that we are all able to represent ourselves as persons in community who are taking educational action in the world.

This chapter discusses these points, and is organised, as before, into the themes of the potential significance of your action research for yourself, for others and for the world. It also highlights the importance of getting recognised by the community of researchers, as follows:

1. The potential significance of your action research for yourself
2. The potential significance of your action research for others
3. The potential significance of your action research for the world
4. Getting recognised by the community of researchers

In this book I have deliberately focused on learning as the basis of action. Taking action without understanding your reasons and purposes can lead to untold misery for self and others. Taking action with as much foresight and knowledge as possible can contribute to wellbeing. Understanding and learning are at the heart of what we do as responsible people in community with others and the world. So at this point I shall stop speaking about practice and theory as separate entities (as has been the case earlier when analysing them) and start speaking of them as integrated, as they are always are (I hope I have emphasised this throughout, too). Here, then, I speak about the significance of your action research for your own practices and theorising.

1. The potential significance of your action research for yourself

Through doing your research and taking action in your own thinking, you can show how you have learned to do things differently and better. Your new learning has fed back into new action, which has in turn generated new learning. This is an ongoing process and has become a way of life. You are able to stand back, analyse and comment on the processes involved. In more abstract terms, you can comment on the significance of your own story and how your interpretations have enabled you to re-think and re-act in light of your reflections. Schön and Rein (1994) speak about this as a process of 're-framing', when you create new intellectual and action frames to help deal with problematic situations. They write about policy frameworks but their ideas are equally relevant for people's everyday lives. They say that discourses to do with reframing:

> ... are constructed around the central idea of a reflective conversation. Participants in such a conversation must be able to put themselves in the shoes of other actors in the environment, and they must have a complementary ability to consider how their own action frames may contribute to the problematic situations in which they find themselves. (p. 187)

At this point it may be helpful to articulate the difference between the lifeworld of people, which is to do with how they live their everyday lives, and the system(s) they develop to organise that lifeworld (an idea developed by Habermas, 1975). 'The lifeworld' is about real-time practices and learning; 'system' is to do with how people organise and formalise their lifeworlds as structures and processes. This can take the form of councils and procedures, and rules and regulations. However, because working with systems is such a common experience among people, they tend to forget that systems were created by and contain real-world people and are processes by which people interact with one another. They learn to think of systems as reified (turned into 'things') rather than processes. Often, says Habermas, once people have put systems in place they forget about them. Consequently, the system takes on a life of its own: it becomes detached from the people who created it and floats somewhere above the lifeworld. The point is, however, that people can change what they have made and recreate it to their own advantage. This is what action research is about. 'The world is not entirely given', says Nixon (2012: 33), 'but made through our understanding of it – and, as Marx went on to argue, if the world is what we make of it, then we can seek to make it a better world.'

The implications are that if we wish to change the socio-political systems that others and we create, we need to put ourselves in others' shoes and imagine new worlds that would benefit everyone, difficult though this may be.

Below are several examples of how people learned to act differently through learning to think differently. The examples are taken from the master's dissertations of teachers, the first and second in Ireland, the third in South Africa; and from work in Latvia and Cambodia. Texts like these, produced through our collaborative efforts to establish practice-based forms of research in local settings, have gone some way to contributing to the current impetus for educational change in those settings, and a move towards individual and organisational self-evaluation and improvement.

Thérèse Burke (1997) writes:

The critical self-reflective aspect of my [research] required me to look at who I was and where I was situated, both personally and professionally as I approached my twenty-fifth year of teaching ... This recognition of my own professional development complements my own theory of learning difference. I no longer view the child as the sum of all her parts, but as an individual with her own ontological and epistemologi- cal needs, a person who can engage with others and use her potential to learn at this moment ... I am now conscious of what I would like to name as an 'epistemological equality' between myself and my students. I do not have a monopoly on knowledge: mine is not the only way of knowing ... This was a significant learning experience for me as a practising teacher. There can be a smugness about those in education, myself included, who suggest that the values of the school system are the only values that matter, and that what it offers is the only way to be. I challenge this assumption. I believe the theory of individuality which is at the basis of an understanding of learning difference makes a nonsense of this. When I reflect on who and how I was in the past, I realise that I would always have paid lip service to this theory, but now I know its truth and I claim it as an educational value of my own.

Moira Cluskey (1997) writes:

[Having undertaken my master's studies] I now journey into the second half of my teaching life, essentially the same person but with a new perspective. I am not as anxious and awe-struck about the changes those years may bring because I believe I have developed good research techniques which will help me to learn from those situations. I agree with Lomax (1994) who sees the informal inquiry of many other reflective teachers as 'only a basis for the more rigorous and reflective ways in which action researchers work'. I have always been a reflective teacher who sometimes found my practice fell short of my desires, but I lacked the tools for conducting a systematic enquiry into that practice. I wanted to improve but felt helpless about how to do so. I had been imbued with the notion that those in authority knew a 'right way' to teach in any given situation but had omitted to teach me it. Nor had I ever found the answers to my problems in any of the in-service courses I had attended - stimulation, yes, but the power to act, no. Now, through my engagement with action research, I have been empowered to act - to engage in a systematic enquiry of my practice and to change it.

> But I do wonder if I would have made that breakthrough, would have persisted in follow-
> ing through on a plan of action, had the promise of accreditation for my effort not been
> in the background. It provided an added stimulus and purpose to my enquiry. If the state
> values its teaching profession it must devise a system which accredits and encourages
> teachers to improve their practice and to provide a quality educational experience for
> their students.

Texts such as those by Thérèse and Moira have led to widespread reforms in the provision of new forms of professional education for teachers.

> Gerhardus Adams (2008) from the Khayelitsha group in South Africa writes:
>
> By engaging in this research project I have become aware of my shortcomings as an
> educator, my strengths and the potential contribution I can make to the education profes-
> sion. I believe that by attempting to live my values in my practice, I will not only improve
> myself as an educator but will also encourage others to do so ... I hope to produce an
> account that will make my values of respect for others, social justice and enquiry learning
> explicit, and provide authentic explanations and descriptions of my own learning that can
> be understood by others.
>
> I believe in the worth and dignity of all human beings, devotion to excellence and the nur-
> ture of democratic principles and social justice. Essential to those values is the protection
> of the freedom to learn and to teach and the guarantee of equal educational opportunity
> for all. I will strive to help each learner realise his or her potential as a worthy and effec-
> tive member of society.
>
> The education profession is vested by the public with a trust and responsibility requiring
> the highest ideals of professional service. In the belief that the quality of the services
> of the education profession directly influences the nation, I hope to make every effort
> to raise professional standards, to promote a climate that encourages the exercise of
> professional judgement and to achieve conditions which attract persons worthy of the
> trust to careers in education.

Look at what these colleagues, like you, have learned to do. They and you have learned to challenge and resist the influence of disabling discourses and systems. You have changed your self-identification from being 'just a teacher' or 'just a plumber' to being a competent theorist. Your theories of practice are rooted in your capacity to understand and appreciate the emancipatory power of your thinking. Like Hannah Arendt (1958), you have accepted the responsibility of thinking: in her terms, to be 'present' both in the social world and in your own mind. You are aware of your responsibility not just to watch the sufferings of others on television, as Susan Sontag (2003) describes, but also to find ways of realising your capacity to do something about it. If you cannot go direct to the world's trouble spots you can at least get your degree, which will authorise you and give you the institutional legitimacy to challenge those authoritarian systems and disabling discourses that influence the perpetuation of trouble spots. This will give you the public authorisation to try to influence your workplace practices.

But yours is more than a politics of dissent: it is a form of activism. You have turned yourself into an activist practitioner. Sachs (2003) speaks about an activist teaching profession that is unafraid in challenging unjust forms of policy or curriculum; authors like Nadine Gordimer and Doris Lessing write about injustice in apartheid states; singer-songwriters such as Bruce Springsteen and Joan Baez write protest songs that challenge injustice. Classic and popular literatures are full of stories of heroes, some famous, some not. According to Arendt, says Kohn (in Young-Bruehl and Kohn, 2001: 229), 'it is not knowing what justice is, but rather thinking about justice, culminating in the individual act of judgement, that lets justice appear in the world'. You also deserve to be in a hall of fame: this happens when your name appears on the list at your graduation ceremony. You know what you have done, and you can hold yourself accountable for it. You should celebrate your accomplishments and be proud of yourself.

Now consider how your research can benefit the learning of others.

2. The potential significance of your action research for others

You can influence people's learning by contributing to their understandings of how to improve their lifeworlds. Through reading your dissertation about how you have changed your practices and influenced others in your workplace, other people can see how to do something similar in their own contexts. They will not do the same as you, because each person and context are different but they can learn and adapt. Importantly, they can see that they need not put up with unsatisfactory conditions or disabling discourses but can take action to change these. At an immediate level they can change their own discourses.

> Linda Pavītola , Lāsma Latsone and Dina Bethere did this: they conducted their action research with higher education lecturers and doctoral students in Latvia, to explore why there was so little apparent awareness of the need for openness and criticality. Being critical, in their view, is key to social wellbeing: they write (2016: 96):
>
> > Criticality can ... be viewed as a means of understanding and making meaning from experience. This is a positive philosophy rather than skeptical, and the focus on testing the validity of findings according to particular criteria underpins new ideas and releases creative energy (Korol, 1981). Criticality includes an explicitly articulated intention to change reality: it raises critical research questions and develops questioning attitudes (Niehaves and Stahl, 2006).
>
> They found that government-mandated technical issues, such as a need to publish research papers, appeared to be prioritised, and that institutions tended to maintain a culture of silence where people kept themselves to themselves.
> These days they continue to work towards influencing new cultures of collaboration and dialogue:
>
> > The outcomes of our research will, we hope, contribute to extending theoretical and practical knowledge about the power of research to promote positive attitudes towards

the principles of criticality and openness, and to establishing a sustainable research culture within and beyond borders of individual research institutions. (2016: 108)

Linda, Lāsma and Dina continue to work tirelessly towards opening up institutions for increased intercultural understanding and dialogue.

It is the same for you. Through making your work public, and explaining how and why you are doing so, you are sharing workable ideas that encourage others in workplaces to say 'I can do this too'. Perhaps the greatest gift you can give to others is both the encouragement to develop a new vision and also the idea that a new vision is possible. You are saying to people 'It doesn't have to be like this. You are capable of rethinking the way things are and changing them'. You are showing your faith in yourself and them that you can find ways to create your own new futures. By providing your account of practice you are giving others ideas about how they can do so too.

If you are in any doubt that encouraging a sense of open vision and providing the means to realise it are the overall purpose of your work, stop and think about the relationship between your action research and any report of bullying, whether on a personal or international scale. Bullying is usually the direct outcome of a lack of acceptance of the Other, a monumental hubris that allows some people to think they are more deserving of their place on earth than others. Read any newspaper, or the literature of Amnesty International: see how relationships of power and their outcomes of pain weave themselves through pages. Listen to the rhetoric of politicians and read between the lines. 'We want people to be free', you hear. Free for what? Free to continue serving power? Go into your workplace. See how relationships of power permeate discourses. In which direction does the power lie? Who tells others what to do? How do they do this? Do they blatantly coerce, or do they manage to get people to perform according to institutional requirements, and even come to believe that performing appropriately was their own idea?

Things do not need to be the way they are. The most amazing thing about you is that, by even considering the possibility of doing your action research, you hang onto your sense of vision that there is another way. By doing your action research you can find that way. By making your account public you are saying to people 'You can do this too'.

This is how your research can benefit learning for the world.

3. The potential significance of your action research for the world

This is where you can influence practices in the wider world at the level of systems. At a minimum you can show how your learning has the local potential for helping others develop systems that will be more appropriate for their needs than existing ones; at a more complex level you can explain how your learning has exponential potential. This idea of realising exponential potential is termed 'impact' in some policy contexts; the Higher Education Funding Council for England (HEFCE) defines the 'impact' of higher education research as 'an effect on, change or benefit to the economy, society, culture, public policy or services, health, the environment or quality of life, beyond academia' (see www.hefce.ac.uk/rsrch/REFimpact/), and this is how it is often defined in other contexts too. I have elsewhere (McNiff et al., 2017) defined this differently, pointing out that the term 'impact' often conjures up images of violence and is therefore probably more appropriate to those discourses (including policy discourses) that themselves do violence to practitioners; it becomes part of the Newspeak (Orwell, 1989 [1949]) of the new managerialism (Deem et al., 2007). In contexts about educational processes, however, it would probably be better termed 'influence'.

However, the point of 'impact' or 'influence' is that you can show the processes of 'passing on the knowledge': you do not keep knowledge to yourself or for use only by your immediate circle but ensure that you pass on that knowledge to others for their use. This becomes your personal and collective responsibility and privilege.

Here is an example to show how knowledge can be passed on for wider benefit and the improvement of practices.

> In Chapters 5 and 6 and elsewhere I referred to the work of the Tromsø [Land]Mine Victim Resource Centre (TMC), initiated in 1999 by a small group of Norwegian medical and healthcare practitioners committed to reducing the mortality rate among local citizens living in low resource settings and especially in war and conflict zones, including Afghanistan, Burma, Eastern Angola, Northern Iraq and Cambodia. The high level of mortality was often maintained because injuries, including those resulting from abandoned landmines, were too often treated inappropriately by local people: for example, it was standard practice to apply a tourniquet to prevent bleeding, the effect of which was a restrained blood supply to whole limbs and thereby frequent unnecessary amputation. Most people died from blood loss, given that injuries are usually incurred far from available health services. The Norwegians taught the local people more appropriate life-saving methods: for example, packing wounds with gauze, securing dressings with elastic bandages to prevent blood loss, and giving the patients intravenous fluids, painkillers and antibiotics. Those trained locals were now identified as medics; each was equipped with a refillable back pack containing the necessary emergency equipment. The most capable among these local people taught the next group who in turn were quickly able to take over the training. Every medic then trained groups of first helpers to assist them in their districts; this came to be known as the 'chain of survival' (Husum et al., 2000). They also introduced the practice of maintaining injury charts to document the treatment of patients. Statistical evidence shows that the mortality rate of mine victims dropped from 40% to around 10% following the adoption of these new recommended procedures, together with a higher degree of limb retention (see Edvardsen, 2006; Husum, 2003; Husum et al., 2000).
>
> In every setting they worked in, the Norwegians and professionals from the countries they were already in set up a Village University, where they taught locals the basics of scientific research. This helped the locals to produce appropriate reports of what they had achieved that could be passed on to people in other places.
>
> By the time this book is published, Odd Edvardsen, Margit Steinholt, Peter McDonnell and I will have revisited the same locals in Cambodia and helped them learn how to do action research into their own practices. We aim to provide ongoing support for as long as it takes, and publish the accounts of the local people, in their own right as authors, to celebrate the excellence of their practice-based knowledge. These are commitments for life: but, for me, there is no better way of spending a life than by contributing to helping those less privileged than oneself to enrich their own lives through learning.

Now consider how you can get recognised by the community of researchers by showing how your research can contribute to new thinking and new theorising.

4. Getting recognised by the community of researchers

You can get recognised by the community of researchers by explaining how your action research is not just about contributing to new learning about practices but also about contributing to new learning about theory.

Through doing your research you have challenged the dominance of abstract forms of theorising and the hegemony of a traditionalist academy. You can show in practice what Stringer speaks about, that when explaining their theories to others practitioners use 'experience-near concepts – terms people use to describe events in their day-to-day lives (rather than, e.g. theoretical concepts from the behavioral sciences) – to clarify and untangle meanings and to help the individuals illuminate and organize their experiences' (Stringer, 2007: 96). He continues, also quoting Denzin:

> 'Interpretation is a clarification of meaning. Understanding is the process of interpreting, knowing, and comprehending the meaning that is felt, intended, and expressed by another' (Denzin, 1989: 120). The purpose of interpretive work, therefore, is to help participants to 'take an attitude of the other' (Mead, 1934), not in a superficial, mechanistic way but in a way that enables them to understand empathetically the complex and deeply rooted forces that move their lives. (Stringer, 2007: 96)

You are doing this: you are influencing the idea of what counts as theory. You have changed the way in which 'theory' is understood: you do not just produce ideas about something but also show through what you do what meaning you give to your life. Theory resides not only in libraries or in formal lecture theatres where 'official' theorists cite the literatures to talk about other literatures: it also exists on the street, in the public square, as you explain to others why they should take your work seriously and consider doing something similar. This kind of debate is what Geras (1995, drawing on an idea developed by Oakeshott, 1962, and referring to the body of work of Richard Rorty) calls 'the conversation of humankind': it moves the literatures of theory out of the realm of abstraction and into the world of everyday practices (as in, for example, de Certeau, 1984).

> As a further example of the realisation of the principle of 'passing on the knowledge', Karen O'Shea (2000) from among the group of Irish teachers writes about the potentials for practitioners to contribute both to practice and to theory:
>
> > [My dissertation tells] how I set about influencing a national curriculum. It aims to contribute to the field of human rights and citizenship education by illuminating the curriculum development process and highlighting how it can benefit from personal reflection and collaboration.
>
> *(Continued)*

(Continued)

[My dissertation] documents how I, by seeking to become an agent of change in my own context, was drawn into a deeper exploration of my values, which in turn challenged me to explore my understanding of my practice. I reached a stage in my research where I described my educational practice as a reflective, value-based community activity that seeks to encourage the development of a more just society within which all can reach their fullest potential. Thus the research highlights how understanding can be generated through the process of action and reflection.

From my research I suggest that educational practice is generative in nature in that it is in a continual state of growth and development. In conclusion, I explore the implications of my learning for educational theory and practice, in particular for the development of communities of learning and ongoing teacher education. I suggest that teacher education is a lifelong process and that developing an understanding of one's practice provides an ideal starting point for ongoing professional development.

Perhaps your most important contribution, now at the level of influencing thinking about and for theory, is to challenge the idea of fundamentalism or absolutism, that there is no one Big Book of Answers. Absolutist thinking permeates all forms of human discourses including moral absolutism and political absolutism: it is assumed that there is an ultimate source of truth. In epistemological terms, the idea implies, as outlined on page 43 that there is one specific answer to any question, that this answer may be found if you look for it, and that everyone will agree with it. It also assumes that people will agree with the idea of fundamentalism itself. It permeates the discourses of leadership, educational practices and values-based forms of enquiry. Many authors have challenged the concept, with good reason: Berlin (2002) says that when you impose your idea of freedom on other people it stops being freedom and becomes a form of tyranny; Easterly (2013) speaks of 'the tyranny of experts' in the form of those official aid agencies who conduct their work on the basis that they know what is right for locals. The imposition of absolutist forms of theory and practice is doubly disabling because 'ordinary' people (now positioned as recipients) become deskilled and lose confidence in their own capacity to do things for themselves, including think. Absolutism is a form of fundamentalism, where people become so entrenched in an idea that they lose sight of the bigger picture.

It does not have to be like this. Commenting on the work of the Highlander Centre, Chambers remarks that it:

contributed the seminal insight that local people with little education ... had far greater abilities for analysis, action, experimentation, research and monitoring and evaluation than had been supposed by outside professionals, or by themselves. (2008: 299)

This insight also emphasises the key observations of authors such as Lyotard (1984) and Cochran-Smith and Lytle (2008) that practitioners' local theories of practice are as valid as the grand theories of scholarly literatures; it also reinforces Easterly's (2013) view that development work, rather than proceeding from a 'blank slate' perspective, should respect locals' capacity to work within and transform their existing culture for social improvement. And it not only challenges views expressed, for example, by Hattie (2015) that teachers and other shopfloor practitioners cannot do research, it also reveals those views as both misled and misleading.

This is where we came in: by restricting the idea of theory as a discipline conducted only by 'official' academic practitioners, and by imposing an abstract form of theory as the only legitimate kind, those same academic researchers destroy the very thing they claim to have nurtured, that is, the wellbeing of practitioners. Nor do they all perceive what they are actually doing. In the same way as inquisitors burned people's feet for their own good, some academic practitioners insist that imposing a view of the superiority of abstract theorising is for practitioners' own good. No. While it can contribute significantly, it is not the only answer. You already have the answer in your capacity to theorise your own practice. Your theory is in your practice: this counts towards the common good, when you talk with others about what they are doing, and work together to find and negotiate better ways that are in everyone's interests. And, as I have said throughout, taking this stance is in itself a form of fundamentalism and presents a logical conundrum in that you can never arrive at a foundation story because all stories are underpinned by other stories. Yet we all have to ground our views and values somewhere; perhaps the saving grace here is to remember that we are part of the bigger picture and contribute to its creation. So my absolutist stand is that we all need to encourage one another to see that we live in a dialogical world, but can create our own theories of practice that show how we promote solidarity with others. Hay (2006) speaks about 'something there': we cannot define it, but there is something that gives us our sense of humanity, which, if we deny it, makes us less than we should be, less than human.

However …

The fact remains that you are in an institutional academic system that you have actively bought into: you have paid good money to study for your degree. Having done so, you have no option but to obey the rules if you wish to be recognised. But you can still get your own way by finding ways to manoeuvre within the rules, especially when you come to write your dissertation. It becomes a question of skilfully mapping onto existing patterns the story that is your action research, and doing it so well that no one could deny you the award. And this now becomes the focus of Chapters 18 and 19.

Summary

This chapter has outlined some key issues in demonstrating the legitimacy of your knowledge claim. Establishing legitimacy is an important aspect of the politics of knowledge and involves demonstrating the potential significance and implications of your action research for yourself, for others and for the world.

The next chapter considers how demonstrating the legitimacy of your research may be achieved through writing your dissertation.

EXERCISE

- Are you confident about the potential significance of your research for yourself, for others and for the world? It may be considerable: discuss with a critical colleague how they see the significance of your research, and write out your own opinion. Show this to your colleagues and ask for their feedback.

PART VI

How do I represent and communicate my knowledge?

This part is about writing up your research and communicating it to a reader. Writing a story and communicating it are different things and involve different practices. The chapters explain the differences and also offer ideas about how to organise your ideas into a form that will be acceptable to an academic readership while maintaining the integrity of your work.

This part contains the following chapters:

At this point in your enquiry you are asking, 'How do I write up my story? How do I communicate it to a particular readership?' The chapters give detailed advice on how to do this.

Thinking about writing your dissertation

This chapter is about getting ready to write your text. It emphasises the importance of seeing writing itself as a research process and part of your overall research project. You therefore need to factor preparation time into your overall action plan: the more preparation you can do, the greater the likelihood of your producing a high quality, comprehensible and self-explanatory text. This is essential because the only thing your reader knows about you is what they read on the page: you have to tell them what you want them to know. Do not assume that they will work out your meanings for themselves, nor is it their job to do so. It is your responsibility as a writer to explain things to them so that they will see what you mean, clearly and without effort.

Achieving this kind of quality means thinking carefully about what writing involves, and using this knowledge to produce a text that your reader will appreciate fully and without effort.

Thinking about writing involves a range of different aspects, including understanding what goes into a text (its content), how to construct a text (its form), and how to produce a text (the writing process itself). Crucially it involves appreciating that a text includes offering explanations as well as descriptions of your practice: and this in turn means appreciating the different methodological practices involved, including designing, planning, production, analysis and synthesis and meta-reflection, and then explaining to your reader how you have undertaken them. The practices themselves take the form of acting, reflecting on the action, taking new, more informed action which is now subject to further reflection ... and so on in an ongoing spiral. You move into new spaces of more refined thinking, which informs a more refined form of action, which informs ... This process of action and reflection also implies that the quality of your overall practice moves towards a manifestation of how you understand 'the good'. Also remember that, although these matters are presented here as separate issues for purposes of analysis, they are always dynamic and integrated as part of your dynamic and integrated life.

A useful strategy for achieving this kind of dynamic action-reflection process can be to think about working in and across conceptual spaces. The term 'conceptual spaces' is adapted from a paper by Gärdenfors (2004) and has been developed in relation to other fields by Bereiter and Scardamalia (1987). Here I use it to refer to the different notional spaces in your head where various ideas or sets of ideas are located. It is rather like when you think of a house with different rooms, each of which has a separate purpose and function: you have a kitchen for cooking, a living room for relaxing, a bedroom for sleeping, and so on. You move across these different spaces for different reasons and to achieve different purposes. Similarly, in writing you have different spaces for different tasks. Using the metaphor can help you decide which aspects of writing to focus on over time, and how to write to achieve specific purposes.

The chapter discusses three of these spaces and what they involve, as follows:

1. Working in and across conceptual spaces: from 'what next?' to communicating with a reader
2. Working in and across conceptual spaces: designing and planning
3. Working in and across conceptual spaces: the writing process

1. Working in and across conceptual spaces: from 'what next?' to communicating with a reader

Early work in the 1980s from researchers such as Hayes and Flower (1980) and Bereiter and Scardamalia (1987), as reported by Sharples (1999), shows that very young children think and write mainly in terms of 'what next?': they write, 'We did this, then we did that, then we did …' ('We saw the lions, then we saw the tigers, then we saw the elephants and then we went home'). Their speech and writing take the form of recounting a chain of events; they do not necessarily reflect on the originating circumstances, outcomes or implications of those events, nor do they think in terms of explaining what they mean to their listener. They tend simply to say what has happened: in more analytical terms, they offer descriptions of what they have done. This same practice, while conducted at a much more sophisticated level, also tends to be one of the most common errors that beginning adult researchers make when writing their dissertations: they produce an account that stays mainly at the level simply of saying what they did. They produce a descriptive account as a straightforward chain of events without a clear explanatory framework to help the reader see the point of the story. The text appears as a 'what next?' list of actions. This kind of writing, important though it is, does not necessarily get a degree. To get a degree you need to add further explanatory, scholarly and reflexive frames that embed the descriptive narrative. You also need to think in terms of writing for a reader. This means that two processes are involved: (1) writing at multiple levels and (2) communicating with a reader.

Writing at multiple levels

First consider how your research text can take the form of writing at multiple levels. In my books *Writing and Doing Action Research* (2014) and *Writing Up Your Action Research Project* (2016c), I have suggested imagining the writing of a research text as working from a simplistic basic descriptive level to a more complex higher meta-reflexive level. I have also suggested using the metaphor of an airport concourse, or a shopping mall, with escalators moving from lower to higher levels. As you, the researcher, move up and down these levels, you adopt different identities: you become different 'I's, depending on the job in hand, and your different 'I's talk about different aspects of your research, as follows:

- **At Level 1** you say what you did in your research: you asked 'What is my concern?' and told your reader how you began a research project based on this question.
- **At Level 2** you bring in your explanatory 'I': your explanatory 'I' looks down to your descriptive 'I' and explains to the reader what you were doing.
- **At Level 3** your researcher 'I' enters to test the validity of the claims that your Level 2 'I' is making: your researcher 'I' reflects on the quality of your Level 1 descriptions and your Level 2 explanations.
- **At Level 4** your scholarly 'I' adds scholarly aspects in terms of linking your explanations with themes from the literatures.
- **At Level 5** your critically reflective 'I' critiques any provisional conclusions you are drawing, on the understanding that whatever you say is always already located in the cultural norms of the times in which a researcher does their research.
- **At Level 6** your dialectically critical 'I' locates everything within what you are thinking and experiencing, but now from your current situatedness.
- **At Level 7** your meta-reflexive 'I' considers the entire text you have produced so far and imagines ways of evaluating and improving it. This brings you to a new beginning, where you consider how to address the new questions that your writing has generated.

These ideas are further refined in newer work (McNiff, 2017).

Communicating with a reader

Now consider how to communicate with a reader: this means that you move across horizontal spaces, from saying to communicating, as follows.

Again use a metaphor. Think about a space where you store content and another space where you send the content out: for example, think of a supermarket that has storage space for goods and a retail space for selling the goods; or a post office that has storage space for letters and a despatch room for sending out the letters. In the same way, think of the content of your text (what you are going to write) and how you are going to communicate this content (send it out) to your reader. To illustrate this, think of a time when you needed to communicate the same information (content) to an adult and to a child: you would say the same thing but communicate it in different ways, as, for example, in Table 18.1.

Now use the same idea in relation to your research:

- First think about describing what happened while you were doing the research: you describe the different actions or steps you took, who you involved, what their and your reactions were, and so on. You recount the story in terms of a chain of events: you say 'We did this and we did that'. In everyday language this would perhaps be referred to as telling a story, where 'telling' is meant as 'recounting' or 'narrating': you give an account of events, you write a narrative account. At this point you work in a content space.

Table 18.1   Saying what is happening to an adult and to a child

Content/what you say	Communicating the story to an adult	Communicating the story to a child
Joe (husband and father) has to tell his wife and child that he will be away on business for a week.	Joe explains to his wife: 'The company has asked me to be away for a week and I have to go. It could be an interesting assignment, and it could mean promotion. What do you think? Is it all right with you?'	Joe explains to his two-year old son: 'Daddy has to go and do some work in another city and be away for a week. That means six sleeps and I'll try and phone every evening and you can tell me all your news and what a good boy you have been and how you have helped Mummy. And when I come back we'll all go out together for the day.'

- Now think about how you are going to tell the story to your reader. This means deciding how to move from the content space where you give an account of events into a communications space where you talk with a reader. Your job is to communicate the content to a reader or a listener, as set out in Table 18.2.

Table 18.2   From content to communication

Event/what happened	Content space: Saying what happened	Communication space: thinking about how to tell the story to a reader	Revised text
You decided on the research issue of student participation.	You write: 'I decided to focus on student participation as my research issue.'	You think: 'How do I communicate what the research issue was to my reader? I need to be clear about this so that the reader will immediately understand what the research was about.'	You now write: 'I decided to focus on student participation as my research issue, as this is a major concern among our staff. Students seem reluctant to engage with their own learning.'
You say why this was a research issue.	You write: 'I decided on this focus because participation is basic to good learning practices.'	You think: 'It is important to clarify the reasons for the research so that the reader can appreciate its significance and possible use value. But this means that I need to explain the relationship between participation and deep learning. This then means I have to refer to the literatures where other people have talked about participation and deep learning.'	You now write: 'I decided on this focus because participation is basic to good learning practices, as exemplified by research conducted by Brown and Black (2014) who demonstrate the relationships between student participation and deep learning.'
You set out a research design.	You write: 'I thought about how to conduct the research in order to address the research question.'	You think: 'The reader needs to understand why I thought about designing the research as I did, so that they can see that I thought it through carefully myself and was reasonably clear about its importance. I need to explain that this focus was part of a deliberate process of considering and negotiating my personal values with others' organisational values.'	You now write: 'I thought about how to conduct the research in order to address the research question. It also involved focusing on the values that informed my research, and taking care to negotiate my personal values with my organisation's values.'

Here you move across the different conceptual spaces of saying what happened to communicating this information to a reader and making clear why the shift is necessary. This kind of shift is core to good writing-for-communication: you do not just outline what you did and assume that your reader knows what you are talking about; you explain to your reader why you did what you did so that they can see the reasons and purposes that informed your actions. In other words, you move from saying what you did to describing and explaining why you did it and what you hoped to achieve, also as linked with and grounded in the literatures.

The differences outlined here are central to the process of producing a text in such a way that a reader will see immediately what you are getting at. They may also be understood in terms of the lovely idea of a writerly text and a readerly text (Barthes, 1970).

WRITERLY TEXTS AND READERLY TEXTS

A writerly text (according to Barthes) is when a writer writes (produces a text) for themselves. They know what they mean: they write it down so that they will not forget ideas or because they wish to sort out those ideas before sharing them with anyone else. You would probably do this when producing a first draft: you would write out ideas, move words and sentences around, insert new ideas and so on. The aim here is to produce a text that sets out what you did in terms that make sense to you (but not necessarily other people). Other forms of writing would also qualify as writerly texts, including a diary, a shopping list or a 'things to do' list. To return to the example of the intelligence building on page 192, you write in your own code which, at this point, no one else necessarily understands; they would have to download and interpret this. A skilled writer, on the other hand, writes in such a way that their text would immediately be comprehensible to anyone in the building, but this means producing a readerly text, as follows.

A readerly text is when you wish to communicate your meanings to a reader. This involves writing so that your reader will see, immediately and effortlessly, what you are getting at. It is a matter of decoding your own messages so that the reader will see your meanings. Your decoding process amounts to offering descriptions (what you did, which is still weighted in favour of narrating a series of events) and explanations, which involves giving reasons and purposes, saying why you did what you did within a specific context, and some of the possible implications. It also involves building arguments and themes that will run through the text: you would explain why, for example, participation is important in terms of what other literatures say about the need for participation. This process also amounts to setting out the main conceptual frameworks for your study (namely identifying the main themes and topics that you were investigating).

But you are not yet finished with the process: you also have to reflect on and evaluate what you have written, and whether you have achieved your aim of writing for a reader.

Evaluating your communicative practices

These action–reflection processes move you towards meta-reflection, where you reflect on the content (what you have written), on the process (how you have written it) and whether you have succeeded in communicating your messages. This may also be understood in terms of an action–reflection cycle as part of a cycle of cycles, as in Figure 18.1.

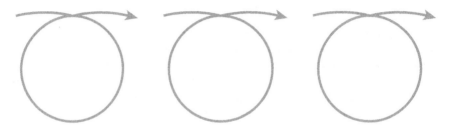

Figure 18.1   A traditional action-reflection cycle of cycles

It is possible to understand the model depicted in Figure 18.1 as a process of acting, reflecting, modifying, evaluating and re-planning at different stages of any action–reflection process (in this chapter the process refers to writing), and also seeing this as part of a generative transformational evolutionary system where the learning from one element transforms into a new element, the learning from which transforms into new spirals of action and reflection (as in Figure 3.1).

This process is never-ending, bounded only by the limits of life. Life itself becomes a process of enquiry, where new questions generate answers that always already contain new questions within themselves. We interpret meanings from what others and we ourselves do, and we use those meanings to inform new actions. We renew our practices, and ourselves, through linking thinking and action on a continual basis.

Now consider the different though interrelated spaces of designing and planning.

2. Working in and across conceptual spaces: designing and planning

Writing also involves the different processes of conceptualising, designing a text and planning a text. The processes are different in that, broadly speaking, designing means having a mental image of what the finished product will look like while planning involves imagining how you might achieve the design. This again becomes a process of moving back and forth across different conceptual spaces in that both processes involve different but complementary mental capacities, as outlined here.

Designing

Designing involves imagining what a product might look like in its final state: you can have a visual image of a boat, an aural image of a piece of music or a tactile image of a hammer. Chefs use their olfactory senses to create new dishes and dancers use their kinaesthetic senses to stay balanced. The production of most artefacts involves multiple senses: a bookbinder sees an idealised image of a book, listens to the processes involved in binding it, feels its weight in their hand, smells the paper, gauges how a reader will handle it. You also design your text from different sensory perspectives: the appropriateness of its length, the balance of its chapters, the integrity of its contents, the lightness of its style. You also have an overall perspective of the responses it will evoke in your reader and how it might be used. Designing involves thinking about the questions: What is your vision? What is your overall conceptualisation? What will the final product look and feel like? And as well as exercising judgement about its balance and aesthetic quality, you also consider the pragmatic issues of whether it will give practical information that has use value for others.

Planning

Planning involves how you are going to achieve your design. It also involves multiple processes, including a focused strategic process and a practical, logistical process.

Take the example of an organiser who is drawing up plans for an outdoor music festival. They also think in terms of designing, strategic planning and logistics, as follows:

- In designing the festival they ask questions such as: What kind of music do we want? Which musicians? How many stages will there be?
- They then move to strategic planning where they ask: Where will the festival be? What number of visitors will we attract? What permissions do we need?
- They also think about logistics, including: How will people be transported to and from the event? What supplies of food and drink will they require? How many car parks do we need? How many toilets?

The idea of moving across the conceptual spaces of designing and planning are key to producing a successful text, because now you are thinking of producing a readerly text that will immediately speak to a reader's experience. It means asking questions such as the following:

In relation to design (what the finished product will look like) you ask:

- What will my dissertation say? What will it represent? What should the reader get from it?
- Will it focus on scholarly debates in the literatures or will it be a case study? Will it be a personal narrative? Why will it take this form?
- What will it look like? Will it be a thesis of 80,000 words or a smaller volume of 20,000?
- What kind of language will it use? Will it use a first- or third-person form?

In relation to more strategic planning, you ask:

- What do I want to say?
  - What key messages do I wish to communicate? What are the central issues in my text? What is their importance? Why should my reader listen to me?
- Who do I want to say it to?
  - Who am I writing for? Who do I anticipate will read my text? Will it be my supervisor, an examiner, my peers? Knowing your audience influences your choice of style and content.

- Why do I want to say it?
  - What is important about my text? What will people learn from me that they cannot learn from anyone else? What is the burning issue I wish to communicate?
- How am I going to say it?
  - What style will I adopt? How will I speak to my reader? What tone of voice? How do I anticipate that they will interpret what I am saying?

In relation to logistics it means thinking about the criteria by which your dissertation will be judged: these usually include the following, though individual institutions have their own criteria:

- The dissertation makes a contribution to knowledge of the field (at doctoral level the contribution must be original; at undergraduate or master's level it can show understanding of the field but not necessarily be original).
- The dissertation demonstrates critical engagement: this means engagement with the literatures and with your own thinking. 'Critical' means interrogating assumptions and explaining to and showing your reader that you do not take things for granted but raise questions about possible conclusions.
- The dissertation is error-free and includes a full list of references.
- The dissertation contains an account of innovative practice.

Addressing the criteria and working at a logistical level means asking questions of the form:

- What do I need to know in order to produce my dissertation? What subject knowledge do I need? What research knowledge?
- What do I need to do to achieve the assessment criteria? Whom do I need to consult?
- What literatures do I need to refer to in order to fulfil the requirements?
- How many chapters will my dissertation contain? What will they say? How many words will the chapters contain?
- How much time do I give to writing?

Asking these kinds of practical questions requires you to draw up an action plan, or several separate action plans for the production of your dissertation (see also Chapter 19). It can be helpful to produce action plans such as the ones in Tables 18.3, 18.4 and 18.5. Keep these plans flexible and adjust them as the need arises and according to your own progress.

Table 18.3 Design of my dissertation

Appearance of dissertation	Extent
Overall length	40,000 words
Number of chapters	7-8
Number of words per chapter	5,000-6,000
... and so on	

Table 18.4   Time required for writing my dissertation

Writing phase	Time required for writing
For production of dissertation	12 months
For production of individual chapters	1 month per chapter
For revision of text in light of supervisor's feedback	Two months
...and so on	

Table 18.5   Action plan for writing my dissertation

Action	January	February	March
Planning overall dissertation: number of chapters	✓		
Consulting supervisor	✓	✓	✓
Consulting the literatures: intensive reading	✓		
Working with the data		✓	
... and so on			

Also aim to keep a writing diary to record what you have done and what you still need to do. Working with action plans allows you to tick off tasks as you complete them.

Now consider what is involved in the writing process itself.

3. Working in and across conceptual spaces: the writing process

The writing process itself also takes the form of a series of action–reflection cycles, as part of the overall action reflection process of producing a dissertation. It contains the following phases: again, although these are presented here as discrete for purposes of analysis, in reality they take a back-and-forth, integrated form. This is especially the case when, for example, you develop new insights via the writing process itself.

Different phases in the writing process

The writing process tends to take place in your production space, which involves working with ideas and structures as well as with the practical tools of the trade such as pens and pencils and computers and printers. It is generally agreed that the writing process includes the following phases.

Composing

This refers to the actual action of writing. As with everything else, it takes the form of an action–reflection process that involves multiple rounds of drafting, reading, revising and re-drafting, until you are reasonably satisfied that you have produced the text that best communicates the realities of your practices; this includes the learning generated through the experience of those realities. Writers tend to develop their own strategies for drafting and redrafting. My practice is to think about ideas over time: this can last from a day to several months or years, depending on the job in hand. I often think about one issue parallel to writing about other well-thought-out issues. When I begin writing I write in longhand or direct onto the computer; both strategies involve a lot of reading of the text as it appears followed by critical revising and re-reading. I also print off what I have produced and edit the printed version: somehow I see things more closely on a printed document than on a screen, but it has to be emphasised that people have their own preferences and ways of working. I then type up the amended text and repeat the process multiple times. Once I have a reasonably completed version of a section or of a chapter, I send it to colleagues for their critical review. (A reminder that, on the matter of critical colleagues, try to build up a circle of these colleagues who are willing to work with you, and always acknowledge their help as often as possible.)

Sometimes people think that their first draft will be their final draft. This is seldom the case. Even the most experienced writers will produce multiple drafts for any text, which is one of the reasons why it is important to write from the start: the day you begin your research programme is the day you also begin writing, even if this takes the form of a reflective diary.

Composing a text also requires competent self-organisation. Draw up an action plan for how you are going to produce your text and try to stick to this, though do adjust it if the circumstances require. Keep a record of the different versions you produce: always label and date new drafts and place everything in the same folder. I also keep the typescripts of earlier versions of a text until the final version is published: earlier versions can often contain nuggets of gold that will sometimes get lost in later revised versions. Remember to back up your computer documents and keep these on one or two memory sticks. You never know when you may accidentally drop your computer or spill a cup of tea over a keyboard.

Most important of all, aim to enjoy the process. Do not think, 'Oh, here we go again: another day of slog' (though probably everyone has days like this): think instead, 'Here is another day to showcase my talent, contribute to other people's thinking, and get my cap and gown'.

Editing and revising

This stage requires reflection, analysis and a possible re-think of the text you have produced so far. It involves reading your text both for content and meaning and for style. Approach this with a critical eye and check that it reads fluently. Listen to the voice in your head as you read: if it doesn't sound right, or if you don't understand something you have written, neither will anyone else, so change this so that it makes sense.

Editing can happen at different levels. You do light editing of sentences as you go, such as checking for spelling and grammar, choosing forms of words and generally tidying up the text. You do more serious editing at the level of paragraphs and sections, when you begin to move text around. This can often happen at the level of chapters when you cut and paste chunks of text from one place into another. This also requires intensive and frequent reads of the entire text; it can be difficult to keep the details of chapters in your head so maintain a summary of points in an accompanying paper or electronic notebook.

Revising is more serious in that it requires a disciplined and focused critique of what you have written. You will need to be honest with yourself and check that the entire chapter or dissertation hangs together coherently. If anything is adrift, put it right and then check and check again that it makes sense. If possible, ask a critical friend to read your text, and act on the advice they give. Be prepared to do the same for others: you need one another so form good alliances and be generous with your time and feedback.

Polishing

This is when you show (rightly) that you are prepared to take pains to get your text absolutely right. Some writers spend hours working with a text: they take out any repetition of words, make sure that the cadence of each sentence sounds just right, and check that the text provides a pleasurable and inspirational read. Ginger Rogers is reported to have asked Fred Astaire, 'Why do you practise so much?' He replied, 'To make it look easy.' It is your job to make it look easy.

Checking and proofreading

Learn how to proofread. Proofreading involves checking the accuracy of every word of your text for spelling and appropriateness, and every sentence for its meaning. You can do this in several ways: you can read the text to yourself, silently or aloud, and mark off each word as you go; you can ask a colleague or family member to proofread it too; you can proofread together; and you can pay a professional proofreader to read it. Take extreme care, if you chose to hire the services of a copyeditor, that they do not comment on the overall content of your text: this could be seen as guiding your writing, which would be beyond the expectations of a copyediting service, and if this should come to the attention of your supervisor or the validating institution, you could well be disqualified for dishonest practice.

Now the question arises, what does it take to produce a text that you can be proud of and does justice to your own intellectual strengths?

How do you produce a text you can be proud of?

Here is a range of strategies to help you produce a text you can be proud of.

Practise!

The most important advice is to practise. Over and over again. You learn to swim through swimming; you become a better swimmer through practising swimming. You can get better at a task through practising physically and mentally. Or use the strategy of mental rehearsal. Considerable research has been conducted to show that when practitioners, including athletes and musicians, rehearse their performances in their minds, their real-time performances are enhanced. When I am scheduled to do a presentation I run the video of the presentation in my head for several days; when it is time to do the actual presentation I act out the video. We all develop strategies that enable us to give of our best, not our second best. Practising and rehearsing are well-known practices. (And a note on spelling: in British English, the noun is spelt as 'practice' and the verb as 'practise'; in US spelling the spelling 'practice' is used for both verb and noun.)

Start before you are ready

This advice comes from Stephen Pressfield (2011) and makes good sense. If you wait until you are ready you will wait for ever. This applies to general life processes as well as to the practice of writing. Start anywhere; whatever you produce will get changed anyhow, so just start. Also do not feel you have to write chapters in the order in which they will appear in your final text: write anything and fit it into the overall text as different sections come off the computer. Just get on with it and don't look for excuses not to write.

Maintain regular contact with your text

Work with your text on a regular basis. If you leave it even for one day you will lose touch with it and waste valuable time reconnecting. Even if you write 50 words, write something and keep the text alive in your head and on your desk. It can sometimes help to set yourself a regular schedule for writing but different people work differently. Observe and get familiar with your own writing practices, and build up a momentum. Remember, however, that everyone has off-days, so use these to top up your reading or talk with colleagues about ideas or their research process. Do not use the fact that these days exist as an excuse not to write: be disciplined with yourself and do it.

Enjoy it

Aim to enjoy the process of writing. Writing original ideas can be exhilarating and draw on a creative sense that you may not have been aware of. Also remember that this may be the one and only chance you have to write something imaginative and scholarly where you can be sure of a captive audience who will pay close attention to your ideas. Just go for it and enjoy the process.

Why do you practise so much? To make it look easy.

Why do you write so much? Because it is enjoyable.

Summary

This chapter has been about getting ready to write your dissertation. It has emphasised that writing should be seen as a research process in itself, as part of the wider process of doing your research project. It has introduced the idea of working in and across conceptual spaces, in relation to designing and planning your dissertation, and in relation to the writing process itself.

A distinction has been made between telling a story and communicating with a reader, and outlines have been given of the different stages involved in the production of a text.

The next chapter outlines what a dissertation should look like and how this may be achieved.

EXERCISES

- Are you comfortable with the idea of different conceptual spaces? Can you see how this concept may be useful to you in your research?
- Are you clear about the difference between telling a story and communicating that story to a reader? Being able to articulate the difference is important.
- Explain to your colleagues how you can show the different levels in your research. Explain especially why your explanation is an explanation and not only a description.
- Check that you have explained how writing your research has involved moving through the different stages of composing, editing and revising. Also check that you are aware of the importance of thorough proofreading.
- Explain to your colleagues what is involved in learning to be a good writer.

Writing up your dissertation

Having spent time thinking about writing up your project, you now need to get on with it. You need to produce an account of the actions you have taken and what you have learned through doing so. However, it is not just a case of writing your research story: remember that you are in an institutional context with its own norms and traditions, and that yours may be among the many institutions that have turned action research into a standardised form that suits their traditions. So check with your supervisor what the institutional expectations are, and consult your handbook for guidance about how your dissertation should be written and how it will be judged. It is vital that you have the assessment criteria to hand, because you must fulfil these to get your degree. To repeat, your first priority at this point is to get your degree; you can use it for your own, possibly activist purposes later.

This chapter gives advice about how to do this. It contains the following:

1. Presenting your dissertation: possible structures and frameworks for writing
2. Criteria for testing the validity of knowledge claims
3. Some dos and don'ts

1. Presenting your dissertation: possible structures and frameworks for writing

The standard structure for writing a traditionalist research project is as follows:

- Abstract.
- Introduction.
- Aims and objectives.

- Literature review.
- Methodology and methods.
- Findings/preliminary results.
- Discussion.
- Conclusion.
- References.

You can find this structure everywhere, including on the Internet where you can read advice from different institutions about how to structure your report.

More elaborate structures that provide variations on the theme are also available in the literatures, including the following examples.

From Phillips and Pugh (2005: 60):

- Introduction (including aims).
- Literature survey (background theory as a review of the relevant literature).
- Method (data theory including a description of what has been done).
- Results (focal theory including what was found).
- Discussion (development of focal theory and suggestions for future work).
- Conclusions (summary and contribution).

From Murray (2002: 116–17):

- Introduction/Background/Review of literature:
    - summarize and evaluate books, articles, theses, etc.;
    - define the gap in the literature;
    - define and justify your project;

- Theory/Approach/Method/Materials/Subject:
    - define method, theoretical approach, instrument;
    - method of inquiry;
    - show links between your method and others;
    - justify your method.

- Analysis/Results:
    - report what you did, list the steps followed;
    - document the analysis, showing how you carried it out;
    - report what you found;
    - prioritise sections for the thesis or for an appendix.

- Interpretation/Discussion:
    - interpret what you found;
    - justify your interpretation;
    - synthesise results in illustrations, tables, graphs, etc.

- Conclusion/Implications/Recommendations:
    - for future research;
    - for future practice;
    - report issues which were beyond the scope of this study.

Institutions that expect these kinds of structures also expect the exercise of certain linguistic conventions, including:

- the text is written in an objective and dispassionate style;
- the passive voice is preferred;
- the report is written in the third person (the researcher did ...);
- there is little personal reflection;
- the work is presented as if you always knew what you know now: there is no reflection on personal learning.

These attributes belong to traditionalist forms of research but not, of course, to action research where there is a strong emphasis on personal involvement, taking action, and the use of the first person 'I'. The question then arises, is it possible to fit an action research account into a standardised structure? The answer is yes, and here is how to do it.

I have said throughout that the common-sense form of an action enquiry is something like:

What is my concern?

Why is this a concern? ... and so on, as outlined below.

If you are in a traditionalist institution you will have to fit this action research story into an accepted standardised frame: how to do this appears below as Structure 1. If you are in an institution that accepts action research, you can use action research questions to structure your report: how to do this appears below as Structure 2. Check with your supervisor what will be the best way to go and then draw on all the advice offered in this book to achieve the nominated criteria for assessing quality in a report (outlined below).

Here are the two possible structures.

Structure 1: Fitting an action research report into an accepted standard structure

The main headings for your report are:

- Abstract.
- Introduction.
- Background.
- Contexts for the research.
- Literature review.
- Methodology.
- Analysis.
- Research findings.
- Discussion.
- Conclusion.
- References.

Here is an example of how to fit your action research story into this structure.

Abstract

An abstract is a summary of what the research was about and its main findings. The abstract is about 200–300 words. It is not the place to use quotations or offer descriptions of practice. The abstract sets out the claim to knowledge, shows how its validity may be tested, and presents the main research findings. Say that this is work in progress, which you are now offering for public testing and critique.

Introduction

Introduce yourself and your research, and say where that research was located. Immediately tell the reader what you believe you have achieved (that is, state your claim to knowledge, probably in terms of having generated your personal theory of a particular aspect of your practice). Explain why you wanted to do the research in terms of wanting to find ways of living more fully in the direction of your values. Say why you adopted an action research approach: do not go into detail here as these ideas will be developed in your methodology chapter. Set out your conceptual frameworks (the main fields or key ideas that informed your research, such as justice, gender or ecological sustainability). Relate these issues to your values. Explain how your research possibly contributes to your field in terms of ideas for new practices and new theories. Give a brief summary of your chapters. Tell the reader anything specific you want them to know as they read your report.

Background

Set out the background to the research in terms of why you wanted to do it, and relate this to your values. You may have experienced bullying or marginalisation in the workplace, of yourself or someone else, and this has led you to find ways of creating more collegial practices. Perhaps you wanted to evaluate your practice and see whether you were living in accordance with your own values.

Contexts for the research

Set out the contexts for your research; perhaps analyse them in terms of specific categories such as the following.

Personal contexts

What was going on in your personal/professional life that inspired the research? Why did you want to investigate the situation you were in? How can the reader see your situation as it was?

Theoretical contexts

Explain how you related your research issue to the literatures. Why did you relate to the work of Paulo Freire (1972)? How did you relate to issues of ecological sustainability in the work of Zimmerman et al. (2001)? Were issues of gender, 'difference' or political action important? Show how you drew on the literature to develop and test your own thinking. The concepts you are dealing with come to form your conceptual frameworks.

Policy contexts

What was happening in terms of policy formation and implementation that affected you and your research? Could you work in a way that was consistent with your values? Or not? Did policy allocate funding to the groupings you were supporting? Was there a policy on assessment that was inappropriate for the work you were doing? How did policy support your own preferred way of working (or not)? Could you do anything about it? Could you contribute to policy through your research?

Any other relevant contexts

Mention here any other relevant contexts. Perhaps you are a member of a wildlife trust (significant if you are researching environmental issues); or you are in the police service (relevant for researching how to improve practices in rehabilitation centres). If you are partially sighted or a member of a political action group, say so. Let the reader see why your contexts are important to your research.

Literature review

Outline your key literatures. Do not just give a list of titles and a brief description of the text: aim rather to link your ideas with what you read in the literatures. Do not name drop, as in the fictional 'Brown (1993) said this, Black (2014) said that', or 'It is evident that this is a major issue (Black, 2014; Brown, 1993; White, 2002)'. If you use such citations, say briefly what was important about what Black, Brown and White said. Also make sure you have read any work that you reference: your examiner may know the work of Black very well and want to see what you have to say about it. Make sure you demonstrate critical engagement with the literatures: this is a main assessment criterion for academic work.

Methodology

In this section you will outline how you planned and carried out your research. Give details of the following (you may prefer to swap the plan/design and methodology sections if it suits your purposes):

- The research plan in terms of the following:
    o timescale for the research;
    o location for the research;
    o research participants: reasons for choosing them;
    o resources needed;
    o ethical issues, including permissions sought: include blank copies of letters requesting and granting permission in your appendices.

- Methodology:
    o why you used an action research approach rather than another;
    o how you monitored your actions and learning and, wherever possible, other people's actions and learning;
    o data-gathering strategies and forms of analysis and interpretation (see also below).

Gathering, analysing and interpreting data and generating evidence

Set out how you gathered the data, and which data-gathering techniques you used and why. Explain that you gathered data in relation to your research issue and about your action and learning; say that you did this in order to track changes in the action and look for improvement in terms of the realisation of your values. Explain how you sorted your data into categories of analysis, such as conversations and transcripts, and that you focused progressively as the data began to form patterns about how (and whether) you were influencing other people's and your own learning. Also explain how you analysed and interpreted the data to check whether your values were being realised, and how your values emerged as the standards by which you made judgements about the quality of your work. Show that you understand the difference between data and evidence, by explaining how you pulled out of the data those pieces that you wished to stand as evidence in support of your knowledge claim.

Say whether you found disconfirming data that showed that things were not going as you wished, so you had to rethink the situation. Explain how these data generated powerful evidence for your claim that you learned from your research experience.

Say that you were aware of the need to submit your data and evidence to the critical scrutiny of others. Say how you negotiated with colleagues to act as critical friends and validation groups, how often you met and what kind of feedback they offered on your work. Say whether you acted on the feedback, or not, and why.

Research findings

Now set out what you have found out, both about substantive issues, such as managing your time more efficiently and the need for good timekeeping. Link your findings with your knowledge claim. Explain what you know now that was not known before. You have created your personal theory of practice. You have incorporated ideas from others in the literature and reconfigured that knowledge in terms of your own context. You do not present your findings as final answers so much as tentative theories, which you are now subjecting to testing and critique. You demonstrate research responsibility by regarding solutions as provisional and open to refutation and modification.

One of the most important claims you can make is to have influenced learning for improving practice. This claim can be presented in terms of the following:

- Your own learning: you have become aware of your own capacity for learning.
- Your colleagues have learned from you and are trying things out for themselves.
- People in different professions have learned from you how to work together so that they too can influence learning.

Say that you have contributed to new practices by showing how people can change their own situations. Say that you have contributed to new theory by showing improvement in your own thinking and have deepened insights around your research issue. Through focused learning you have come to know differently; you are making your theory of practice public in order to test its validity and have it accepted as a legitimate contribution to knowledge of the field. Be confident: say that people should listen and learn from what you have done in terms of practice and knowledge generation. Say that you have demonstrated methodological rigour in presenting your research account. Say that you have articulated the criteria and standards of judgement by which the validity of your knowledge claims have been tested. It is as important to say that you have done these things as to have done them.

Discussion

Discuss how your findings might have implications for other people. Perhaps you have encouraged them to think in new ways. Perhaps they will begin to see the world through new eyes. Perhaps their new thinking will inspire them to develop new practices.

One of the most valuable (and difficult) things to do is to persuade people to begin to question prejudices. If you can do this, your research will have been worthwhile. Emphasise that people should be aware of their own capacity for learning, to see themselves always in process, on the edge, never at a point of closure. Express the hope that your work might promote a celebration of open-endedness and lack of certainty.

Conclusion

Tie everything up with a tidy conclusion that restates the main points.

References

Give a full and accurate list of references. Check that all citations used in the main body of the text appear also in the list of references.

Table 19.1 is a summary of and slightly different take on the above. It is adapted from McNiff (2014: 175–6).

Table 19.1   Mapping an action research narrative account onto a traditionalist research structure

Traditionalist research structure	Action research narrative account
Title: Write the title	**Title:** Write the title
Abstract: Write the abstract	**Abstract:** Write the abstract
Introduction, background, research question Write an introduction. Say what the background to the research was in terms of a hypothesis to be tested. Identify the research question. Explain the methodology and methods used.	**Introduction, background, research question** Write an introduction. Describe the focus of the research and issue to be investigated: 'What issue did I wish to investigate? What was my concern?' Explain the methodology and methods used. Describe the background and contexts: 'Why did I need to investigate this issue? Why was I concerned?' Give reasons for the project in terms of the values base of the study. Outline the contexts.
Methods, methodology, data, participants, ethics Explain all aspects of conducting the research, focusing on collecting and analysing data. Say who your research participants were and why you chose them. Issues of ethics.	**Methodology, methods, procedures, data, participants, ethics** Explain which methodology you used and why; say how you gathered data, who your participants were, how you ensured good ethical conduct. Say what you did to find new ways of working to encourage improvement in the social situation you were in. Tell the story of practice; explain how this became a research story. Issues of ethics.
Results, findings Outline results. Analysis of data in order to generate evidence. Produce quantitative and qualitative evidence; explain how you tested its validity.	**Results, findings** Say what happened when trying out new ways of working. What worked and what didn't; offer opinions about why it worked or didn't. Produce quantitative and qualitative evidence; explain how you have tested its validity.
Discussion, critique Discuss findings in relation to evidence; explain relevance as a contribution to knowledge of the field; accepting or refuting established theory.	**Discussion, critique** Discuss findings in relation to the evidence; explain relevance as a possible contribution to knowledge of the field (must be original for doctorates), for research, practice and theory; contributing to new thinking and practices, and new communities of enquiry.
Conclusions, summary Summarise main points, revisit research question; conclude by restating the importance and significance of the research for the field.	**Conclusions, summary** Summarise main points, revisit research question(s); conclude by restating the importance and significance of the research for the field and for your own and others' continuing learning.
References Give a full and accurate list of references, paying attention to academic conventions.	**References** Give a full and accurate list of references, paying attention to academic conventions.
Scholarly aspects Engage critically throughout with the literatures. Do a literature review. Develop arguments drawing on key concepts in the literatures; offer critique and different, new conceptions as appropriate.	**Scholarly aspects** Engage critically throughout with the literatures. Do a literature review where necessary and possibly at intervals throughout the text. Develop arguments drawing on key concepts in the literatures; offer critique and different, new conceptualisations as appropriate.

(Continued)

Table 19.1   (Continued)

Traditionalist research structure	Action research narrative account
Reflexive critique	**Reflexive critique**
Optional.	Compulsory. Demonstrate critical and dialectical reflection at all points, i.e. reflection on own learning, and on potential influence in wider domains.

Structure 2: Using action research questions to structure your report

The main headings for your report are:

- What was my concern?
- Why was I concerned?
- What kind of data could I gather to show the situation as it was and as it developed?
- What did I think I could do about it?
- What did I do about it?
- What kind of data and evidence did I produce to show the situation as it unfolded?
- How did I test the validity of my emergent knowledge claim?
- How did I ensure that any conclusions I came to were reasonably fair and accurate?
- How did I modify my practices in light of my evaluation?

What was my concern?

Say what your research was about: perhaps to find ways of developing collaborative relationships, helping early years children to read, improving leadership practices. This concern became the starting point for your research. You framed your question as 'How do I/we …?': 'How do I/we develop collaborative relationships?' or 'How do I/we improve my/our leadership practices?'

Why was I concerned?

Say how the situation represented the realisation or denial of your values. Doing so means articulating the values that inspire your work such as justice and care for the other. You undertook the research to find ways of staying consistent with your values. You may have been trying to find a solution or just trying to understand the situation better in order to live with it.

What kind of data could I gather to show the situation as it was and as it developed?

Explain that you first undertook some reconnaissance (Elliott, 1991) to establish what the situation was like. You gathered data using different techniques to show the situation as it was: for

example, you interviewed people and used excerpts from your transcripts; you had conversations with colleagues to gauge feelings about the situation. You kept careful records and stored
data under password protection. You used multimedia to gather still and moving images. Say
that you gathered data from at least three sources (triangulation).

What did I think I could do about it?

Outline your options for action. Say which ones you considered and what you decided to do,
whether alone or collaboratively. Explain how you thought about the situation, and how you
could perhaps address it. Were you looking for solutions, or testing out different strategies?

Also say that you were aware of the ethics of involving others within a social context where
your proposed action may have implications for them. How could you safeguard your own and
their wellbeing?

What did I do about it?

Say what course of action you decided on: this was only one possible course of action which
you were ready to change according to the changing situation. Say whether it was problematic
to go forward like this. Identify some of the practicalities. Who did you involve as your research
participants? How did you select them? How long did the research last? What resources did you
need? Also explain how you ensured good ethical conduct. Say that you produced ethics statements and letters requesting permission to do the research, and put blank copies of these letters
in your appendices together with letters granting permission and with names blanked out.

What kind of data and evidence did I produce
to show the situation as it unfolded?

Identify the data-gathering methods used to show the situation as it developed: these may have
been the same or different from those used earlier. Describe what happened and explain why
you think it happened and what was achieved. What was your part in the change? Did you
influence others' learning so that they changed their ways of working? Remember that the focus
of the research is your learning; you are monitoring and recording other people's learning in
relation to your own. You are helping people to think and change things for themselves.

How did I test the validity of my emergent
knowledge claim?

Say that you observed all methodological procedures in stating your claim to knowledge. Identify
your criteria and standards of judgement and explain how these helped you evaluate and test the
validity of your knowledge claim. You alerted your critical friends and validation groups to these,
and emphasised that you were producing explanatory rather than only descriptive accounts of
learning and action.

How did I ensure that any conclusions I came to were reasonably fair and accurate?

Say that you tested and critiqued your provisional conclusions throughout the research and the procedures you put in place to do so. You identified critical friends and negotiated the formation of a validation group to convene at regular intervals and offer critical feedback on your findings. Say what judgements they made, whether they agreed with your findings or asked you to re-think. Explain that you were testing your ideas throughout and not presenting these as established fact. Set out the main recommendations of your validation group and include any reports as an appendix to your report. Say how you acted on their advice and the outcomes.

How did I modify my practices in light of my evaluation?

Say how doing your research has led to new practices and new thinking (and theorising). Whose practice has changed, yours or other people's or both? Can you explain how new practices are improvements on previous ones? Are your values being fully or part-realised? On reflection, could/should you have done things differently?

Say that this endpoint of one research cycle becomes the beginning of a new enquiry to evaluate new practices and improve them where necessary. Do not feel you have to aim for an endpoint or final answer, because there is none. Your research story is about making the journey, not about arriving: we never arrive and have to be satisfied with 'nearly there'. This represents a new beginning that embeds its own intent. Say what your new beginnings involve and how you intend to live now with an eye to the future.

2. Criteria for testing the validity of knowledge claims

Several sets of criteria may be found in the literatures that claim to assess quality in action research. These include Heikkinen et al. (2012), Winter (1989) and Herr and Anderson (2005), as outlined in Chapter 16. Two further sets of criteria may be useful. These are from Habermas (1976) and Foucault (2001) (I have outlined these also in McNiff, 2014: 189–90).

Habermas (1976) identifies the following for judging the validity of knowledge claims:

- Is the claim comprehensible? Does it make sense and sound reasonable to the reader?
- Is it truthful? Is the researcher telling the truth? Do they provide a firm evidence base against which to test the validity of the claim?
- Is it authentic? Does the researcher demonstrate their authenticity by showing, over time and through interaction, that they have committed to living as fully as possible the values they explicitly espouse?
- Is it appropriate? Does the researcher show that they understand how historical and cultural forces form a normative background to the claim?

Linking with this set of criteria is a second set from Foucault (2001), who speaks about parrhesia (commonly understood as 'speaking one's truth'). This involves demonstrating:

- frankness: the speaker believes what they say and communicates the conviction of their commitment to others;
- truth: the speaker knows what truth is and can communicate it to others;
- courage: the speaker accepts the risk of telling the truth;
- criticism: the speaker exercises critique towards self and others;
- duty: the speaker accepts the responsibility of telling the truth.

In relation to these two sets of criteria, you need to show that you have:

- conducted rigorous research: you tested the validity of your ideas within a disciplined methodological and epistemological framework;
- engaged in scholarly enquiry: you tested the validity of your ideas against the ideas of people in the literature;
- told the truth: you went through rigorous validation procedures, to test the validity of what you were saying; you did not expect people simply to take your word for it;
- developed confidence in your personal knowledge: you believed your claims were worthy of merit;
- displayed courage and tenacity: you got your claim validated and legitimated through informed debate;
- exercised provisionality: you believed that you were right, but you acknowledged that you may have been mistaken;
- lived your values in practice: you were prepared to stand up for what you believed in.

Other criteria are available, some of which I have explored throughout: the idea of not seeking answers so much as asking questions is paramount.

3. Some common-sense dos and don'ts when writing

Here are some common-sense dos and don'ts when writing up your research project:

Do

- Make your dissertation interesting and relevant. Aim to engage your reader's attention and interest throughout. Keep it under control and disciplined.
- Engage critically with the literatures and with your own thinking. Be courageous in speaking your mind but be careful not to make unwarranted statements. Be positive: critique the ideas but never the person.
- Keep to the point. Keep your arguments to the point and build them systematically.
- Write in an everyday, easy form of language: not chatty or informal, but normal. Don't use pretentious language: say 'use' rather than 'utilise'.
- Although you can and should use 'I', keep it in moderation. A dissertation is primarily about issues, actions and learning, less about you personally. The reader wants to know what you have learned, not what you had for breakfast.

- Write for that reader. Do not assume they know anything about your study: they don't.
- Keep to a word count. Generally you are allowed 10% over or under the stipulated word limit. Check with your supervisor and handbook. Write the number of words on the front of your dissertation.
- Use a dictionary. Check that your grammar and spelling are impeccable.
- Be prepared to work hard. Be prepared to practise.
- Enjoy the experience.

Don't

- Ramble: keep to the point. Remember to follow the golden thread, and make sure you keep your reader with you.
- Drop names, especially out of context or without explaining what the 'Name' said. If you cite a text, make sure you have read it.
- Make unwarranted statements: your reader will expect to see authenticated evidence for any knowledge claim.
- Take quotations out of context: this can be misleading for your reader. Besides, they may know the text you are speaking about and pick you up on errors.
- Plagiarise: in an extreme form this can lead to severe penalties: in a mild form it will lose you credit.
- Try to be too clever. Write your dissertation as a coherent story. Show how your findings and claims link back to your research question.
- Procrastinate. Start before you are ready. In the time you spend wondering what to do in order to put off writing, you could have written three sentences. Start anywhere and go for it.

The owner of the shop next door to mine, all those years ago, had a mantra: 'Retail is detail'. He was right. You are selling ideas and in presenting your dissertation you are selling yourself. To paraphrase Rorty (2006), take care of the detail and the dissertation will take care of itself.

Summary

This chapter has focused on the business of writing up your dissertation. It has outlined different structures for a dissertation, and how you can map a form appropriate for an action enquiry onto a traditionalist form of structure that will be appropriate for university accreditation.

The next chapter provides a conclusion to the book.

EXERCISES

- Are you comfortable with the ideas of different structures for different kinds of writing? Are you clear about how to structure your dissertation and what goes into the different parts?
- Can you judge the quality of your dissertation yourself? How would you do this? Give your dissertation in draft to a colleague and ask for their critical feedback.
- As a final exercise, produce a good top copy and submit it.

PART VII

How do I show the significance of my knowledge?

This part comprises one final chapter: 'The significance of it all'. It explains how, through doing your research, you have given deeper meaning to your own life, to the lives of others and to the life of the world.

The significance of it all

So, look what you have done.

In her *Men in Dark Times*, Hannah Arendt (1967) showed how, in times of deepest trouble, exceptional people stepped forward to provide a guiding light. You are that exceptional person, within a lifeworld that is potentially always in dark times. Through undertaking your action research, you have given deeper meaning to life: for yourself, for other people, and for the world. You have lit a candle, as they say, instead of grumbling about the dark. Here is what this looks like.

1. Giving deeper meaning to your life

You are making sense of what you are doing personally and are giving deeper meaning to your life in the following ways.

You are showing what it means to live your values in practice

You have thought about what gives meaning to your life and have found ways of showing this in action. Values are not defined by words: you practise compassion, not just define it in words. Your values have come alive through how you live. You remove the spider from the bath; you save the meadow mouse and leave it free to go and you do not expect anything in return. Values emerge when you give your time and energy to helping others or to doing your study.

You have become an actor in the world

You have challenged your own assumptions about the nature of relationships and are clear about your contribution to life. You are not a bystander watching the world go by: you are part of it; you contribute to it as life contributes to you. You use your space on earth well, for your own and other people's benefit. You have moved from being a participant to being an actor in the world; from saying, 'I wish I could do …' to doing it. You have become political by taking action in the world. Through your studies you are contributing to stopping wars.

You have challenged the hegemony of academic knowledge and won

You have shown that you are a powerful knower; you know what you are doing in your salon and your ward and can explain this to anyone. You have read the theories-in-the-literatures and can use these to strengthen your conceptual knowledge. Whether you are a shopfloor practitioner or an academic practitioner, you have contributed to the body of knowledge through the production of your dissertation. You share this knowledge with others so that they can do the same.

You have overcome anxieties about higher education study

You have changed your language to 'I can' and you know what it takes. You have embraced multiple identities: you are still a shopkeeper and you are now also an academic; you are still an academic and you are now also a shopkeeper. It is your choice how you identify yourself but you are no longer constricted by manufactured rules that tell you to remember your place. Your place is where the practical and intellectual action is and you can explain what this means.

You have learned the meaning of hard work and tenacity

Who thought you would do it? Gone are the doubts about achieving an appropriate academic standard: you have exercised self-discipline and stuck with it and done it. Now you can use your qualifications to promote your own and other people's wellbeing. You may still be shy but now you are a person to be reckoned with.

You have brought something new into the world

You have knowingly entered the political world, and you have exercised your influence in other people's thinking. The world is a better place because you are in it and because of your contribution. You encourage others to believe this about themselves. You say, 'Things do not have to be as they are. We can change them'. You work systematically with others to do so; you celebrate small triumphs and set out to do more.

You have set in motion new relationships of power among people

You no longer believe that power is a thing that belongs only to the privileged few. Power is in people's relationships as they talk together about how they should live. You include others and they include you: no matter what the condition of mind and body, or any kind of difference, they are part of you and you are part of them. Life is enriched because you and they share it.

The day will come when I say 'I will die tomorrow'. Perhaps it will be today. I know that my life has been worthwhile.

2. Meaning for others

Your work has meaning for others: you can influence their thinking and actions in the following ways.

You have enabled others to see that it can be done; you have become a trailblazer

Others can see what you have done. They feel your influence in your workplace and in the public square. You have shown them that you can overcome barriers, and they have learned from your example. You have become a beacon: you show others the way and light the path.

You have set precedents in your workplace

You have developed management styles that respect other people's knowledge. You create opportunities for them to contribute. You send round an email saying, 'Cakes at coffee time!' You pair up seniors with juniors; every child is involved in the school play. You promote further study and professional education. You speak about your own achievements and say 'You can do this too'. You have set new achievable precedents; you encourage all to have a go. You give them the courage to try.

You have defended the defenceless

You have defended those who are not able to defend themselves. You have spoken out for disadvantaged people and shown care. You let someone go before you in the post office. You have actively fought bullying in all shapes and forms. You have withstood the intellectual bullying of traditionalist epistemologies and done your action research, and you can show that your work meets appropriate academic standards.

You have influenced other people's thinking and practices

You have explained how you have given deeper meaning to your life and are showing others how they can do so too. Meaning emerges through interaction. You show what this looks like in your dissertation, and you explain its significance. You mind your language; you take your second reaction. You nudge people along and support their thinking as they go.

You have encouraged others to speak and act for themselves

You have made yourself activist and encouraged others to do the same. You are not victims: you are knowledgeable people who can use that knowledge to take action in the world. Others may think they cannot do it; you have shown them that they can. If you can do it, so can they. You have made yourself into an intellectual and practical resource for them to draw on.

3. Meaning for the world

You have influenced new thinking for new practices globally. You have shown how personal enquiry becomes a starting point for personal, social and organisational development. Through putting your dissertation on your website and speaking about your studies at staff meetings and through your blog you show how people can change their thinking and actions and influence others to do the same.

You have demonstrated that practitioners' knowledge and theories are as valid as traditionalist academic ones

Although the world is moving towards increasingly closed forms of thinking and acting you show that it does not need to be like this. You have challenged closed forms and opened up new vistas. You show that all forms of knowledge are integrated in a person's life, that their life is part of others'. You have achieved legitimation for your research and you encourage others to do so too.

You have contributed to a new epistemology

In doing this you have contributed to Schön's (1995) idea of a new epistemology for a new scholarship. You have brought new practice-based ways of thinking into your institution: they will not go away as long as you keep promoting them. You refuse to be coerced or cajoled into remaining silent: you are a knower and you have the degree to show this.

You have contributed to new understandings of 'the university'

Because you are in it, you have turned the university into a workplace where people work together. You have challenged established forms of knowledge and demand evidence for their usefulness in the world. You refuse to allow your action research to become domesticated and mainstreamed: you keep your thinking on the move. You continually interrogate and adjust your current thinking and find new ways forward.

You have made the world a fairer and more compassionate place

Your dissertation shows how you have contributed to making the world a fairer and more compassionate place. The fact that you have produced your dissertation shows what can happen when you challenge established ways of thinking and being. Your dissertation now has its rightful place on university shelves, alongside other traditionalist dissertations. It will soon be joined by those of others whose thinking you are influencing. Put them on your website also: they will not go away.

You have enabled others to say 'I can do this too'

You have helped them to see themselves as knowledgeable and capable practitioners and theorists who are able to take control of their own professionalism and profession. You have helped them to see that things do not need to be as they are. Whatever people have created can be recreated. But you do need to work together: no one can change systems on their own, though they can start the process of change.

You have contributed to reconceptualising the idea of theory

You have shown the legitimacy of practitioners' personal theories of practice in terms of their usefulness for the world. By doing so you have contributed to the idea that theory may take a dynamic, living form as well as its currently dominantly static abstract form.

Here is an excerpt from a transcript of a conversation with Noam Chomsky, in 1995. We were speaking about teachers and teaching: what was said applies equally to every one of us as learners.

> Noam: Teaching [at primary level] ought to be very similar to graduate teaching in the sciences. Teachers might put different questions at different levels but it is not about pouring water into children's ears like filling a bowl of water. Children have to explore. If they are going to learn anything it's going to be by their own exploration. In the course of that they are also going to challenge. If they are not convinced by what the teacher says they should have the right and the confidence to pursue their own convictions. As far as I can see that should happen at all levels.
>
> Jean: It should but it doesn't.
>
> Noam: It doesn't but it can.

You have a voice: speak with it. You have a pen: write with it. Use both to help others see how they can celebrate their talents too, and make their contributions to the world.

References

Abram, D. (2010) *Becoming Animal: An Earthly Cosmology*. New York: Random House.

Achbar, M. (1994) *Manufacturing Dissent: Noam Chomsky and the Media*. Montréal, Québec: Black Rose Books.

Adams, G. (2008) 'Module 6: Practitioner Research and Knowledge Transfer'. Khayelitsha: St Mary's University College MA Programme.

Ainscow, M. (1999) *Understanding the Development of Inclusive Schools*. London: Routledge.

Al-Abdallah, A. (2013) 'From Skills to Knowledge in Basic Mathematics', in J. McNiff (ed.), *Teacher Enquiry Bulletin: Action Research for Teachers in Qatar*. Qatar: Supreme Education Council and Tribal. Available online at www.jeanmcniff.com/userfiles/file/qatar/Qatar_Action_Research_booklet_email.pdf (last accessed 30/10/16).

al-Fugara, S. (2010) 'Developing inclusion in schools: How do I integrate students with additional educational needs into mainstream schooling?', in J. McNiff (ed.), *Teacher Enquiry Bulletin: Action Research for Teachers in Qatar*. Qatar: Supreme Education Council. Available online at www.jeanmcniff.com/qatar.asp (accessed 31/01/17).

Appadurai, A. (1996) The right to research, *Globalizations, Societies and Education*, 4 (2): 167–77.

Apple, M.W. (1993) *Official Knowledge: Democratic education in a conservative age*. New York: Routledge.

Al Shorman, H. (2010) 'How do I help my students in Grade 12 Advanced Chemistry to improve their academic standards?', in J. McNiff (ed.), *Teacher Enquiry Bulletin: Action Research for Teachers in Qatar*. Qatar: Supreme Education Council. Available online at www.jeanmcniff.com/qatar.asp (accessed 31/01/17).

Arendt, H. (1958) *The Human Condition*. Chicago: Chicago University Press.

Arendt, H. (1967) *Men in Dark Times*. San Diego, CA: Harcourt, Brace and World.

Arendt, H. (2006) *Eichmann in Jerusalem: A Report on the Banality of Evil*. London: Penguin.

Argyris, C. and Schön, D. (1978) *Organisational Learning: A Theory of Action Perspective*. Reading, MA: Addison Wesley.

Bakhtin, M. (1981) *The Dialogic Imagination* (ed. M. Holquist). Austin: University of Texas Press.

Ball, S. (2003) The teacher's soul and the terrors of performativity, *Journal of Education Policy*, 18 (2): 215–28.

Barthes, R. (1970) *S/Z*. New York: Hill & Wang.

Bassey, M. (1999) *Case Study Research in Educational Settings*. Buckingham: Open University Press.

Bayat, A. (2009) *Life as Politics: How Ordinary People Change the Middle East*. Cairo: The American University in Cairo Press.

Bereiter, C. and Scardamalia, M. (1987) *The Psychology of Written Composition*. Hillsdale, NJ: Lawrence Erlbaum.

Berger, J. (2007) *Hold Everything Dear: Dispatches on Survival and Resistance*. London: Verso.

Berlin, I. (1990) *The Crooked Timber of Humanity* (ed. H. Hardy). London: John Murray.

Berlin, I. (1997) *Against the Current: Essays in the History of Ideas* (ed. H. Hardy). London: Pimlico.

Berlin, I. (1998) *The Proper Study of Mankind: An Anthology of Essays*. London: Pimlico.

Berlin, I. (2002) *Freedom and Its Betrayal: Six Enemies of Human Liberty*. London: Chatto & Windus.

Bernstein, B. (2000) *Pedagogy, Symbolic Control and Identity: Theory, Research, Critique*. Lanham, MD: Rowan & Littlefield.

Birks, M. and Mills, J. (2015) *Grounded Theory: A Practical Guide* (2nd edn). London: Sage.

Bleach, J. (2013) 'Community Action Research: Providing Evidence of Values and Virtue', in J. McNiff (ed.), *Value and Virtue in Practice-Based Research*. Poole: September Books, pp. 17–32.

Bleach, J. (2016) 'Sharing the Learning from Community Action Research', in J. McNiff (ed.), *Values and Virtues in Higher Education Research*. Abingdon, Oxon: Routledge, pp. 126–40.

Bloom, H. (2000) *How to Read and Why*. New York: Scribner.

Bolt, R. (1960) *A Man for All Seasons*. London: Heinemann Educational.

Bourdieu, P. (1984) *Distinction: A Social Critique of the Judgement of Taste*. London: Routledge and Kegan Paul.

Bourdieu, P. (1988) *Homo Academicus*. Cambridge: Polity.

Boyer, E. (1990) *Scholarship Reconsidered: Priorities of the Professoriate*. Princeton, NJ: Carnegie Foundation for the Advancement of Teaching.

Branson, C., Franken, M. and Penney, D. (2016) 'Reconceptualising Middle Leadership in Higher Education: A Transrelational Approach', in J. McNiff (ed.), *Values and Virtues in Higher Education Research*. Abingdon, Oxon: Routledge, pp. 155–70.

Brinkmann, S. (2012) *Qualitative Inquiry in Everyday Life*. London: Sage.

Brookfield, S. (1987) *Developing Critical Thinkers*. Buckingham: Open University Press.

Brydon-Miller, M. (2008) 'Ethics and Action Research: Deepening our Commitment to Principles of Social Justice and Redefining', in P. Reason and H. Bradbury (eds), *The SAGE Handbook of Action Research: Participative Inquiry and Practice*. London: Sage, pp. 199–210.

Buber, M. (1937) *I and Thou* (trans. R. G. Smith). Edinburgh: Clark.

Bullough, R. and Pinnegar, S. (2004) 'Guidelines for quality in autobiographical forms of self-study', *Educational Researcher*, 30 (2): 13–21.

Burke, T. (1994) *Dewey's New Logic: A Reply to Russell*. Chicago: University of Chicago Press.

Burke, T. (1997) 'How can I improve my practice as a learning support teacher?' MA dissertation, Dublin: University of the West of England.

Butler-Kisber, L. (2010) *Qualitative Inquiry*. Los Angeles, CA: Sage.

Button, L. (1974) *Developmental Group Work with Adolescents*. London: Hodder Arnold.

Callahan, R. (1962) *Education and the Cult of Efficiency*. Chicago: University of Chicago Press.

Carr, N. (2010) *The Shallows: How the Internet is Changing the Way We Read, Think and Remember*. New York: Norton.

Carr, W. (1995) *For Education*. Buckingham: Open University Press.

Carr, W. and Kemmis, S. (1986) *Becoming Critical: Education, Knowledge and Action Research*. London: Falmer.

Chambers, R. (1993) *Challenging the Professions: Frontiers of rural development*. London: Intermediate Publications.

Chambers, R. (2008) 'PRS, PLA and Pluralism: Practice and Theory', in P. Reason and H. Bradbury (eds), *The SAGE Handbook of Action Research: Participative Inquiry and Practice*, pp. 297–318.

Chan, N., Svay, V., Houy, C., Sano, R., Edvardsen, O. and Ingstad, B. (2014) 'Community Workshop: A qualitative study on a rural workshop run by mine amputees in Samloth District, Cambodia.' Paper presented at Seminar on the Presentation of Research Findings, Battambang Provice, Cambodia. June 2014.

Charmaz, K. (2014) *Constructing Grounded Theory* (2nd edn). London: Sage.

Chevalier, J.M. and Buckles, D.J. (2013) *Theory and Method for Engaged Inquiry.* Abingdon, Oxon: Routledge.

Coghlan, D. and Brannick, T. (2014) *Doing Action Research in Your Own Organization.* London: Sage.

Chomsky, N. (1965) *Aspects of the Theory of Syntax.* Cambridge, MA: Massachusetts Institute of Technology.

Chomsky, N. (1969) *American Power and the New Mandarins.* New York: Pantheon Books.

Chomsky, N. (1986) *Knowledge of Language: Its Nature, Origin and Use.* New York: Praeger.

Chomsky, N. (1987) 'The Responsibility of Intellectuals', in N. Chomsky (ed. J. Peck), *The Chomksy Reader.* London: Serpent's Tail, pp. 59–136.

Chomsky, N. (1991) *Media Control: The Spectacular Achievements of Propaganda.* New York: Seven Stories.

Chomsky, N. (1992) *Chronicles of Dissent.* Stirling, Scotland: AK Press.

Cluskey, M. (1997) 'How can I facilitate learning amongst my leaving certificate applied students?' MA Dissertation, Dublin: University of the West of England.

Cochran-Smith, M. and Lytle, S. (2008) 'Teacher Research as Stance', in P. Reason and H. Bradbury (eds), *The SAGE Handbook of Action Research: Participative Inquiry and Practice,* pp. 39–49.

Coghlan, D. and Shani, A.B. (eds) (2016) *Action Research in Business and Management.* London: Sage.

Collins, J. (2010) *Bring on the Books for Everybody.* Durham, NC: Duke University Press.

Crawshaw, S. and Jackson, J. (2010) *Small Acts of Resistance.* New York: Sterling.

Creswell, J. (2007) *Qualitative Inquiry and Research Design.* Thousand Oaks, CA: Sage.

Dadds, M. (1995) *Passionate Enquiry and School Development: A Story about Teacher Action Research.* London: Falmer.

Dadds, M. and Hart, S. (2001) *Doing Practitioner Research Differently.* London: Routledge.

Darbey, L., McNiff, J. and Fields, P. (2013) *Evidence Based Handbook: Guidance Case Studies.* Dublin: National Centre for Guidance in Education. Available online at www.ncge.ie/uploads/Evidence_based_handbook-final.pdf (last accessed 30/10/16).

Davids, N. and Waghid, Y. (2017) *Educational Leadership in Becoming.* Abingdon: Oxon: Routledge.

De Certeau, M. (1984) *The Practice of Everyday Life.* Berkeley, CA: University of California Press.

Deem, R., Hillyard, S. and Reed, M. (2007) *Knowledge, Higher Education, and the New Managerialism.* Oxford: Oxford University Press.

Denzin, N. and Lincoln, Y. (1998) *Collecting and Interpreting Qualitative Materials.* Thousand Oaks, CA: Sage.

Department for Business, Innovation and Skills (2016) *Success as a Knowledge Economy: Teaching Excellence, Social Mobility and Student Choice.* London: HMSO. Available online at www.gov.uk/government/uploads/system/uploads/attachment_data/file/523396/bis-16-265-success-as-a-knowledge-economy.pdf (last accessed 30/10/16).

Derrida, J. (1997) *Of Grammatology.* Baltimore, MD: John Hopkins.

Dewey, J. (1933) *How We Think.* Boston, MA: D.C. Heath.

Dweck, C. (2006) *Mindset: The New Psychology of Success.* New York: Ballantine.

Dyrberg, T. (1997) *The Circular Structure of Power.* London: Verso.

Early Learning Initiative (ELI) (2012) *Submission to the Joint Committee on Jobs, Social Protection and Education on Educational Disadvantage.* Dublin: National College of Ireland.

Easterly, W. (2013) *The Tyranny of Experts.* New York: Basic Books.

Edvardsen, O. (2006) 'En nettverk av førstehjelpere i det mindelagte Nord-Irak.' Masters Dissertation. Tromsø: University of Tromsø.

Edwards, D. (1998) *The Compassionate Revolution.* Totnes, Devon: Green Books.

Eig, J. (2010) *Get Capone.* New York: Simon & Schuster.

Eikeland, O. (2006) Condescending ethics and action research: An extended review article, *Action Research*, 4 (1): 37–47.

Elliott, J. (1991) *Action Research for Educational Change*. Buckingham: Open University Press.

Ellis, V. and McNicholl, V. (2015) *Transforming Teacher Education*. London: Bloomsbury.

Engeström, Y. (1987) *Learning by Expanding: An Activity Theoretical Approach to Developmental Research*. Helsinki: Orienta-konsultit.

Fairclough, N. (2003) *Analysing Discourse: Textual Analysis of Social Research*. Abingdon, Oxon: Routledge.

Fairclough, N. (2015) *Language and Power* (3rd edition). Abingdon: Routledge.

Feldman, A. (2003) Validity and quality in self-study, *Educational Researcher* 32 (3): 26–8.

Festinger, L. (1957) *A Theory of Cognitive Dissonance*. Stanford: Stanford University Press.

Feynman, R. (2001) *The Pleasure of Finding Things Out*. London: Penguin.

Foucault, M. (2001) *Fearless Speech*. Los Angeles, CA: Semiotext(e).

Frankl, V. (1963) *Man's Search for Meaning*. New York: Pocket.

Freire, P. (1972) *Pedagogy of the Oppressed*. New York: Seabury.

Fromm, E. (1956) *The Art of Loving*, World Perspectives (Vol. 9). New York: Harper & Row.

Furlong, J. and Oancea, A. (2005) *Assessing Quality in Applied and Practice-Based Research: A Framework for Discussion*. Oxford: Oxford University Department of Educational Studies.

Gadamer, H.-G. (2004) *Truth and Method* (2nd revised edn). London: Continuum.

Gärdenfors, P. (2004) Conceptual spaces as a framework for knowledge representation, *Mind & Matter*, 2 (2): 9–27.

Garnett, J., Costley, C. and Workman, B. (eds) (2009) *Work Based Learning*. Middlesex: Middlesex University Press.

Gee, J.P. (2005) *An Introduction to Discourse Analysis* (2nd edn). Abingdon: Routledge

Geertz, C. (1973) *The Interpretation of Cultures*. New York: Basic Books.

Geras, N. (1995) *Solidarity in the Conversation of Humankind*. London: Verso.

Gibbons, M., Limoges, C., Nowotny H., Schwartzman, S., Scott, P. and Trow, M. (1994) *The New Production of Knowledge*. London: Sage.

Gibbs, C.J. (2006) *To be a Teacher: Journeys towards authenticity*. Auckland: Pearson Prentice-Hall.

Giroux, H. (2003) *The Abandoned Generation*. New York: Palgrave Macmillan.

Glenn, M. (2006) 'Working with collaborative projects: my living theory of a holistic educational practice'. PhD, University of Limerick, 2007. Available online at www.jeanmcniff.com/glennabstract.html (last accessed 30/10/16).

Goethe, W. (1988[1790]) '*Die Metamorphose der Pflanzen*', reproduced as 'The Metamorphosis of Plants' in D. Miller (ed.), *Goethe: Scientific Studies*. New York: Suhrkamp.

Graff, S. (2003) *Clueless in Academe*. New Haven, CT: Yale University Press.

Gray, J. (1995) *Enlightenment's Wake: Politics and Culture and the Close of the Modern Age*. London: Routledge.

Greenwood, D. and Levin, M. (2007) *Introduction to Action Research* (2nd edn). Thousand Oaks, CA: Sage.

Guattari, F. (2008) *The Three Ecologies*. London: Continuum.

Gungisa, N. (2008) 'Module 6: Research and Knowledge Transfer'. Khayelitsha: St Mary's University College MA Programme.

Habermas, J. (1975) *Legitimation Crisis* (trans. T. McCarthy). Boston, MA: Beacon.

Habermas, J. (1976) *Communication and the Evolution of Society*. London: Heinemann.

Habermas (1987) *The Theory of Communicative Action Volume Two: The Critique of Functionalist Reason*. Cambridge: Polity.

Habermas, J. (1998) *The Inclusion of the Other* (edited by C. Cronin and P. De Greiff). Cambridge, MA: MIT Press.

Harré, R. and von Langenhove, L. (1999) *Positioning Theory*. Oxford: Blackwell.

Hattie, J. (2015) *What Doesn't Work in Education: The Politics of Distraction*. London: Pearson. Available online at http://visible-learning.org/wp-content/uploads/2015/06/John-Hattie-Visible-Learning-creative-commons-book-free-PDF-download-What-doesn-t-work-in-educa tion_the-politics-of-distraction-pearson-2015.pdf (last accessed 30/10/16).

Hay, D. (2006) *Something There: The Biology of the Human Spirit*. London: Darton, Longman and Todd.

Hayes, J.R. and Flower, L.S. (1980) 'Identifying the Organisation of Writing Processes', in L.W. Gregg and E.R. Steinberg (eds), *Cognitive Processes in Writing*. Hillsdale, NJ: Lawrence Erlbaum.

Heikkinen, H., Huttunen, R., Syrjäläm, L. and Pesonen, J. (2012) 'Action research and narrative inquiry: five principles for validation revisited', *Educational Action Research*, 20 (1): 5–21.

Helyer, R. (ed.) (2015) *The Work-Based Learning Student's Handbook* (2nd edn). London: Palgrave.

Heron, J. and Reason, P. (2001) 'The Practice of Co-Operative Inquiry: Research "with" rather than "on" People', in P. Reason and H. Bradbury (eds), *Handbook of Action Research*. London: Sage, pp. 179–88.

Herr, K. and Anderson, G. (2005) *The Action Research Dissertation*. Los Angeles, CA: Sage.

Higgs, J. and Titchen, A. (2001) *Practice Knowledge and Expertise in the Health Professions*. Oxford: Butterworth Heinemann.

Hiim, H. (2015) *Læreren som forsker: Yrkespedagogiske perspektiver* ['The Teacher as Researcher: Perspectives on Vocational Pedagogy'] (edited by O. Eikeland, H. Hiim and E. Schwencke). Oslo: Gyldendal Akademisk Forlag.

Hiim, H. (2016) 'Educational Action Research and the Development of Professional Teacher Knowledge', in E. Gunnarsson, H. P. Hansen, B. Nielsen and B. Steen (eds), *Action Research for Democracy*. Abingdon, Oxon: Routledge, pp. 147–61.

Hillesum, E. (1983) *An Interrupted Life: The Diaries of Etty Hillesum* (trans. A. Pomerans). New York: Pantheon.

Hunt, C. (2016) 'Why Me? Reflections on Using the Self In and As Action Research', in J. McNiff (ed.), *Values and Virtues in Higher Education Research*. Abingdon, Oxon: Routledge, pp. 48–63.

Husum, H. (2003) *Tracks of blood: Studies of trauma and trauma systems in the rural South*. Tromsø: University of Tromsø.

Husum, H., Gilbert, M. and Wisborg, T. (2000) *Save Lives, Save Limbs*. Penang: Third World Network.

Ilyenkov, E. (1977) *Dialectical Logic*. Moscow: Progress.

James, M. (2013) 'Developing a theopraxis: How can I legitimately be a Christian teacher-educator?' PhD thesis, Leeds: University of Leeds.

Jenkins, R. (1992) *Pierre Bourdieu*. London: Routledge.

Jørgensen, M. and Phillips, L. (2002) *Discourse Analysis as Theory and Method*. London: Sage.

Kahneman, D. (2011) *Thinking Fast and Slow*. London: Penguin.

Kemmis, S. (2006) Participatory action research and the public sphere, *Educational Action Research*, 14 (4): 459–76.

Kemmis, S., Hardy, I., Wilkinson, J., Edwards-Groves, C. and Lloyd, A. (2011) 'On being "stirred" into practice.' Unpublished manuscript. Charles Sturt University, School of Education, Wagga Wagga, Australia.

Laclau, E. and Mouffe, C. (1985) *Hegemony and Socialist Strategy: Towards a Radical Democratic Politics*. London: Verso.

Lankshear, C. and Knobel, M. (2011) *Literacies: Social, Cultural and Historical Perspectives*. New York: Peter Lang.

Lather, P. (1991) *Getting Smart: Feminism research and pedagogy with/in the postmodern*. London: Routledge.

Lewin, K. (1946) Action research and minority problems, *Journal of Social Issues*, 2 (4): 34–46.

Lewin, M. (1993) *Complexity: Life on the Edge*. London: Phoenix.

Lovelock, J. (2006) *The Revenge of Gaia*. London: Penguin.

Loy, D. (2010) *The World Is Made of Stories*. Boston, MA: Wisdom Publications.

Lyotard, J.-F. (1984) *The Postmodern Condition: A Report on Knowledge*. Manchester: Manchester University Press.

MacBeath, J. (2006) *School Inspection and Self-Evaluation: Working with the New Relationship*. Abingdon, Oxon: Routledge.

Macmurray, J. (1961) *Persons in Relation*. London: Faber and Faber.

Marlin, R. (2002) *Propaganda and the Ethics of Persuasion*. Ontario, Canada: Broadview.

Mason, J. (2002) *Researching Your Own Practice: The Discipline of Noticing*. Abingdon, Oxon: Routledge.

Mason, M. (ed.) (2008) *Complexity Theory and the Philosophy of Education*. Oxford: Blackwell.

McCarthy, M. (1994) 'Teaching an English Novel to First Year Students', in J. McNiff and Ú. Collins (eds), *A New Approach to In-Career Development for Teachers in Ireland*. Bournemouth: Hyde Publications.

McDonnell, P. (2017) *What Happened to Nursing?* Poole: September Books.

McDonnell, P. and McNiff, J. (2016) *Action Research for Nurses*. London: Sage.

McLaughlin, C. and Ayubayeva, N. (2015) 'It is the research of self experience': feeling the value in action research, *Educational Action Research*, 23 (1): 51–67.

McNiff, J. (1989) 'An explanation for an individual's educational development through the dialectic of action research'. PhD thesis, Bath: University of Bath.

McNiff, J. (2000) *Action Research in Organisations*. London: Routledge.

McNiff, J. (2003) 'Peace Education and Other Stories of Violence'. Paper presented at the Ben Gurion University of the Negev, February. Available online at www.jeanmcniff.com/items.asp?id=82&term=peace+education.

McNiff, J. (2010) *Action Research for Professional Development: Concise advice for new and experienced action researchers*. Poole: September Books.

McNiff, J. (2013) *Action Research: Principles and Practice* (3rd edn). Abingdon: Routledge.

McNiff, J. (2014) *Writing and Doing Action Research*. London: Sage.

McNiff, J. (2016a) *Action Research for Professional Development: Concise Advice for New (and Experienced) Action Researchers* (2nd edn). Poole: September Books.

McNiff, J. (2016b) *You and Your Action Research Project* (4th edn). Abingdon, Oxon: Routledge.

McNiff, J. (2016c) *Writing Up Your Action Research*. Abingdon, Oxon: Routledge.

McNiff, J. (2017) *Writing Research: Researching Writing*. Poole: September Books.

McNiff, J. and Collins, Ú. (1994) *A New Approach to In-Career Education for Teachers in Ireland*. Bournemouth: Hyde Publications.

McNiff, J., Edvardsen, O. and Steinholt, M. 'Discourses in development work and the construction of identity'. Under review.

McNiff, J., McGeady, L. and Elliott, M.R. (2001) *Time to Listen: An Evaluation*. Final Project Report. Available online at www.jeanmcniff.com/items.asp?id=76

McNiff, J., McNamara, G. and Leonard, D. (eds) (2000) *Action Research in Ireland*. Poole: September Books.

Mathien, T. and Wright, D.G. (eds) (2006) *Autobiography as Philosophy*. Abingdon, Oxon: Routledge.

Mellor, N. (1998) Notes from a method, *Educational Action Research*, 6 (3): 453–70.

Meyer, J., Ashburner, C. and Holman, C. (2006) Becoming connected, being caring, *Educational Action Research*, 14 (4): 477–96.

Mitchell, M. (2006) *Michael Polanyi*. Wilmington, DE: ISI Books.

Mouffe, C. (2013) *Agonistics: Thinking the World Politically*. London: Verso.

Mpondwana, M. (2008) 'Module 6: Practitioner Research and Knowledge Transfer'. Khayelitsha: St Mary's University College Practitioner Research MA programme.

Murray, R. (2002) *How to Write a Thesis*. Buckingham, UK: Open University Press.

Naser, S. (1998) *A Beautiful Mind*. New York: Touchstone.

Nixon, J. (2012) *Interpretive Pedagogies for Higher Education*. London: Bloomsbury.

Nixon, J., Buckley, A., Cheng, A., Dymoke, S., Spiro, J. and Vincent, J. (2016) 'The "Questionableness" of Things: Opening Up the Conversation', in J. McNiff (ed.), *Values and Virtues in Higher Education Research*. Abingdon, Oxon: Routledge.

Noffke, S. (2009) 'Revisiting the Professional, Personal and Political Dimensions of Action Research', in S. Noffke and B. Somekh, B. (eds), *The SAGE Handbook of Educational Action Research*. London: Sage, pp. 6–23.

Noffke, S. and Somekh, B. (eds) (2009) *The SAGE Handbook of Educational Action Research*. London: Sage.

Norbye, B., Edvardsen, O. and Thoresen, A.-L. (2013) 'Bridging the Gap Between Health Care Education and Clinical Practice Through Action Research', in J. McNiff (ed.), *Value and Virtue in Practice-Based Research*. Poole: September Books, pp. 69–78. Available online at www.septemberbooks.com/valueandvirtue.asp (last accessed 30/10/16).

Oakeshott, M. (1962) *Rationalism in Politics*. New York: Basic Books.

Orr, D. (1992) *Ecological Literacy*. Albany: State University of New York Press.

Orwell, G. (1989 [1949]) *Nineteen Eighty-Four*. London: Penguin.

O'Shea, K. (2000) 'Coming to know my own practice'. MA dissertation, Dublin: University of the West of England, Bristol.

Patton, M.Q. (2002) *Qualitative Research and Evaluation Methods* (3rd edn). Thousand Oaks, CA: Sage.

Pavītola, L., Latsone, L. and Bethere, D. (2016) 'Perspectives on Criticality and Openness in Educational Research in the Context of Latvia', in J. McNiff (ed.), *Values and Virtues in Higher Education Research*. Abingdon, Oxon: Routledge, pp. 94–109.

Pearson, J. (2016) 'Physical mis-education: The power of performance and assessment': Paper presented at the Sixth International Conference on Value and Virtue in Practice-Based Research. York: York St John University.

Phillips, E. and Pugh, D. (2005) *How to get a PhD* (4th edn). Maidenhead: Open University Press.

Polanyi, M. (1958) *Personal Knowledge*. London: Routledge and Kegan Paul.

Polanyi, M. (1967) *The Tacit Dimension*. New York: Doubleday.

Popper, K. (2002) *The Poverty of Historicism*. London: Routledge.

Pressfield, S. (2011) *Do the Work!* The Domino Project, Do You Zoom, Inc.

Pring, R. (1984) *Personal and Social Education in the Curriculum*. London: Hodder Arnold.

Putnam, R.D. (2000) *Bowling Alone: The Collapse and Revival of American Community*. New York: Simon and Schuster.

Rafferty, A. (1996) *The Politics of Nursing Knowledge*. London: Routledge.

Rafferty, A. (2010) Why does fear and loathing surround nursing degrees?, *Nursing Times*, 2 March. Available online at www.nursingtimes.net/why-does-fear-and-loathing-surround-nursing-degrees/5012118.article (last accessed 30/10/16).

Reason, P. and Bradbury, H. (2001) *Handbook of Action Research: Participative Inquiry and Practice*. London: Sage.

Reason, P. and Bradbury, H. (eds) (2008) 'Introduction', in P. Reason and H. Bradbury (eds), *The SAGE Handbook of Action Research* (2nd edn). London: Sage, pp. 1–10.

Reid, C. and Frisby, S. (2008) 'Continuing the Journey: Articulating Dimensions of Feminist Participatory Research (FPAR)', in P. Reason and H. Bradbury (eds), *The SAGE Handbook of Action Research*. London: Sage, pp. 93–105.

Ricoeur, P. (1992) *Oneself as Another* (trans. K. Blamey). Chicago: University of Chicago Press.

Rolfe, G. (1998) *Expanding Nursing Knowledge*. Oxford: Butterworth Heinemann.

Rorty, R. (1989) *Contingency, Irony and Solidarity*. Cambridge: Cambridge University Press.

Rorty, R. (1999) *Philosophy and Social Hope*. London: Penguin.

Rorty, R. (2006) *Take Care of Freedom and Truth Will Take Care of Itself*. Stanford: Stanford University Press.

Rowell, L.L., Bruce, C., Shosh, J.M. and Riel, M.M. (eds) (2016) *The Palgrave International Handbook of Action Research*. Los Angeles, CA: Palgrave Macmillan.

Rowlands, M. (2005) *Everything I Know I Learned from TV*. London: Ebury.

Russell, S. (1996) *Collaborative School Self-Review*. London: Lemos and Crane.

Sachs, J. (2003) *The Activist Teaching Profession*. Buckingham: Open University Press.

Said, E. (1994) *Representations of the Intellectual: The 1993 Reith Lectures*. London: Vintage.

Said, E. (1997) *Beginnings: Intention and Method*. London: Granta.

Said, E. (1999) *Out of Place*. London: Granta.

Schön, D. (1983) *The Reflective Practitioner: How Professionals Think in Action*. New York: Basic Books.

Schön, D. (1995) Knowing-in-action: the new scholarship requires a new epistemology, *Change*, November–December: 27–34.

Schön, D. and Rein, M. (1994) *Frame Reflection*. New York: Basic Books.

Sen, A. (1999) *Development as Freedom*. Oxford: Oxford University Press.

Senge, P. (1990) *The Fifth Discipline: The Art and Practice of the Learning Organization*. New York: Doubleday.

Senge, P. and Scharmer, O. (2001) 'Community Action Research: Learning as a Community of Practitioners, Consultants and Researchers', in P. Reason and H. Bradbury (eds), *Handbook of Action Research, Participative Inquiry and Practice*. London: Sage, pp. 238–49.

Sharples, M. (1999) *How We Write: Writing as Creative Design*. London: Routledge.

Sinclair, A. (2017) 'Developing a curriculum for ecoliteracy'. Working Papers, York St John University.

Siv, S., Houy, C., Ray, S., Edvardsen, O. and Ingstad, B. (n.d.) 'Safe motherhood: a qualitative study on the impact of maternal waiting houses in rural areas of Battambang and Pailin Provinces, Cambodia', TMC, Battambang.

Solvason, C. (2016) 'Ethicality, Research and Emotional Impoverishment in a Technological Era,' in J. McNiff (ed.), *Values and Virtues in Higher Education Research*. Abingdon, Oxon: Routledge, pp. 33–47.

Sontag, S. (2003) *Regarding the Pain of Others*. London: Penguin.

Sowell, T. (1987) *A Conflict of Visions: Ideological Origins of Political Struggles*. New York: Morrow.

Stenhouse, L. (1981) What counts as research?, *British Journal of Educational Studies*, 29 (2): 103–114.

Stenhouse, L. (1983) Research is systematic enquiry made public, *British Educational Research Journal*, 9 (1): 11–20.

Sterling, S. (2001) *Sustainable Learning: Revisioning Learning and Change*. Bristol: Green Books.

Stiglitz, J. (2002) *Globalization and Its Discontents*. London: Penguin.

Stringer, E. (2007) *Action Research* (3rd edn). Los Angeles, CA: Sage.

Taber, K. S. (2013) Action Research and the Academy: seeking to legitimise a 'different' form of research, review article, *Teacher Development*, 17 (2): 288–300.

Taylor, F. (1911) *The Principles of Scientific Management*. New York: Harper & Brothers.

Thomas, G. (1998) The myth of rational research, *British Educational Research Journal*, 24 (2): 141–61.

Todorov, T. (1999) *Facing the Exteme: Moral Life in the Concentration Camps* (trans. A. Denner and A. Pollack). London: Weidenfeld & Nicolson.

Torbert, W.R. (2001) 'The Practice of Action Inquiry', in P. Reason and H. Bradbury (eds), *The SAGE Handbook of Action Research, Participative Inquiry and Practice*. London: Sage, pp. 250–60.

Toulmin, S. (1992) *Cosmopolis: The Hidden Agenda of Modernity.* Chicago: University of Chicago Press.

Townsend, A. and Thomson, P. with the 'Get Wet' team (2015) Bringing installation art to reconnaissance to share values and generate action, *Educational Action Research*, 23 (1): 36–50.

Waldrop, M. (1992) *Complexity: The Emerging Science at the Edge of Order and Chaos.* London: Penguin.

Walker, R. and Solvason, C. (2014) *Success with your Early Years Project.* London: Sage.

Wambura, J. (2016) '"Normalising the Cut": Language and female genital mutilation practices in Kuria, Kenya'. Paper presented at the Sixth International Conference on Value and Virtue in Practice-Based Research, July, York St John University.

Wenger, E. (1998) *Communities of Practice: Learning, Meaning, Identity.* Cambridge: Cambridge University Press.

Wheatley, M. (1992) *Leadership and the New Science: Learning about Organization from an Orderly Universe.* San Francisco, CA: Berrett-Koehler.

Winter, R. (1989) *Learning from Experience.* London: Falmer.

Winter, R. (1998) Managers, spectators and citizens: where does 'theory' comes from in action research?, *Educational Action Research*, 6 (3): 361–76.

Winter, R. (2002) Truth or fiction? Problems of validity and authenticity in narratives of action research, *Educational Action Research*, 10 (1): 143–54.

Winther, S. (2016) 'Safe patient transitions from an intensive care unit to general wards'. Paper presented at the Sixth International Conference on Value and Virtue in Practice-Based Research, July, York St John University.

Wood, L. (2013) 'Developing Virtuous Leaders: An Action Research Approach to Improving School Leadership in a South African Context', in J. McNiff (ed.), *Value and Virtue in Practice-Based Research.* Poole: September Books, pp. 54–68. Available online at www.septemberbooks. com/valueandvirtue.asp (last accessed 30/10/16).

Yin, R. (2009) *Case Study Research: Design and Method* (4th edn). Thousand Oaks, CA: Sage.

Young-Bruehl, E. and Kohn, J. (2001) 'What and How We Learned from Hannah Arendt: An Exchange of Letters', in M. Gordon (ed.), *Hannah Arendt and Education: Renewing Our Common World.* Boulder, CO: Westview, pp. 225–56.

Zimmerman, M.E., Callicott, J.B., Sessions, G., Warren, K.J. and Clark, J. (2001) *Environmental Philosophy: From Animal Rights to Radical* Ecology (3rd edn). Upper Saddle River, NJ: Prentice Hall.

Zinn, H. (2005) *A People's History of the United States: 1492–Present.* New York: Harper Modern Classics.

Index

Made in the USA
Las Vegas, NV
08 May 2021